AD LIB:
REPEAT TO FADE

INTRODUCTION

BACK AND TO THE LEFT.....1

ACT ONE.

AD LIB

NOT ALL THERE.....4
MY PARENT'S RANDOMLY AVERAGE
RECORD COLLECTION.....12
CHILDREN'S FAVOURITES.....24
VENUS IN BLUE JEANS.....32
POP LIFE.....36
DISCOTHEQUE.....41
SPREAD IT. SPREAD IT.....46
BOSS RADIO.....50
CLASS.....54
SWITHUNTIME AND TIDE.....60
STOP TALKING!.....64
OVERSPILL.....70
BLACKBERRY WAY.....76
RAINBOW CHASER.....80
GROCER BOY.....87
ROUGH BOOKS.....94
WATERING CANS WALKING DOWN TAVISTOCK STREET.....100
THE NARROW WAY.....107
AD LIB FILTH.....110
AH-AH YAWA EM EKAT OT GNIMOC ER'YEHT.....118
PECULIAR.....124
THROUGH THE RECESS,
THE CHALK AND NUMBERS.....133

ACT TWO.

REPEAT

PAVILIONS OF THE SUN.....144
BIG LOAD GOING SOMEWHERE.....151

ACT THREE.

FADE

THERE'S A GHOST IN MY HOUSE.....169

INTRODUCTION

BACK AND TO THE LEFT

We were driving down from Manchester to Luton Hoo to see Kraftwerk play a rare live gig. It was May 1997. A bright, sunny Saturday. Caroline, my girlfriend, was at the wheel and I was navigating the last leg of the journey through Dunstable, negotiating, in as much as you need to negotiate, a long straight road punctuated by a series of mini-roundabouts. My eyes were fixed firmly on the AA map and the remainder of the route ahead, but as we cornered yet another roundabout the left side-sweep of my peripheral vision registered a crescent of shops. What occurred next happened in a micro-flash. Guided by some unconscious impulse I jerked my head in reverse J.F.K. mode back and to the right, and looked across to the opposite side of the road. There, waiting to greet me like a daylight ghost, was the football ground, long abandoned by the looks of it, of the ACDelco works team. South Midlands League, Division One. Circa 1960s.

I hadn't been to this precise location for 30 years or more. Nor, up until the moment it happened, was I expecting to see ACDelco's football ground. From memories that lay as derelict and dormant as the ground itself, I'd misremembered the ACDelco factory as being located in Luton, not Dunstable, so inasmuch as I had thought of the place at all, which was next to never, I wouldn't have been expecting to see it here, in this fleeting moment on the A5, with my mind elsewhere, heading to Luton Hoo to see Kraftwerk play live. And yet with that one impulsive twitch I was transported back to my childhood.

I was probably last there in October 1966, perhaps only ever there in October 1966. I walked across the road from the ground to the crescent of shops with my friends, to buy or possibly steal sweets, before watching my home-town team, Albion Sands, play an away game. It was here, huddled in a fawn windcheater, cradling a transistor radio, standing in the shadow of the ACDelco factory's impressive Art Deco frontage, that I first heard *Good Vibrations* by the Beach Boys. My life is littered with such moments, trigger mechanisms for memorials to the past, a glance a glimpse and gone again. Just as the archaeology of old Dublin can be reconstructed from James Joyce's *Ulysses*, I can rebuild my youth in the rubble of reminiscence.

We drove into the manicured grounds of Luton Hoo with Joey Beltram's *Energy Flash* blasting out of the car cassette player on an old Sami B show, taped off Sunset Radio ("the Kickin' FM"). As we cruised unimpeded down a grassy track towards the parking area, our arrival could only have been announced more momentously if we'd had a bunch of our scally mates hanging out the windows armed with klaxons. No one accidentally steps in front of a car when Joey Beltram's *Energy Flash* is playing at full volume.

Kraftwerk were reliably retrograde. No new material. Just them and an à la mode slide-show. Heritage futurism. After the star attraction had done their greatest-hits thing we wandered about for a bit, bumping into Manchester mates who had also made their way down. Someone mentioned that the bouncers were being nasty. A warm May afternoon had turned into a chilly clear-skied evening and the extras from *Deliverance* who had been hired to man the gates were stopping habitually underdressed rave girls from going out to their cars to fetch cardies on the pretext that they were bringing in drugs. This same excuse was then being used to intimately body search those they had let out in case they were working as scantily clad drug mules and had stuffed the contraband down their fluffy bras.

As the Luton night grew colder we hung about for a bit, small-talking. Rob out of Stereo MC's walked by, looking like Catweazle and kicking up a trail of cartoon dust. Just after midnight we decided that we either had to investigate ways of staying up all night or submit to the lure of our unattended bed 150 miles away. We drove home.

We passed ACDelco's old ground again, now shrouded in shadows and silhouettes. There is something overpoweringly poignant about abandoned stadia, the uncut turf grass grown high, thistles forcing their way through cracks in terrace steps, stands and former tea huts leaking and rusting away, the ghosts of long-forgotten footballers chasing the ball out there in the dark where the goal posts used to be and where I stood as a boy of 11, going on 15, going on seven, depending on sugar intake and the phases of the moon. Many of the dream places of my past are similarly populated by phantoms, post-industrious, reduced to ruins, paved, parked upon. The C90 of life, taped over and taped over and taped over. Even the road we drove on, the former Watling Street, had once been an old English dirt track, charted by the ancient Britons, regulated by the Romans, and now stuccoed with mini roundabouts. Memory is like this, layers multi-layered upon layers, the foundation long forgotten until disinterred by some chance encounter.

I was momentarily wistful for those Saturdays of my childhood spent watching my small-town team play their small-time football. This phase of my life pretty much ended in 1970 when I was 15. John Peel's *Top Gear* moved from Sunday evenings to Saturday afternoons, thus presenting a culture clash that took a few messy months to resolve. For a while I combined both worlds and took my radio to matches. I wasn't the only one, and the compromise cut both ways. I have clear memories of going to Hyde Park free concerts in the early 70s and seeing people with ears pressed to match reports or final scores while Canned Heat or King Crimson were playing. In my case an accord was reached the day a friend turned ugly and drop-kicked my radio along the touchline. I can't recall the precise moment, but I suspect it was when John Peel said "and now another song from that Incredible String Band session." It was a turning-point in my life, the moment my leisure habits shifted and all my available funds stopped going on football and started going on gigs and records instead.

We drove on into the night. Road signs flashed past for Totternhoe, Eaton Bray, Barton-le-Clay and other satellite towns and villages that played in the South Midlands League in the 1960s, and which I probably visited no more than once or twice. As we skirted the edge of Milton Keynes we found ourselves in the middle of a rave convoy. Now we both grew wistful for a dance life recently aborted (other ghosts, other reasons). Trapped in the phalanx of slow-moving vehicles, we thought briefly about following the scent, just for old time's sake. Eventually the convoy snaked off the A5 and headed down a B Road towards Whittlewood Forest. It probably made the local papers and the regional news bulletin. I watched in the wing mirror as the last flickering tail-light disappeared into woodland, heavy-hearted as we denied ourselves the energy flash of an all-night rave party. We drove on into darkness and didn't talk for a while.

All this from one memory spasm. Paths of enchantment and roads that go nowhere. Synapses sizzling with overload. All emanating from a half-glimpsed row of shops and a boy so alive in the long ago. Back and to the left and then to the right. And now on into the labyrinth. What else shall we find?

ACT ONE.
AD LIB

Who will show a child as it really is? Who will place it in its constellation and put the measure of distance in its hand?
Rainer Maria Rilke, *Duineser Elegien.*

It's the particular curse of adolescence that its events are never adequate to the feelings they inspire, that no unadorned retelling of these events can suggest the feelings.
Edmund White, *A Boy's Own Story.*

NOT ALL THERE

When I was four, I used to sit in my back garden and watch Jacob carry a wind-up gramophone down to his shed, where he would play The William Tell Overture on a 78rpm record to his hens. Jacob was the boy next-door-but-one, and was, as grown-ups told you in lowered tones, "not all there". But the part of him that was there was down his garden playing *The William Tell Overture* to his hens because his mother swore that it increased their productivity. I particularly liked it when the gramophone records began to slow down and Jacob had to wind the crank handle. Grooooooeeeeerrrr-groooooooeeeeeeee the machine would go as *William Tell* fluctuated between slightly too slow and slightly too fast, only ever adjacent to the correct tempo, a bit like Jacob himself. When he wasn't away at his special school for the not especially special, Jacob and I played.

Next door to Jacob's was Webb's, or Wubbse's as I pronounced it. Wubbse's was a small haulage yard, just large enough to accommodate two lorries. Every afternoon when me and Mum got back from the shops, I used to race down the garden and stand on our small compost heap to watch Wubbse's lorries being loaded for Covent Garden market. Late in the afternoon when the big gates were open and the yard was empty, Jacob and I would scavenge for bruised or discarded vegetables. Then we used to load the goods into our toy barrows and sell them to each other. If there weren't any vegetables to be had we made do with bricks, stones and clumps of mud. I quickly learned Jacob's bricks, stones and clumps of mud conversion rate, which ones were spuds, which ones were onions etc. We spent entire afternoons like this, trading pretend produce till we were called in for tea.

One afternoon I loaded Jacob's barrow with too much brick-cabbage and mud-potato and it toppled over on the path, spilling the wares. Jacob looked at me, then looked at the wares. "You cunt. You cunt," he said. "You are a cunt." Then he went in.

Days passed. Who knows how many, given the elasticity of child time? It might have been a month. It could have been the very next afternoon. I was at my grandparents'. Down the garden watching Grandad attend to his cage birds, fascinated by the dead moths and butterflies entangled in the aviary mesh, their wings crumbling to powdery dust when touched. When I went in Mum and Grandma were talking in the scullery. I said "Mum, what's a cunt?" There was a brief disconcerted silence.

– Who taught you that word?
– Where did you learn that word?

Once the betrayer's deed was done, much calming ensued. I was after all innocent and merely at the beck and call of an older boy. I didn't see Jacob for a while after that. When I did he chided me sheepishly, dim grin turning to scorn on his lips. "You mustn't tell on me. You mustn't." Soon after that I started school, and my playing days with Jacob came to an end.

****

I come from Bedfordshire, the bit you go through to get somewhere. Too far north to be the Home Counties, too far west to be East Anglia, too far southeast to be the Midlands, but not far enough southeast to be the South East.

Black earth moistened by marshland rolls out across the Fens, ripples into hillocks and a limestone ridge. These are the flatlands, bland acres of inconspicuous countryside: mostly crop-farming, rarely a sheep or cow. Hills are so rare we elevate them to the status of tourist attractions: Dunstable Downs, for instance, which we occasionally used to drive out to on Sundays, and where the highlight of the afternoon was to gaze at a hang glider caught in an air pocket. Other than that, it was endless arable: miles of spuds, sugar beet and Brussels sprouts. A place to grow up small. Big skies though. Huge oceanic domes of sky.

I have rarely encountered a writer who approaches my part of the country with anything other than a tourist's gaze. Psychogeographers, would-be Bill Brysons, Holy Grail-seekers hoping to locate the heartland and prejudices of Middle England: they all skim the periphery like the A1 skims the western edge of town. However, barely a paragraph or two into Helen McDonald's *H is for Hawk*, I knew I was in for the long glide. It was that mention of the shotgun-peppered road signs that did it. Being shot at with an air rifle was a rite of passage when I was a kid. If you hadn't had your short-trousered legs peppered by the time you were ten, you were obviously indoors reading *Look and Learn* or watching *Top of the Form* and not making your wary way into a world where indolent farm boys and gasworks-gang thugs took target practice as and where they pleased. This was the random everyday malevolence of rural life. Although McDonald's journey takes her further into the Fens and closer to the roar of the airbases, she fashions a cartography utterly familiar to me. Within a few pages I was in the broken light and cold-shadowed woodland with her, treading soft dunes, pine-needle carpets and frosted ground, smelling the same damp air. I lived in that ramshackle wildness she described, invented all my childhood games in it, and rarely explored spinneys and coppices with a sense that any of it was out of bounds.

Draw a map of no-man's land and it would look like this. Flatten out the ridges until one bump remains. And a beach. A town with a beach many miles from the sea. Where the floodwaters subsided aeons ago they left a low crop of sand hills rising from the bog. The town nestles in their shelter, taking its name from them – Albion Sands – and its soil. Dig three feet down and the earth is as yellow as the sun. Caesar's men had a camp there in the Roman days. Not Caesar himself, but he sent some men. Remnants of their narrow pathways and ancient tracks still wind in unbroken circles round the back of the hills. In less sentimental times, evidence of their presence – coins, pots, bowls, bones, amulets – was unceremoniously ploughed up and ploughed back in again, year after year, in the surrounding fields.

When publisher John Taylor first visited the poet John Clare at home in Helpston on the edge of the Fens, he was amazed at the contrast between the verses on the page and the unremarkable landscape that greeted him. The 1821 poem *Last of March, Written at Lolham Brigs* essays the rapture of spring, where "bullocks low their liberty" and "larks rise to hail the peeping sun". Clare describes "walls the work of Roman hands" and muses on "paths that age has trampled o'er/the builder's names are known no more." In contrast to Clare's poetic vision, what Taylor encountered was, in his own words, "nothing but a dull line of ponds, or rather one continued marsh, over which a succession of arches carries the narrow highway". Clare projected beauty onto mundanity. It's what you do if mundanity is all that is set before you.

Had I been raised in the Alps or the Lake District I might have grown blasé with every curtain-opening glimpse of it, but blasé is never an option when all you encounter is dredged levels and scrub. You soon learn to project. Your world, exterior and interior, rapidly becomes contoured with superimposition, criss-cross grids of fantasy and myth, negotiations with the unactual.

****

One Sunday. Summer. It had been hot like this for months and I seemed to live outside. Sitting by the white picket fence at the front of Wubbse's yard with my knees tucked under my chin. On my own. No Jacob. Lazily trailing a stick through the dirt, writing a new dirt alphabet. There were very few cars on the Great North Road, and when one did appear it seemed to flash by in silence. I sat there forever in the heat and there was no one else alive. A car passed going south. From an open window a little girl waved and yelled a startling yell. I lifted my heavy head, filled to the brim with the heat. Too slow to catch what she'd said. She disappeared into the shimmering haze still waving. Long after she'd gone I stared into the empty space where she'd been. I've often wondered if she was yelling at me in bossy anger or whether she was shouting a different kind of hello, thrilled with the sensation of being a stranger you'll never meet, little boy, no matter how fast you lift your head next time.

It's an enduring image and I think of it often. That hot day. The shouting girl. She was every future thrill personified. Look up quick and you might just catch a glimpse. Glance too late and the moment has gone.

Sitting on the toilet in the outhouse, legs dangling, trousers round my ankles. Mice dance twice around the mangle and scuttle back to the skirting. Spiders scamper from corner dust to gaps between bricks. The smell of wood rot and Rinso. Day in. Day out. Cold-arsed until I was seven and we left that damp tumbledown cottage and moved to a brand-new council house. Adjacent to the drainpipe in the tiny back yard lived the actual Incey Wincey from the nursery rhyme. I believed that then. Until the world expands beyond your backyard domain, all children do. The world is Platonic. There is only an ideal one of everything. My early memories are like that too. Episodic. Fragmentary. No dots to join. Making it up as I went along.

****

Dad was always away when I was very young. "On the road," Mum called it. Up north a lot of the time. I barely knew him until I was six. Mum brought me up mostly. Mum and her Mum. It was my Grandma (who we always called Grummar) who taught me how to read. Repeating the stories endlessly until the words gradually formed themselves into shapes that made sense and I could read them myself.

When Jacob was away at his special school – for longer it seemed the older I got – I sat out front on next-door's wall, stacked up the empty crates that the milkman often left there and spent entire mornings delivering pretend milk. Always facing south, static in my universe, driving my wall, the traffic a moving backdrop as I inched through time at nought miles an hour.

****

In the corner of the living-room, radiating light, was the big black-and-white television set that Mum and Dad received as a wedding present when they got married in the Coronation summer of 1953. It had wooden doors and looked like furniture. Most working-class families in the 1950s had either a car or a TV, but rarely both. I remained unfamiliar with AA maps, Shell Guides and the golden age of pre-motorway motoring, but I was fluent in *Watch with Mother* and Westerns. Westerns were my first myth world, and my play scenarios were moulded by the preponderance of cowboys that dominated the schedules on both television channels. *Bronco Layne. Tenderfoot. Wells Fargo. Wagon Train. Gunsmoke. Rawhide. Casey Jones* and the *Cannonball Express. Bonanza*'s burning map of Ponderosa. I was proficient in Wild West terminology by the time I started school. Posse. Lasso. Totem pole. Tomahawk. Sioux. Cheyenne. Comanche. Neckerchief. Injun with a J. Next to nursery rhymes, the music I was most familiar with as a child was cowboy-show theme tunes.

****

Dr Barbara Moore was famous for walking the length and breadth of Britain in order to illustrate that a healthy vegetarian diet and walking hundreds of miles were good for you. A member of the Breatharian Movement, she pronounced that she expected to live until she was 150 by subsisting on a diet of nuts and wheatgrass washed down with honey and lemon juice. In December 1959, at the age of 56, she walked the 373 miles from Edinburgh to London. She passed silently past my window in the middle of the night as I lay sleeping. Dad was there then. He must have been because Mum said they stayed up to see her. And then suddenly Dad was there all the time. The way Mum told it, and retold it, a tramp came to the back door late one night asking for food, and it scared her, being there all alone with just me and my little brother.

It's a plausible enough tale. There were many itinerants on the road in those days, although not as many as there once had been, certainly not as many as there were when Laurie Lee walked out early one summer morn in the 1930s on his journey to Spain. Lee encountered men brewing tea by the roadside, men with cardboard suitcases and grass-polished shoes, men carrying their livelihoods in parcelled bundles under their arms as they traipsed the highways and the trunk roads searching in vain for work that wasn't there. I saw similar apparitions drift by the front-room window or past my wall as I delivered my milk and dreamed my dreams. Lee's jobless army passed in a somnambulist blur, faces and frown lines blackened by dirt, expressions worn away by life. Mine did likewise. They rarely spoke, and if they did I was never frightened, not like Mum obviously had been in the dead of night. Soon after the tramp incident Dad stopped being a service engineer away up north and started working at Sunny Smile in Eaton Socon four miles up the road, making plastic injection moulds for baby toys that were sold in Woolworth's. After that we never went short of baby toys.

Early in 1961 work began on widening the Great North Road. Two lanes were turned into four and a row of cottages opposite our house was demolished, as were the local bakery that made the morning-breeze smell of bread, and Mr Lincoln's antique shop – where a huge stuffed grizzly brown bear always sat outside. They all stood on what is now the northbound side of the A1. All trace of their existence was rapidly erased by the tarmacadam gangs.

And then one day we didn't live in the damp cottage any more, with the wallpaper peeling and my mildewed mattress steam-drying by the fire. At half-past-three I began detouring the long way home from Infant school just to watch Dad measuring up in a brand-new house that smelt of fresh paint and wood. I used to sit at the top of the stairs on the bare boards, watching him put pencil marks on walls and across the tops of windows. Waiting for Mum to come and collect me and take me home for tea while Dad carried on measuring and pencilling till it got too dark to continue. Mum, faithful to the grace and favour of parish life, said we had Mrs Plowright the local councillor to thank for our new house. "No, we didn't," Dad explained to me many years later. "We'd been on the housing list for ages and finally got enough points when your sister was born."

We left the Great North Road with the bulldozers rumbling and the wrecking balls demolishing. Our furniture was loaded onto the back of an open truck trailer and we trailed along behind it. "There goes another load," said Mum as a second trailer, piled not so high with our possessions passed us, before we reached our destination.

In the backyard. Incy Wincy drainpipe in the background.

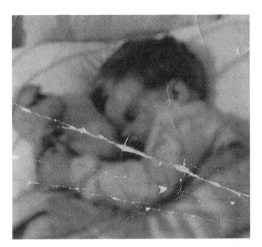

Sleeping downstairs when the bedroom was too cold and damp.

With younger brother Chris in the back garden. Jacob's hen run just visible.

MY PARENT'S RANDOMLY AVERAGE RECORD COLLECTION

Explore the innards of any 1950s record-playing equipment, be it state-of-the-art hi-fi or a hire-purchased radiogram, and you will see a section set aside for record storage. This modest little alcove usually measured about eight by 12 inches and was a direct acknowledgement from the manufacturers that most people didn't buy many records. The discs themselves boasted the ultramodern allure of "Stroboscopic Sound" and "Vitaphonic Stereo". Trade advertisements promised "more exciting standards of clarity and brilliance". LP sleeve notes often devoted more space to the technical specifications of the listening equipment than to details of the musicians featured on the record itself. And yet, despite all this technological advancement, the typical storage capacity of the average record player was somewhere in the region of a dozen or so albums and a similar number of seven-inch singles or EPs.

In the majority of households this unassuming storage facility played host to an amalgam of incongruities. What sat in those alcoves was public taste in all its logic-defying randomly average juxtapositions. My parents had such a collection. Perhaps yours did too. So slow was the rate of expansion in our house that I can still remember every record we had. By the time Beatlemania was in full swing, my parent's collection consisted of a dozen or so items. We had the following singles: *Lover Please* (Decca 1962) and *Funny All Over* (Decca 1963) by The Vernons Girls, *My Old Man's a Dustman* and *Lively* by Lonnie Donegan (both Pye 1960), *Strawberry Fair* by Not Antony Newley (Embassy 1960), *Sun Arise* by Not Rolf Harris (Embassy 1962), and Frank Ifield's *I Remember You* and *The Wayward Wind* (Columbia 1962 and 1963 respectively). Our long-player collection consisted of a single sleeveless 78rpm disc of Wagner's *Tannhäuser* on black HMV, *Pearl Bailey Sings for Adults Only* (Roulette 1959), *The Button-Down Mind of Bob Newhart* (Warner Brothers 1960) and *Rotatey Diskers with Unwin* by Stanley Unwin (Pye 1961).

The Vernons Girls were a female trio named in honour of the Liverpool-based football pools company that employed them. Bold, peroxided and sassy, they embodied the kind of working-class womanhood that prevailed when I was a boy, a world where 17-year-olds weren't girls – they were women. The school-leaving age was 15, and during this time of relatively full employment most ex-Secondary Modern females would have been working, often in skilled or semi-skilled occupations, for four years or more by the time their teens were over. Unless they were married, these young women had disposable incomes and a robust attitude towards pleasure. It's the world that Nell Dunn documented so astutely in *Up the Junction*, and it's an aspect of the 1960s that doesn't get anything like as much attention as it should. These young women owned pop. Pop song echoed their emotional terrain. Its vistas were of feminine proportion. Men ventured into this topography at their peril, as interlopers, as bait. The Vernons Girls were not soppy. They mocked the predatory gaze.

Lover Please, their 1962 cover of a Clyde McPhatter song, sounds reined in and restrained by modern standards, and less Scouse than I remember it from my childhood. In my mind's eye they are giving it the full "loovah please/ please coom baaack," but the delivery is demure, the sentiment muted. The B-side, however, was gear. With the kind of early sixties string arrangement and wavery-pitched sha-la-las that always made me think the record was playing off centre, *You Know What I Mean* is delivered in tones that suggest the lead vocalist is fending off a randy groper even as she sings. With its triple-edged play on "boys are natural twisters" (i.e. duplicitous, good dancers and serial shaggers), the song was predatory to the core, a world-weary missive to the "gerls" who have been there, not particularly regretted it and lived to gossip about it on Monday morning at "werk". The phlegmy "Ooh, wack" that precedes each "Well, you know what I mean" chorus conveys compliance and contempt, then resignation. The fade-out, conveniently inaudible, is filthy. "So I said to him... I said, 'What do yer think yer doing?' Practically twisted me legs off. Couldn't keep up with him."

None of the Vernons Girls discs was a Top 30 hit but they all made the lower reaches of the Top 50, and it was probably the constant playing of these inanely seductive ditties when I was eight or nine that instilled in me a life-long love of girl groups. Surreptitiously the Vernons Girls songs hinted at so much more than the sum of their writhing parts. This was withdrawal-method pop, rife with nudges and innuendo. A song like *Funny All Over* conveys quivering abstinence and forbidden (but not always forsaken) pleasures. It's the world of Mike Sarne and Wendy Richard's *Come Outside*, which *Funny All Over* directly alludes to, as the boy yearns for a grope. There's also a nod to Bobby Darin's *Multiplication*, a song which anthropomorphised animal-kingdom promiscuity to a syncopated Broadway rhythm, and which *Funny All Over* cribs faithfully from break beats to chorus.

I suspect Dad liked The Vernons Girls in the way that he liked Patsy from work when she appeared on the Sunny Smile float at Eaton Socon Carnival in 1964. "Looks a picture, doesn't she?", he said, while Mum pretended not to notice. Patsy was dressed like Tinkerbell in a skirt that showed her arse. Seeking visual evidence of this lingering vignette, I found a photo on the internet, taken from a community archive website. It utterly vindicated my memory. There was the float and there was Patsy. Christmas theme. A winter wonderland. Snowmen made of cotton wool. Everyone in mufflers and mittens. All except Patsy and her friend who bend at the waist, cock a leg and steal a coy glance at the camera. It's those Vernons Girls songs personified, choreographed, freeze-framed.

While I was still a foetus, Lonnie Donegan was busy pioneering a particularly durable brand of British skifflebilly. By the time I started school he was in his Music Hall pop-star prime. *My Old Man's a Dustman* was Number One in the singles chart for five weeks in the spring of 1960, and unusually for a chart topper was recorded in front of a live audience. It's the crackle and cackle of that Gaumont Cinema crowd that used to excite me as a kid. Right from the off, they fill Donegan's comedic pauses with expectant laughter. They whoop and hoot during verses that are littered with casual violence, police snoopers, sexual innuendo (delivered by an octogenarian old lady no less) and undergarments. They punctuate the punchlines with their shrieks, and their electrified counterpoint guided my own responses. I laughed at the child-friendly puns ("'cos there's not mushroom inside!") and the rest of the time I laughed because the grown-ups laughed, laughing along with my parents who were laughing along with the laughers.

Lively, the fifth of six Top 30 singles that Donegan released in 1960, repeated Dustman's formula to the letter, but it lacked the input of a live audience, and left Donegan to do all the work himself. It sounds peculiar now (although it didn't then) to hear him riffing in a vacuum, feeding off dynamics that aren't there, shadow-boxing with the punch-lines and hamming up the delivery in a recording studio devoid of atmosphere. The BBC took a dim view of Lively's amoral tale about burglars tying up their victims and old maids praying for a bit of the other, and banned the song from the airwaves. Corporation programming policy strictly forbid any mention of "the other", particularly if the other was directly aligned to praying to the Lord above for a bit of it. In 1960 that would have been akin to rhyming "the Queen" with "fascist regime".

In May 1960 Mum and Dad took me to see Donegan at Bedford Granada. It was Mum's 30th birthday treat and my first-ever gig, the most people in the biggest room I'd ever been in. We had seats near the front. I still remember that low hum, the sound a large gathering makes, that pre-performance air of expectancy, a noise I didn't hear again until I went to my first football match. I remember the heady scent of perfume and hair lacquer and smoking. Lonnie Donegan came on and made a joke about the Scotsman, the Welshman and the Irishman. I remember laughing because all the adults were laughing. And I don't remember anything after that. I was five-and-a-half. I probably fell asleep.

The official souvenir programme for that special night kicked around the house for years, but eventually disappeared like most mementos do. Priced sixpence, it was illustrated with a cartoon of Donegan's biggest hit: a line drawing of a guitar propped next to a dustbin, obligatory skeletal fish heads poking out from under the lid.

The Frank Ifield records in our collection were Mum's. She liked all the Frankies: Frank Ifield, Frankie Vaughan, Frankie Laine. Some years later, a *Best of Frankie Laine* album on the budget Hallmark label found its way into the randomly average collection. I still see it at car-boot sales. Brown on brown cover. Never played it once. Didn't have *Rawhide* on it.

We often shopped at Woolworth's in Bedford. I remember stacks of consumer non-durables in wire-mesh skips. Toys with razor-sharp corners. Plastic trains and boats and planes. Dolls fumbled and discarded by every passing child. Handled so many times they were frequently deficient in limbs. The trick was to find one with a full torso. I remember tea in the skips too. Quarter-pound Typhoo packets with First Division football squads on the side. If you collected the set you could send off for a colour poster of your team. Poking and prodding at packets with all the other football kids. Rummaging all the way to the bottom of the skip for a Sheffield Wednesday or Everton or West Ham to complete your collection. Also in the skips, piled like so much landfill, were records on the Embassy label. Embassy was Woolworth's own cut-price imprint for those who were not unduly troubled by authenticity. Our version of *Sun Arise* was by Paul Rich. Our *Strawberry Fair* was by Bobby Stevens. It surprises me in retrospect that we didn't have Anthony Newley's original version.

My parents were big Newley fans. Mum mostly for the songs, Dad chiefly for the comedy. I became familiar with Max Jaffa's theme tune to Newley's

Gurney Slade simply because Dad always seemed to be standing there whenever it was on the radio, telling me about a TV programme which had obviously caught his imagination because he never stopped going on about it. And long ago in a far-off land called Bromley a young David Bowie was having a similar epiphany. Mum's contribution to my ripening Newley appreciation was to tell me that on the bit at the end of *Strawberry Fair*, the bit where Newley clone Bobby Stevens went "Won't be round tomorrow (pause), the donkey's (pause) pinched all the strawberries" was in fact a euphemism for "the donkey's pissed on the strawberries". She didn't use the word "euphemism" and she didn't say "pissed" either. She said "piddled". But I understood the inference soon enough. She had quite a scatological sense of humour, did my Mum. Her favoured retort during an argument with Dad was "arseholes", and like a lot of women of her generation frequently used the expression, "It hurt like buggery". One didn't enquire. And in a house that wasn't remotely royalist and never tuned to the Queen's speech on Christmas day, she reasoned that the royals weren't like us because "they even have someone to wipe their arse for them".

Did either of our Embassy facsimiles sound remotely like the originals? How would I have known? I had little or no concept of what an original was. My ears were full of ersatz. This realization was brought home to me when I acquired a Top Six EP in 1964. Distributed by Pye and hugely popular at the time, each Top Six EP contained half-a-dozen cover versions of hits from the recent charts. I had Number Nine in the series: *Oh, Pretty Woman, Where Did Our Love Go, She's Not There, Rag Doll, Is It True?, I'm Into Something Good*. I'm pretty sure that was a tea-packet offer too. Sent off the requisite number of labels and back it came. I was convinced at the time that my EP contained the original versions, although, looking back, the inclusion on the label of publishing details and songwriter credits but not the artist name would have provided damning evidence to a more discerning purchaser. "They aren't the originals," said my mate Gary Rose, fount of all pop knowledge, as he perused the record with a senior's practiced disdain. "Yes, they are," I maintained, not perceiving the difference between what I heard and whatever it was that "original" meant.

One day in 1996, shortly before the IRA drastically redesigned Manchester city centre and the Corn Exchange stall holders were all ejected from their bomb-damaged lots like so many unwanted sitting tenants, I was rooting through the trinkets and treasures and found a copy of my original Top Six EP. Timeworn and scratchy, jettisoned long ago from someone else's randomly average collection, it found refuge in mine. I wasn't expecting a

Proustian reawakening, but nothing had quite prepared me for the auditory chasm between what the nine-year old heard then and what the forty-something heard now. Although the arrangements were reasonably faithful to the originals and the vocals were "in the style of", there was no mistaking what I heard through the dust-encrusted grooves for what Roy Orbison, the Supremes, the Zombies, the Four Seasons, Brenda Lee and Herman's Hermits recorded back in 1964. On closer listen I suspect that the vocals were all done by the same two singers, drawn no doubt from the permanent session pool of those who made their living that way.

The Top Six series ran until 1967. Should I have been so inclined in the Summer of Love I could have bought Top Six 38 with *Penny Lane* and *Edelweiss* on it, or Top Six 42, the last in the series, which contained versions of *Thoroughly Modern Millie* and *San Francisco*. Top Six was the brainchild of Bill Wellings, an Australian ex-pat who later pioneered the

Music for Pleasure Hot Hits series. So popular were these cover-version LPs in the 1970s that the sales criteria eventually had to be rigged just so that MFP (and its cut-price cousins K-Tel and Ronco) could be excluded from the album charts. There are more lauded Aussie ex-pats than Bill Wellings. Germaine Greer, Clive James, Richard Neville and Barry Humphries detonated their culture bombs all over the sixties to great effect. Wellings belonged to the unsung rearguard rather than the avant garde, but it's the rearguard that gets to clean up. Wellings cleaned up all right.

In February 1963 I was entrusted for the first time to choose a record for myself. Standing by the counter in Gale's Electrical Goods shop in the High Street, I studied the Top Ten for that particular week. As with Grand Nationals, it was my understanding that you were supposed to choose the winner, so I chose the Number One record in the singles chart, which happened to be *Diamonds* by Jet Harris and Tony Meehan. As first purchases go it was a zinger, a reverberating two-and-a-half-minute drum and guitar duet with a ghostly background chorus. *Diamonds* typified the instrumental sound of the early 1960s, ubiquitous at the time but soon to be all but eviscerated by the coming of the beat group era. *Diamonds* was a prescient choice: a collaboration between a future backroom supremo (Meehan) and an early rock casualty (Harris) – predilections that would later fuel my own pop yin and yang.

Previous to *Diamonds*, the Number One record had been Dance On by Meehan and Harris's former group The Shadows. The next Number One after Diamonds was The Wayward Wind by yodelling Frank Ifield. It occurs to me now that the main purpose of going to the record shop might have been so that Mum could buy the new Frankie Ifield record and that my entitlement, my formative treasured purchase, may well have been little more than an "Oh well, while we're here" afterthought. If so, it would have been entirely in keeping with my own attitude to record-buying in 1963. At eight years old, owning a record didn't matter that much to me. None of my mates had any records. Pop music obsessed us, possessed us even, but our intuitions didn't need record purchases to validate them. There was of course a far more prosaic reason why we didn't buy records. We couldn't afford them.

From the beginning of April 1963 to the end of June 1964, Merseybeat or derivations thereof would occupy the Number One spot for all but all but nine out of 62 weeks. And it's one of those Number Ones, the last single I can remember my parents buying, that intrigues me most. *Little Children* by Billy J. Kramer and the Dakotas was top of the Hit Parade for two weeks in March 1964. By this time my parents had four little children of their own, the last of which, my youngest brother, had arrived in the January of that year. Was *Little Children* a wistful purchase, I wonder? A palliative for Mum's crippling post-natal depression, a weary acknowledgement that, saddled with four kids, and now in their mid-thirties, the leisure game was up? Did they sigh knowingly when Kramer sang the line "I wish they would take a nap little children", with that irritated emphatic snap on the word "nap"?

One day in 1963 I rushed home early from Saturday morning pictures to read my *Valiant* comic, which Mum always brought back from the shops. This particular week's edition had a free gift, a glossy black-and-white football booklet featuring photos of Garrincha, Pele, Di Stefano, Puskas and all those other exotic foreign footballers whose names I already knew as well as I knew Jimmy Greaves or Johnny Haynes. At half past eleven it had seemed worth slipping out of the cinema early for. By 12 o'clock I knew I had transgressed an unwritten code. Such was the annoyance that greeted my premature arrival home, I never attempted anything as rash again. For Mum and Dad Saturday morning was brief respite, one less mewling mouth to feed, one less clattering, chattering presence to placate. As the song said, "Little children/now why don't you go bye bye/go anywhere?" Kramer snarls "go anywhere" as John Lennon would have done. The song is actually about a boy trying to get smoochy with a girl while having to deal with the unwanted presence of her younger siblings, but in our house – and many others, I suspect – its theme was transformed into something more painfully universal.

Mum thought Billy J. was a dish, although she did frequently point out what a big hooter he had and how an unflattering camera angle did him few favours. She also had a penchant for cute-looking boys who chewed gum on Top of The Pops. She clearly thought chewing with devil-may-care insouciance while appearing on prime-time telly was the height of cheekiness. John McNally of the Searchers and Rod Allen of the Fortunes were serial chewers, and my attention was frequently drawn to their masticatory habits. Pop stars were often teased but rarely mocked in our house. My parents liked this stuff. They didn't have an aversion to it. I have often pondered what they were doing buying Billy J. Kramer records in their mid-thirties, but then I cast my mind back to the rave era and remember what I was doing at a similar period in my life. Time and circumstance made it entirely feasible for me to be dancing like Andy Pandy and putting my hands in the air like I just didn't care. The circumstances of their time dictated precisely why they couldn't even if they'd wanted to.

My parents came from the last working-class generation that there was nothing down for. Had they been born ten years later they might have received post-war scholarships and their intelligence would have been rewarded accordingly. Had they been born into the generation after that they would have been me, the beneficiary of a massive expansion in higher education, an era that now seems increasingly like a long-lost golden age. Instead, Dad, born in 1927, undertook an engineering apprenticeship with Perkins Diesel in Peterborough. After his national service with the RAF in Egypt, "mopping up" as he called it, he returned reluctantly to the life of a skilled man, plying his trade first as a servicing engineer, and then as a toolmaker in a succession of factory-bound jobs, few of which ever satisfied him.

Mum, born in 1930, passed her entrance exams to go to secretarial school in Luton. The journey entailed a 60-mile round trip, with no direct route by car, bus or train – there still isn't one to this day. A uniform was required, which was beyond the financial reach of her farm-labouring parents, and there was a war on. And so, like many women of that generation, she buried her dreams, worked briefly as a touch typist at the Meltis chocolate factory in Bedford – but after she married Dad in 1953, again like many of her generation, she gave up paid employment and raised a family instead.

Both of them were wistful about the dawning of the beat group era, and about the fact that it had arrived too late in their lives for them to fully enjoy. I suspect that there were a lot of working-class parents like that – far too busy, cash-strapped or knackered to participate, but by no means dismissive of what they saw and heard developing. It was Dad who suggested to me that Alan Price was the talented one in the Animals and that he was right to leave the band and go his own way. And it was Dad, not a schoolmate or street mate, who first pointed out to me that Brian Jones was playing a different instrument on every Rolling Stones single during the dulcimer, recorder, sitar years. Mum's observations were rarely less impassioned. She detested Cilla Black's adenoidal wail, which she imitated while holding her nose and doing a passable impression. She also disapproved of Dusty Springfield in ways that I didn't understand at the time. The phrase "tomboy" was used prejudicially, I recall. More intriguingly she imparted to me the information, purloined from a copy of *Reveille* or *Titbits*, that Petula Clark and husband Claude Wolff liked nothing better than to walk round their Parisian apartment naked. Such shared intimacies, although infrequent, were treasured insights into her world, a glimpse into another more colourful, more exotic existence, an indication of unattainable dreams and desires. She was also delightfully amoral about the whole Christine Keeler/Mandy Rice-Davies affair, and like a significant proportion of the population was not unreservedly disapproving of the Great Train Robbery either.

Echoes of this desired other life can be garnered from the contents of that Pearl Bailey LP. With its tantalising injunction "performance of this album restricted from airplay" emblazoned on the sleeve, it promised more than it ever delivered to me. I gave it a go, but it never revealed its seductive secrets to ears such as mine. After several cursory listens I remained ignorant of what Pearl had left at the Astor and indeed of what the Astor might actually be. I rarely ventured far beyond that opening track, and consequently my reluctance to engage with Bailey's version of Cole Porter's *Let's Do it* or Rodgers and Hart's *I Want a Man* kept the great American songbook at bay for several years. Perhaps it was that title For Adults Only that put me off. I didn't interpret it as saucy. To me it was merely synonymous with "boring grown-up stuff".

More to my taste were the comedy albums they had. Comedy was a great unifier in my house. Galton and Simpson were gods. So too was Phil Silvers. We were largely BBC viewers rather than ITV when it came to humour, far more inclined towards Bilko and Steptoe than *Bootsie and Snudge*. Like many of his generation, Dad was devoted to the Goons; like many of her generation, Mum said her husband laughed too loud in cinemas. It's true, he did laugh loud, but not often and not just at anything. Dad was very discerning with his comedy. He urged me to watch *The Telegoons* when it started, so I did just to please him. After a few weeks he conceded that it wasn't a patch on the original radio show and ditched it, and I was allowed to admit that I didn't find it funny either. Stanley Unwin appealed to Dad's keenly developed sense of daft, as did Victor Borge, Stanley Baxter and Morecambe and Wise. Bob Newhart appealed to his appreciation of American sophistication and the comedy of the unsaid. I didn't have anything like that understanding of inference as a kid but I played the Newhart album until I half grasped what was going on.

(Memory flash)
One day coming home from Junior School a boy was sitting on the wall outside his house. A big old Citroen bulldog car sat there too, dark blue, tires deflated. He was bored and on his own and asked me if I wanted to come in.

"Alright."

He got out all his Dad's records of comedians and American jazz bands. Thick cardboard sleeves. Unfamiliar names. He put on Bob Newhart's The Driving Instructor and asked if I thought it was funny. He had an intensity I'd never encountered before in a child. "Do you think this is funny?" He kept asking me that, and whether I got the joke. His disappointed face suggested that he had detected something absent in me. Whether he was looking for confirmation in me that The Driving Instructor was or wasn't funny I still don't know. His Dad came in, seemingly pleased that his son had got a playmate, no matter how briefly. There was no sign of a Mum. They didn't live there long, and eventually the cottage was bulldozed. I never saw the boy again and I didn't meet anyone else with that kind of earnestness and passion for quite some time, but by and by I've been meeting that boy or someone like him ever since.

Record charts only measure over-the-counter purchases. They tell you little about the meaning and value attached to those records, or about the ways in which their messages were assimilated and shared. Similarly, my parent's minuscule record collection doesn't even begin to suggest the broadness of their tastes. Dad was big on Ray Charles, Mel Tormé, and Sinatra and his fellow Rat Pack cronies, but as far as I'm aware he never owned a single record by any of these artists. He was pleased when Strangers in the Night went to Number One in 1966, and puffed up proudly when Dean Martin's mellifluous version of Gentle on My Mind got the boozy old crooner back in the pop charts in the spring of 1969, but he never went out and bought either disc.

Mum's tastes were wide-ranging, and her knowledge of music from the pre-rock'n'roll era was extensive. She liked to dance, and Glen Miller orchestrated her wartime youth. She could recite all those nonsensical tongue-twisters like *Gilly, Gilly, Ossenfeffer, Katzenellen Bogen by the Sea*, and "I'm the girl that makes the thing/that drills the hole that holds the ring/that drives the rod that turns the knob/that works the thing-ummy bob." Whenever there was a "name that tune" spot in a TV show she could name that tune. When *Sale of the Century* started on Anglia TV in 1971, and resident organist Peter Fenn reinterpreted evergreens from the past – often, it seemed to me, in the style of Karlheinz Stockhausen – Mum could identify them within a couple of rubato-heavy bars. *"Surrey with the Fringe on Top"* she would cry. Or *"76 Trombones in the Big Parade"*. "You can't possibly know that!", I would say, amazed at how she could extrapolate such information from Fenn's avant-garde adaptations. But she could and she nearly always did.

There's just one randomly average acquisition I haven't mentioned, a 45rpm one-sided flexi-disc of Humphrey Lyttelton and his band playing Lyttelton's composition *Swingin' on the Gate* coupled with the band's arrangement of *Jeanie with the Light Brown Hair* (another Peter Fenn favourite). It came free with the Summer County Margarine vouchers Mum saved up and sent off. I remember that you had to put a heavy coin on the pick-up arm so that it wouldn't skip. Typical of the trad sound that dominated the light-entertainment airwaves of my childhood, it was soon discarded. As with the Top Six EP, as with many of my childhood toys and games, the Summer County Margarine single flashed before my eyes again in the car-boot afterlife. There it was among the rummage, in pristine condition, too. Clearly never left unattended in a houseful of kids. Clearly never skimmed across the room like ours was. I paid my 20p, took it home and played it. There was no Proustian bliss, no memory scent, merely a reminder of how much trad jazz I was forced to endure in my youth.

It seems fitting that a margarine-label flexi-disc was Mum's last purposeful pop acquisition. A flexible, disposable by-product of a flexible, disposable culture. I couldn't imagine a time when I would own thousands of these things, or have entire walls of my house dominated by towering vinylscapes as I do now. As a kid I played the records in our randomly average collection, replayed them, slowed them down to 33 1/3, speeded them up to 78, put them back in the wrong sleeves, left them out of the sleeves altogether. The sleeves got lost or torn or drawn on. The ancient mistreated gramophone needle blunted but continued to plough its knackered way through worn and dust-encrusted grooves. Eventually the records jumped or stuck, were discarded, were forgotten. When the stylus packed up altogether I attempted to play them with a needle plucked from Mum's pin-cushion. The original needle was never replaced and the radiogram reverted to just being a radio. It wasn't until 1969 that we got a new record player, and so for the peak years of the swinging sixties I absorbed my flexi-culture in other ways. Most people did.

CHILDREN'S FAVOURITES

In Housewives' Choice *this morning I heard a so-called "funny" about a chap who was alleged to be deformed to the extent of having three legs. This reminded my wife who was listening with me in the car that she had heard a record earlier this week about a chap who only had a head.*
(BBC Written archive)

The Trad versus Modernism skirmish played out in a variety of forms during the 20th century, most clannishly in jazz in the 1950s, most visibly in the schisms between figurative and abstract art, and revivalist and brutalist architecture. Similar factionalism informed dance, film and theatre; humour, poetry, gardening, food – indeed every last vestige of cultural life. But nowhere did these warring forces manifest themselves more vigorously than in our pliant infant bodies.

The revival in Scottish country dancing and the "Music and Movement" philosophy were actively promoted in schools during the 1950s, and I was the beneficiary of both initiatives. At Infant School I whirled around in a borrowed tartan skirt to strathspeys and reels. At Junior School, a wireless set would be carried into the hall and we would throw interpretive shapes to the musical abstractions of the *Rhythm and Melody* radio program. The aim of the Scottish country-dancing revival was to reinvigorate indigenous folk customs, and was part of a concerted post-war effort to recreate the country dances of the 18th century Scottish Assembly Room. Music and Movement was a progressive amalgam of the holistic philosophy of the Hungarian composer Zoltán Kodály and the Eurhythmics system of harmonious physicality devised by the Swiss musician and educationalist Émile Jacques-Dalcroze. We explored the former activity by observing as best we could strict tempo and toe-to-toe footwork. We embraced the rhythmic vocabulary of the latter by galumphing around pretending to be elephants or by striking voguish poses as trees of unspecified genus. And all the time we gaily twirled or interpretively stomped we remained blissfully unaware that our lithe young bodies were raging physical battlefields between opposing pedagogic forces. At Infant School we gave public displays of country dancing on the lawns of The Limes, a large fête-hosting house with generous gardens that stood in Bedford Road, opposite the Rec. Musical accompaniment came courtesy of a wind-up gramophone operated by the head mistress. Little did we know at the time that we were participating in a process of invented tradition, the same selective revivalism that gave us clan tartans and kilts.

The cut-glass accents of those Music and Movement radio presenters, Marjorie Eele and Rachel Percival, are as indelibly stamped upon the brains of a generation as the equally shrill enunciators who presented *Andy Pandy* or *Listen with Mother*. Our free-style M&M was occasionally supplemented by the *Listen, Move and Dance* series of LPs that HMV released between 1962 and 1966. Arranged by Vera Gray and performed by Desmond Briscoe and Daphne Oram, two of the pioneering spirits behind the BBC Radiophonic Workshop, the LPs featured Gray's short adaptations of modern orchestral pieces as well as Briscoe and Oram's musique concrète creations. As children we were well-disposed towards this kind of avant-gardery, and the atonal sound sculptures produced by Briscoe, Oram and their exploratory ilk met with little resistance. Prejudice against such abstractions was and remains an adult prerogative. In this respect we grow out of, not into, our bodies, and we soon lose touch with the intuitive experimentalism of our childhood physiology.

I don't ever remember listening to the radio when we lived in that small cottage on the Great North Road. There must have been one somewhere – disguised as furniture, no doubt – but my entertainment came predominantly from the reassuring monochrome glow of the TV. All that changed when we moved to our brand-new council house. From 1962, my Saturday mornings fell into a regular pattern: breakfast at the table, *Children's Favourites* on the wireless, Saturday morning pictures at the Victory Cinema. Suddenly the radio, a teak-cased Bush radiogram that sat in the corner of the living-room, seemed to be on whenever the TV wasn't. *Children's Favourites*, a weekly request show, went out on the Light Programme between nine and ten on Saturday mornings and served up an amazingly varied diet of music. By the time I started listening to it, the show was way past its Nelly the Elephant prime. The long-serving presenter Derek "Uncle Mac" McCulloch was nearing the end of his reign, and the last fortified buttresses of Reith's kingdom were looking tired and tarnished. An instructive element was still evident in much of what was aired on *Children's Favourites* – classical music and traditional folk songs were played, in accordance with Sir William Haley's idea of the listening community as "a broadly based cultural pyramid slowly aspiring upwards" – but the foundations of that cultural pyramid were now largely bolstered by pop music. The days when a stentorian listening committee could agonize over whether a flea was a suitable subject for a song, or a producer could be issued with a reprimand after an inappropriate swing version of The Eton Boat Song was broadcast on the show (both actual examples taken from the BBC written archive), were fast coming to an end.

A children's song in the post-war years meant *How Much Is that Doggy in the Window, Three Billy Goats Gruff* and *The Teddy Bears' Picnic*. By the early 1960s it was just as likely to be a light-hearted novelty item sung by a well-known family entertainer or comedian. Items like *Any Old Iron* by Peter Sellers, *Hole in the Ground* and *Right Said Fred* by Bernard Cribbins, *Please, Mr Custer* and *My Boomerang Won't Come Back* by Charlie Drake, *Don't Jump Off the Roof Dad* by Tommy Cooper, *When You Come to the End of a Lollipop* by Max Bygraves and *My Brother* by Terry Scott were the staple diet of my childhood. These and many others like them – in turn amusing, hilarious, irritating, incomprehensible – were mainstays of the *Children's Favourites* playlist. Terry Scott's 1962 playground hit *My Brother* was a classic case of an innuendo-laden song escaping the censor's clutch. It was one of the most subversive items ever played on Children's Favourites, alluding as it did to genital graffiti, and concluding with a set-piece which suggested that the incorrigible kid brother has recently been holding a piece of shit in his hand. With hindsight I have come to realise that *Children's Favourites* was one of the most bizarrely eclectic shows I have ever listened to on the radio. Its regular ensemble of oddities, grotesques, incompetents and malcontents provided the perfect accompaniment to the dysfunctional cast of characters I encountered in my comics and the cartoons I watched on telly.

In amongst all the novelty pop and pre-teen miscellany I hear the authoritative voice of my Dad, pronouncing "This is proper music, boy" from behind his Saturday morning sports pages. He meant Ray Charles's *Hit the Road Jack*, Mel Tormé's *Comin' Home Baby* – stuff like that. He was right, of course, as I later came to appreciate. It's all part of the curse of having a hip dad. What amazes me now is that *Children's Favourites* played Ray Charles and Mel Tormé at all, but play them it did. Where else would I have heard barnstorming gospel-tinged R&B and sophisticated syncopated swing ballads at eight years old?

My pop year zero being when it was, a time when instrumentals still featured heavily in the pop charts, meant that initially at least beat music manifested itself primarily as moodscape. In the beginning was not the word but the wordless twang. Instrumentals were a self-contained language, and the emotions they evoked were only ever arbitrarily related to their titles. I still have as much trouble associating a Shadows tune with its title as I do remembering that the Magritte painting with the apple in front of the face is called *The Son of Man*. *Children's Favourites* played an abundance of instrumentals. The Shadows, the Tornados, the Spotnicks – these were my big beat inventory. This was also where I first heard surf instrumentals – before I even knew what surf was. Records like *Wipe Out* by the Surfaris, *Walk Don't Run* by the Ventures, *Pipeline* by the Chantays and *Let There Be Drums* by Sandy Nelson moulded my audiosphere. I didn't even know what half of these records were called until I later heard them played as oldies on the pirate stations. (At a time when rock'n'roll culture was less than a decade old, an "oldie" in 1966 could be something from the previous year.)

Despite the BBC's long-standing distaste for the "Americanisation" of British culture, *Children's Favourites* represented a form of benign détente. This was where I first heard Alan Sherman's *Hello Muddah, Hello Fadduh*. As with most American items at the time, I didn't get much of the slang or any of the parodic references. I didn't know it was based on the melody of Ponchielli's *Dance of The Hours*, I just heard a loud American shouting at me about how bad Summer Camp was. (I didn't know what Summer Camp was either.) Sherman was part of that great wave of bellowing Americana that sound-tracked my early sixties, just another rasping foghorn alongside Stubby Kaye and Tubby Kaye (who for a long time I conflated into one big shouty entertainer), and all the other perspiring fatsos who filled my TV screen and radio. The King of Brash was Stan Freberg. *Children's Favourites* played *Yellow Rose of Texas* and *Battle Hymn of the Republic*, both in their conventional march-time arrangements and Freberg's crazed anarchic variations. They also played his early 1950s spy spoof *Little Blue Riding Hood* with its cod Micky Spillane argot and its censor-defying "Is that a subpoena in your pocket?".

Some of these American records – *Beep Beep* by the Playmates for instance – were simultaneously creepy and droll. The BBC of course played the advertising-free version with the references to Cadillacs and Nash Ramblers replaced by limousines and bubble cars. Children's Favourites also played moody noir theme tunes like Nelson Riddle's *Route 66* long before I knew what moody noir was, but in playing them it ensured that I eventually did. The programme also regularly aired *Take Five* by Dave Brubeck long before I knew what jazz was. I have a clear memory of hearing *Take Five* on Children's Favourites during the blizzardy winter of 1962/63. I am standing between the dining-room table and the radiogram, riveted to the spot by the lengthy duet between Dave Brubeck's repeated piano figure and Joe Morello's percussion. The dialogue begins around the 1:50 mark and ends at 4:20 with the reintroduction of the main theme. I couldn't distinguish a crochet from a quaver at the time. What I do remember is being utterly beguiled by the fact that something went on for that long in the middle of a record. What makes this recollection even more intoxicating is that I can remember remembering that this was not the first time I had heard *Take Five*. There is a distinct element of "Oh, this is the record with that long bit in the middle" about the evocation.

The theme tune to *Children's Favourites* was the brisk, ebullient *Puffin' Billy* by the Melodi Light Orchestra. Also featured regularly was the grandiose *Coronation Scot* by Vivian Ellis, originally recorded as library music, and lovingly quoted by The Electric Light Orchestra at the end of their 1972 debut single 10538 Overture. *Children's Favourites* also played Nancy Whiskey's version of *Freight Train* and the exuberant *The Runaway Train* by the not-so-exuberant Liverpudlian Bing Crosby soundalike Michael Holiday, who died of a drug overdose in 1963 long before his much-loved children's song hit the buffers. Altogether more surreal was *(The Railroad Comes through) The Middle of the House* by Rosemary Clooney, a record which terrified me as a kid. Clooney's thigh-slapping do-si-do delivery is markedly at odds with the pay-off at the end of the gruesome verses where unwelcome bill collectors and relatives are lured into mutilation. Clooney's hale and hearty manner was placid compared with some of the shrieking harridans that Children's Favourites introduced me to. These female counterparts to the Stubby and Tubby school of fairground hucksters were personified on TV by the deranged, perma-mugging Lucille Ball. On *Children's Favourites* the style came braying into my Saturday-morning living-room in the shape of brash show tunes like *Don't Bring Lulu* by Dorothy Provine and *Second Hand Rose* by Barbra Streisand. The undertow of hysteria that runs through these records was compounded by the fact that I rarely had any idea what these people were singing about, or why, or to whom.

That feeling of being sung at, not to, manifested itself frequently on *Children's Favourites*. For every god like Danny Kaye or Anthony Newley there was someone singing songs that were an adult's idea of a child's world. You pick up on these things quickly as a kid. A dim recollection lurks at the perimeter of my memory of an uncle playing me *March of the Mods* by the Joe Loss orchestra. I can remember the boredom I felt as I watched the needle make its way far too slowly towards the centre of the record. Wrongly assuming that I had enjoyed the experience he then put the needle back to the beginning and played it again. *March of the Mods* was a perennial on *Children's Favourites*, as were *Don't Let the Rain Come Down* by Ronnie Hilton, *Down Came the Rain* by Mitch Murray, *James (Hold the Ladder Steady)* by Carol Deene, songs that were incomprehensible and annoying in the same way that whole portions of the adult world were incomprehensible and annoying.

In order to check the reliability of these memories I called up a selection of programmes as broadcast from the BBC Written Archive. I looked at playlists from the summer of 1962, when I first started listening to the show, through to February 1964 when our Saturday morning picture palace closed down. There they all were just as I remembered them. There were the surf instrumentals. There was *Bo Diddley* by Buddy Holly. I had no idea that Buddy Holly was dead at the time, and for a while assumed that Bo Diddley sang a song called Buddy Holly to return the favour. Russ Conway, Bert Weedon and Max Bygraves were ubiquitous, as was Chubby Checker's *Let's Twist Again*. I was an enthusiastic little twister and a vigorous advocate of the short-lived craze. In this and indeed in all other matters related to dance, Chubby Checker was for all too brief a period my mentor and guide.

Similarly instructive was *Speedy Gonzales* by Pat Boone. My entire knowledge of Mexico at this time was derived from that record and from the Hanna Barbera cartoon character El Kabong, the Masked Avenger/Zorro-style alter ego of Quick Draw McGraw and a seminal influence on my frequent attempts to maim my sister by bringing a toy plastic guitar down hard upon her head while shouting "El Kabong!" in the style of my hero.

Perry Como rather than Bing Crosby or Frank Sinatra was the *Children's Favourites* adult crooner of choice, although Frank Sinatra's High Hopes did get an occasional airing. *I Feel Pretty* from West Side Story was a hardy perennial, as were selections from The Wizard of Oz, South Pacific and Sound of Music. There was a smattering of classical music: repertoire staples like Handel's *Water Music* and *Swan Lake*, and light orchestral arrangements of *Sabre Dance* and suchlike. Along with *Take Five* there were nifty big-beat instrumentals like *African Waltz* by Johnny Dankworth and *Baby Elephant Walk* by Henry Mancini. There was also another, altogether more desolate, piece that I will forever associate with the programme, the mournful, elegiac theme from the film *The Legion's Last Patrol* by Ken Thorne and his Orchestra. There were Western themes, *Bonanza, The Big Country, Guns of Navarone.* There were exotic sounds by Arthur Lyman and Martin Denny. And there was a surprising amount of music that conveyed the beckoning allure of adult sensuality: *Casanova and Romeo* by Petula Clark, Eartha Kitt's *I'm Just an Old Fashioned Girl* etc. When Rosemary Clooney wasn't knocking through the wallpaper-thin fabric of my psyche with her terrifying *Railroad*, she was enticing me, with the inducement of candy, to *Come On-A My House.*

Items I had happily forgotten until I saw them playlisted included *A Scottish Soldier* by Andy Stewart and the cloying original-cast recording of *Mums and Dads* from Lionel Bart's Blitz! With deference to that cultural pyramid slowly aspiring upwards there was an abundance of "trad. arr." folk. *Highland Wedding* (heel to heel and toe to toe) was played in an arrangement by Johnny "Z Cars" Keating. (The much-played *Z Cars* theme itself was based on an old Liverpudlian playground rhyme *Johnny Todd.*) Other folkish fare included *Soldier Soldier Won't You Marry Me* by Jimmie Rodgers, *John Henry* by Harry Belafonte, and *I Know an Old Lady* and *Ugly Bug Ball* by the House Un-American Activities Committee-appeasing Burl Ives. There was murder ballad *Tom Dooley* by the Kingston Trio, and the teasingly ambiguous *Puff, the Magic Dragon* by Peter, Paul and Mary – which would subsequently be cited as an inducement to drug-taking. Most of the folksy *Green Green/Walk Right In* stuff washed right over me at the time, but *Three Wheels on My Wagon* by the New Christy Minstrels irritated me in a way that only eight-year-olds can be irritated. (Who knew then that the group's singer Barry McGuire would be growling portentously within a couple of years about *The Eve of Destruction*?) What was it about *Three Wheels on My Wagon* that irked me? Was it an intuitive resistance to enforced singalong, all that "Green grow the rushes-oh", Scout-hut jamboree stuff? Was it the first stirrings of discriminatory faculties and the onset of taste? Was it simply the fact that hootenannys and "Higgety, haggity, hoggety, high" were alien to my experience and my vernacular? But so too were weasels that went pop and bubble cars that couldn't get out of second gear, and I rooted enthusiastically enough for them, so where did this first flowering of recalcitrance spring from and why did it manifest itself in the way that it did, by lining up the communal campfire bonhomie of folk music in its cross hairs like so many green bottles? Was it a sense that I was being preached to? Probably not. Children are preached at all the time. Perhaps it was just a growing awareness that this was not my noise, and not my noise in the same way that so many other adult-sanctioned scenarios were not my noise. The much-played *Those Lazy-Crazy-Hazy Days of Summer* by Nat King Cole, *The Alley Cat Song* by David Thorne, for instance.

Somewhere in amongst all the choreographed idiocy and the dress rehearsals for an adulthood way beyond childhood comprehension, a musical universe was being born without me realising. You see all the unrealities lined up before you and you select your unreal. And the unreal I chose and which chose me was pop. Gradually its noise begins to separate itself from the other noise, and above all I have *Children's Favourites* to thank for this formative experience. It was the alphabet blocks of my musical education. By the end of 1963 the show was just as likely to feature *The Hippy Hippy Shake* as *Mr Froggie Went A'Courtin'*. Merseybeat sat like a Trojan Horse outside the compound, and once it was invited in it displaced everything else and gave me a whole new beat lexicon to learn. But those initial building blocks, so readily discarded, are never truly set aside. They remain part of a continuum, part of an evolution, part of me. *Children's Favourites* imposed on me a broader spectrum of music than anything I would have sought out for myself at eight. For years I've paid lip service to the idea that I was barely out of *Alice in Wonderland* and *Wind in the Willows* before psychedelic pop was upon me. But perhaps more pertinent is the fact that thanks to *Children's Favourites* I went from *My Brother* and *Any Old Iron* to *Happy Jack* and *I'm a Boy* in barely a hopscotch skip and jump.

The song spell cast itself in all kinds of other worldly ways. In the long-ago land where I once lived, songs were recitations that turned into incantations. They came fashioned in fa-la-lees and fol-de-rols, in Thumbelinas and Poppa-Piccolinos. They said "Come fish, bite fish", and told me "Shrimp boats is a-comin' ". They lulled strange cadences in unfamiliar accents. They sparked the imagination and shaped a child's world in ways that were not always intended. No wonder some of us turned out the way we did. *Children's Favourites* fed us *Sparky's Magic Piano* and *The Laughing Policeman* by Charles Penrose. It gave us Elton Hayes' interpretation of Edward Lear's *The Owl and the Pussycat*, sung with inflections that bear more than a passing resemblance to those later adopted by Ivor Cutler. It gave us *That Noise* by Anthony Newley, the blueprint for everything that David Bowie thought worth pursuing at one time. It gave us the bewitching, hypnotic *Inchworm* by Danny Kaye, which was, as it turned out, just one way among many of measuring the marigolds.

VENUS IN BLUE JEANS

Vic the flick lived at the bottom of our road. His front garden was always full of stock cars which he raced every Sunday at Brafield stadium in Northamptonshire. In the evening they came back battered and mangled, and on Monday Vic and his mates would gather to assess the damage. As the week went on the cars would assume their shape again. Mended and welded. Bumpers restored. New panels bolted. Numbers freshly painted on the side. "Drive on Discol" emblazoned on the bonnet. The following Sunday the cars would disappear, and the process would begin all over again.

In the great culture war of the early 1960s Albion Sands was a Rocker town. You saw plenty of motorbikes, oilskins and leathers, but not a trace of a Vespa. There were Teddy Boy remnants in all their finery but never a hint of Italian chic. In my mind's eye I see Vic with the same sideburns and teased-up quiff as his mates. However, a little archive research reveals him to have been a bit of a John Osborne. Same rounded oval face, same quietly confident smirk, the derisive devil may care gaze of a man who regularly rolled over at high speed on hot shale and shingle while strapped inside a welded metal box and protected by little more than a white boiler-suit. Vic, it transpires, was a well-respected rider on the circuit, racing competitively from 1962 to 1969. He drove and crashed his quintet of souped-up 1930s Fiat-bodied Y-type Fords from Walthamstow and Harringay to Plymouth and St Austell. He spent the decade tinkering with aquaplane heads and close-ratio Wooler gearboxes. The vernacular of the petrolhead was quite unknown to me then, and remains equally impenetrable to me now. All I know is that when Vic revved the cars up in his front garden they sounded like rockets taking off.

Across the road from Vic's was a row of derelict cottages that we used to play in until they knocked them down, and next to the row of cottages was Mrs Cook's shop. Mrs Cook and her assistant liked to chat with their customers, and some days I waited so long to be served that I used to memorise all the brand names to relieve the boredom. I can still recite the peas on the second shelf – Farrow's, Clark's, Morton's, Batchelors – and the associations that went with them. Farrow's was the cartoon bird in the television advert pecking the earth and a voiceover saying: "Sorry, mate, you're too late. The best peas went to Farrow's." Clark's was the Dave Clark Five with the grinning drummer and the stomping beat. Morton was a football team in Scotland. Bachelors was "Son, you'll be a bachelor boy", a record I initially associated with those peas on the second shelf rather than Cliff's marital status. I remember asking someone's Mum once what a "bachelor boy" was. I was up the High Street after school. The record must have been playing on a shop radio. As far as I could tell from the lyrics a bachelor had something to do with turtledoves, but the woman told me it was someone who hadn't married.

Cliff's 1962 hit and those tinned peas on a corner-shop shelf formed one of my earliest literary convergences, one of the first times I remember making a conscious connection between a pop lyric and a lexicon that might lie outside that lyric. On that occasion it didn't get any further than peas, and the facility remained undeveloped for years. I didn't have taste then. There was no good or bad or degrees of greatness. I had very little use for the adjectival either. "Brilliant," "smashing" and a dash of Norman Vaughan's "swinging, dodgy, doubtful" did the job for me pretty much until I sat the 11+. Nouns were where it was at. I used to love Bobby Vee's *The Night Has a Thousand Eyes* simply for the imagery: the night, the stars, the eyes. That was how my mind worked then. Joining the dots like the constellations in the sky to form bigger patterns until eventually they formed me.

Slowly music began to choreograph my life. There was a record by the Four Lads called *Standing on the Corner (Watching All the Girls Go By)*. It came out in 1956 long before I was conscious of music, but it was still played regularly on the radio in the pre-beat-group early sixties. I'd never actually seen men standing on corners watching girls go by, but the song shaped my perception of what that might entail. It rendered in fantasy form a world that was as real to me as any other real that was available at that time. I might well have seen the song acted out on some early pop show, *6.5 Special* perhaps, which launched in February 1957, and which Mum reliably informed me I used to sway away to the minute its "Over the points, over the points" theme tune commenced. If it wasn't *6.5 Special* it could have been any one of a number of light-entertainment programs which I would have seen on our big old black-and-white set. Doubtless it would have involved four-part formation whistling, hats worn at jaunty angles, cheeky grins and stage-set lamp posts, which "men" – aged anywhere between 18 and 48 – swung and clung to as they dramatised their chirpy tableau. Gradually this kind of masque play consolidates itself in a child's mind and codifies how a life might be lived, or at least how an impression of life might be acted out. This was the nature of my earliest exposure to music. Records were two-and-a-half-minute choreographed fictions. It wasn't necessary for me to have seen someone acting out, say, the words to *Walk On By*, her walking down the street and starting to cry "each time we meet". It was enough just to know that a record existed where that happened. The sentiment existed purely in song form and was self-contained, a theatrical fabrication. I don't ever remember trying to "relate" to lyrics when I was young. I took the myth world of pop purely on trust, as a magic other place. That was empathy enough for me.

Walking back to Junior School after dinner. At the entrance to Dog Shit Alley my path was blocked by a couple snogging. They were there every day for what seemed like weeks. A lunchbreak liaison. Leaning against a high brick wall. An invisible sign saying: "Grown-ups: Do not disturb." Although their intimidating physical presence barred me from the alley, I was fascinated by them. She smothered in his embrace. He pressed into her, all muscularity and animal grace. Both of them in blue jeans. Her hair hid her face. Their legs moved in motion. Mark Wynter's song *Venus In Blue Jeans* was in the Top Ten at the time, and there was Venus in my alley, heavy petting in broad daylight, acting out for real the earth angel desires that the song could only hint at.

Walking to school one winter's morning I stopped and watched for a while as Mr Feltwell auctioned off his nursery land. The greenhouses were dismantled and stacked up on lorries, leaving the outline of their foundations in the soil. All the machinery of labour was transported a short distance across to the other side of the A1, where Mr Feltwell resumed his business on a much larger plot. Gardeners gathered in early-morning droves and bought items on the nod. All that remained by the time I walked home from school at half past three were the unsold lots: rusty tools, bundles of canes tied up with twine, a few cracked and chipped flower pots. Descriptions written in smudged ink on beige tickets flapping in the chill wind of a January afternoon.

Houses were to be built on the vacated land, but for the entirety of my youth no-one ever did come and build them. The cratered undulations and heaped-up soil left by the removal gangs gradually weathered into a new uncultivated landscape. Tufts turned to mounds, thistles turned to thickets, brambles wove new enclosures, and the weeds grew wild and wavy. Every summer the field ripened, bolted and burst; thistledown flew and reseeded where it settled. Dandelion fluff tumbled in a blur of whiteness, drifting over tangled knots of nettles. After dark, courting couples discreetly bedded down in the newly unattended pasture, flattening the meadow grass in the hillocks and hollows. Many were felt well in Feltwell's. The sheds and outbuildings crumbled, beams grew unsafe to climb on, and were climbed on. Shards of greenhouse glass cracked underfoot, growing more muffled as neglect inched ever upwards year-on-year and nature reclaimed the place.

The perimeter fence that ringed the field came away slat by loosened slat. Soon it was more gap than slat, until eventually it was all gap and unenclosed terrain. And still no one came to build. One day, in a small corner that led from Church Path into Dog Shit Alley, I decided to walk a short cut. I strayed from the footpath and trampled through the tall grass just to cut seconds from a journey. There was nothing to do with those seconds I would save but I saved them anyway, fashioning the grass into the pattern of my footfall. In their book *Edgelands: Journeys into England's True Wilderness*, Paul Farley and Michael Symmons Roberts called such impromptu diversions "desire paths". The Americanisation of the term is "desire trails". These new trajectories, the authors point out, can be seen everywhere that wildness reigns. "A record of collective short cuttings", they evolve in opposition to prescribed routes and planners' best intentions. Although astute in their recognition of the random patterns of the uncharted, the authors are incorrect in one small detail. "Nobody decides to make a desire path," they maintain. I did. Motivated by little more than the boredom of regular routine, I worked on mine every day. In time, as the grass flattened and the route widened, more people followed my shortcut until gradually evidence of a clear trodden track curved across that corner of the field. Old ladies on bicycles began bicycling through it. Soon it was wide enough for prams and pushchairs to be pushed through it as everyone else began saving seconds that didn't need saving. But my feet had been there first. For as long as Feltwell's field stood empty, everyone trod a path that I had started.

POP LIFE

At the height of Beatlemania, Cook's shop sold penny liquorice, and gave away a free Beatles gemstone ring with every stick. We spent our pocket money pennies until our fingers were full. All us rough boys preening like girls with jewellery gleaming on every Ringo'd finger. Genuine three-carat plastic.

We all spoke fluent Bedfordshire, a blend of London and Norfolk. We mangled vowels, elongated syllables and chewed words into misshapes; unnecessary consonants we did away with entirely. "Didn't" was pronounced "dint". "And all" was "an' all". ("An aarl" if your accent was broad.) A glottal stop the size of a gobstopper put paid to the f and the t in afternoon. "Stop grizzling" meant "Stop crying". "Learn" often came out as "larn", as in: "You won't larn nuffing if you don't pay attention." "Telling" came out "taling", as in: "I'm a-taling you, boy." If food disagreed with you it "give you misery". Until I was ten, I thought the words of the Lord Prayer were: "For Thine is the kingdom, the pa and the glory." That's how "power" was pronounced when two hundred Bedfordshire schoolchildren chanted it in morning Assembly. I reasoned that Pa must be God. Adult Bedfordshire was spoken in tones both warily mordant and airily mournful, as if with a sob in the voice. Many a response began with a ponderous ruminating "w-e-l-l," with a rise and fall in the inflection. Grandad regularly sent me down the garden to get "grunsil" for his cage birds, and it was only years later when I read D.H. Lawrence (or it might have been Thomas Hardy) that I realised the yellow-headed weed was actually called groundsel. Grandad said "arl" for "oil", "smook" for "smoke" and "chimley" for "chimney". The past tense of snow was "snew". When he imitated a posh person he did so in the tones of Stanley Holloway. Grandma used "cockalorum" to describe someone who was full of their own self-importance. She called you a "daft appath" if you were being a daft appath, and told you not to talk "sorft" if you were talking sorft. By 1964, Mum had become our street's resident Gratton's catalogue rep to earn a little of what used to be called "pin money". One day a neighbour sent her daughter Pauline round to pay her weekly subs. She was intercepted by our dog Beauty in the back yard. We were alerted by Pauline's cries of: "She's licking me be-oind!" So comical was her plea, so exaggerated were her vowels even by rustic standards that Mum was still repeating the phrase in jest years later. My own Bedfordshire accent has been all but eradicated. I can still get two syllables out of the word oil (oy-ell) when I lapse, but accents get travelled and educated out of you, so there's barely a trace now of the boy who used to say "the pa and the glory".

I reasoned that Jimmy Dunn's dad must be a spy. I had no evidence for this other than the fact that he wore a beret. "There goes Mr Moonstrike," I would say as he pedalled off down the road on his rusty bike, off on some secret mission no doubt. There was a drama on the BBC at the time called *Moonstrike*, and some of the actors in that wore berets too, so it all added up. Much of the series was filmed at the disused Aerodrome just up the road at Tempsford where several of the old Nissen huts and much of the runway was still intact when I was a kid. During the Second World War, special-duties squadrons were based there, and it was from Tempsford that many of the secret night missions were flown into occupied Europe. Agents and their supplies were parachuted in under cover of darkness. It was all top secret, and it all happened two miles from where I lived. Even people who worked at the Aerodrome didn't know the full extent of the espionage, and the hidden history of this secret war within a war is still only slowly being revealed. Between February and August 1963, the *Moonstrike* TV series offered an action-packed version of these clandestine events in 27 weekly parts. I remember very little of the series now, just one episode where the Germans lined up some women and children against a wall. A Mum hugged her child and the child turned and faced the camera, looking right through the lens and into our living-room. Then you heard the sound of gunfire. "They did that," said Mum, who could be economical with words when she needed to be.

Me and the Ellery twins, Peter and Paul, were walking past the Infant School, the year after we left. It was playtime, and a girl came to the railings and said: "You pretend to be the Beatles and we'll chase you." So we went in through the main gates and ran around the playground with half the school screaming and running after us while we pretended to be the Fab Four. Eventually a teacher came out to see what all the commotion was about. "You don't go to this school anymore," she said politely as she led us back to the gate.

John Waller's Dad started to take me and John to see Bedford Town play their Southern League football on Saturdays. They played at the Eyrie and were nicknamed the Eagles. We used to stand there in the fog which was everywhere that winter, glistening on hats, scarves and mittens. On Tuesdays I used to look in the Beds Courier for the match report. There would usually be a photo and a bland caption. Players suspended in mid-air, heads touching, shirts caked in mud. I used to try and spot myself among the spectators shrouded in the misted background.

Gary Rose was my pop oracle. He seemed to know the Top 30 off by heart and would recite chart positions to me as we walked to school on Tuesday mornings. "*House of the Rising Sun* has come straight in at Number Six," he would say. The next week he would say: "*House of the Rising Sun* has gone to the top of the Hit Parade." Gary knew the rules for everything, and when he didn't know the rules he just made some up. "They're not chisels. They're semi-chisels," he would say, pointing at shoes and evaluating their degree of pointiness. Gary's scale went: winkle-pickers, semi-winkle-pickers, chisels, semi-chisels, semi-semi-chisels. "There's no such thing as semi-semi-chisels," I argued. Gary maintained that there was. He would loom in and out of my face all the way to school, excitedly babbling his favourite songs. "*Hubble Bubble Toil and Trouble*," he would go and over again, making sure you knew there was a record that went like that. "Have you heard *Google Eye*?" he asked. "It goes: 'Google eye, google eye, google eye, google eye'."

It simply hadn't occurred to me that Gary was getting his Hit Parade information from the Daily Mirror. To me he was a conduit for some higher power, the fount of all pop wisdom. I only glanced at the sports pages. I hadn't thought to look further inside the paper, but inspired by Gary I did, and the chart became my oracle too. They serve now as a memory grid, as powerfully evocative as any day-to-day diary would have been, had I been the kind of person who might keep a diary. I can gaze at a random Top 30 from March 1964, say, or July 1969, and can tell you exactly what I was doing. What I was doing was of little consequence, but the records root me to a time and place, and the memories have endured. It's precisely because

I was doing so little of consequence that they have endured. My early life is like one of those TV cartoons I used to watch, *Top Cat* or *Snagglepuss*, where you see the moving backdrop going round on a loop: the same buildings, the same flora, fauna and firehose. All that changed was the soundtrack, and that was updated virtually on a daily basis. Everything else is stasis and me basking in the aural splendour of each new listening experience, lost in the visceral moment where one minute a record didn't exist and three minutes later you couldn't imagine a time when it hadn't existed. What do certain records remind me of? They remind me of hearing that certain record. The memories are entirely self-contained. Just a time, a place, a piece of music and the connectivity between the three.

What was I doing when President Kennedy died? I was waiting for Harry Worth to start on the telly, but a newsreader came on instead. I thought for a moment that he would just make an announcement and they'd show Harry Worth as usual, but as the clock ticked ever closer to 7.35 it began to dawn on me that the programme wasn't going start on time, perhaps wasn't going to start at all. I can shrink the entire time-frame of that world-changing event to my anxiety-measured minutes as a newsreader continued talking gravely and the adults in the room looked on with concern. "He looks like he's been crying," said Mum, and for years I assumed that the newsreader must have been Robert Dougall, who with those doleful baggy eyes usually did look like he had been sobbing. But in Dougall's autobiography *In and Out of the Box*, he makes it clear that he was due to receive a television award at the Dorchester that night, and the newsreader who denied me my weekly appointment with Harry Worth was John Roberts.

London Cousin sent some hand-me-down T shirts. One had a big brown "G" on it and a side strip showing men swinging golf clubs with words written in explosion bubbles: "Swing! Tee! Iron! Drive!" The other T shirt had a big blue "B" for Bowling. I understood more of the words on the golf one but I preferred the B for Bowling one.

Brian Dylan was tall and wiry and spoke fluent Hanna Barbera. "Like, what's the time, Boo-Boo?", he would say, and someone would have to run in and see what the time was. "Oh, my toe bone!", he would exclaim theatrically when the cricket ball landed on his foot, even when it didn't hurt and he was just saying it to get a laugh. When his Mum called him for his tea he would go, "Uh, exit stage right," and execute a Snagglepuss cartoon turn. I worshipped him in the way that nine-year-olds often worship 13-year-olds. Brian's parents were elderly and formal compared with everybody else's, and we weren't ever allowed in his house, but one day I showed an interest in the groups he kept talking about, so he invited me into the inner sanctum. He had pop-star posters on his bedroom wall, the Swinging Blue Jeans, the Hollies etc. On a bedside table, in photo frames shaped like Love Hearts, were pictures of the Merseybeats and the Searchers. "They're for girls really, but boys can have them too," he explained. "You have to send off tea coupons."

– Are you a Mod or a Rocker?"

I was up the Rec, dangling upside down from the roundabout bars, monkey-legged, bat-winged.
– Are you a Mod or a Rocker?"

More insistent this time. It was the older boys. The boys who carried knives and took stuff off you if you didn't learn to keep your mouth shut when you found stuff. They looked menacing, circling the roundabout as my head trailed inches from the cinders. They made me sit upright and threatened to push me round so fast I'd fall off. This didn't scare me but I didn't dare tell them that. They would only find some other punishment. You learn that as well.

– Are you a Mod or a Rocker?"
Or a mocker. Or a mid. Or a semi-mid.

They looked at my B for Bowling T shirt.
– You must be a Mod. Get him.

They wore blue jeans. They were Rockers. They told you who they were. Then they told you who you were. I became me by default in the hot playground sun, gripping the bars with the roundabout whirling faster and their faces all blurring into one big ugly Rocker.

Mum bought a Beatles tea tray. It went on the Flatley clothes drier between the cooker and the sink. I don't ever remember it being used as a tea tray. We just stood the kettle on it. It steamed away and boiled over onto the tray every day. And with the constant scraping and the hard-water lime scale corroding, the image of the Beatles slowly, slowly flaked away. A scratchy circle of silver spread outwards from the centre, leaving less of the Fab Four as time went by until eventually there was just some of John's hair, Paul's chin and George's teeth. Most of Ringo survived.

Outside the Eyrie after the football. An overcast Saturday. A man with a transistor radio playing *Walk On By*. Looking at the man and the radio as he walked by. The man. The radio. The walking by. The space between us. Him walking by as the radio played *Walk On By*. And it was all about the moment and the space between moments. And it all connected in that perfect moment with everything in harmony and the radio playing *Walk On By*.

Or it could have been *My Guy*.

DISCOTHEQUE

We sang rounds in class. Frerer jacker. Door may voo. We sang Hey-ho here we go. Donkey riding. Donkey riding. Michael Finnegin. Chinnegin. Beginnegin. And I play the piccolo. Picca-picca-piccolo. We learned descant and harmony but what I liked best was the hymns. Singing them in prayers. Singing them in the school choir. I liked the shapes they made and the imagery they evoked. *As with Gladness Men of Old. From All that Dwell below the Skies. Immortal Invisible God Only Wise. The Head that Once Was Crowned with Thorns. Who Would True Valour See. One Here Will Constant Be. The Tall Trees in the Greenwood. The Meadows where We Play. There Is a Green Hill Far Away*. (Like D.H. Lawrence in his essay *Hymns in a Man's Life*, I dreamed a green hill in my head.) I liked the marching hymns, the Crusade hymns, the mission hymns, the battle hymns. *Oft in Danger. Oft in Woe. Ride On, Ride On in Majesty. When a Knight Won his Spurs. Onward Christian Soldiers*. And the ones where you could hold a long note with a lungful of breath. Glor-or-or-or-or-or-oria. Hosanna in Exchelsea.

There had to be a minute's silence for Winston Churchill at all the football matches. A minute is a long time to a boy, but he bows his head all the same. Everyone was quiet apart from the coughing. In the Sunday paper it said that a woman shouted out "What about the war widows?" and was led away by a policeman. I think it was at Everton.

Straight after school, up to Ted Weston's for a haircut. It's getting on for four o'clock and the wireless plays *Volare, I'm Forever Blowing Bubbles,*

Alexander's Ragtime Band, and that one about the fox going to town-o. When the *Music While You Work* dance orchestra plays them they all seem to have identical arrangements and all sound the same. Three old men are waiting for a haircut. They communicate in mumbles, grumbles and bulldog growls. They discuss the racing results from Kempton, Plumpton, Brampton. Big hand stuck at three. Little hand stuck at fifty-nine. Weather-beaten faces scowl at you through a Woodbine fog. All waiting to hear who came second at 100 to 8 in the 3:45. Now the wireless plays *The Camptown Ladies Sing this Song Doo-dah Doo-dah*. They sing it like they do on the *Black and White Minstrel Show*. Looming up at you from the front of the screen, smiling through big teeth.

The ubiquitous sound of trad jazz and BBC dance orchestras was the bane of my childhood. Banjos plunking. Brass blaring. Pizzicato strings plucking. The old men and their Woodbines. The waiting. The boredom, the awful music. It all merges in the fug of a late afternoon as you await your ritual shearing. All those light-entertainment grotesques flash before your eyes in a travesty of postures. Ted Ray and his tight-lipped grimace and the joke is never on him. Reg Varney at the old Joanna, all elbows and arms, wiping greasy hanks of hair from his forehead. Dickie Henderson, who looks like my London uncle and has the same superior air, that way of imparting adult information that is only ever inadvertently for your ears. And the grinning never stops. The warding-off emptiness grin. The this-instead-of-sincerity grin. The showbiz grin. Even when they're on the wireless you can still hear them grinning.

The old men continue to talk in mumbles and grumbles. I sit patiently with a comic in my lap and wait my turn. A selection of reading material fans out on a knee-high glass table. *Buster. Tiger. TV21. People's Friend. Reader's Digest. Horse and Hound*. Some of the magazines were here when I came six weeks ago and will still be here when I return again in six weeks time. Flick. Charlie Peace from the olden days. Flick. *Spot the Clue* with Zip Nolan. Flick. Cartoon with man marooned on tiny desert island with frayed trousers, one palm tree and nowhere to sleep. Snip snip. An old man with a few lonely hairs on his scabby head. Snip snip. Ted Weston says: "Anything off the top?" He hasn't got anything on top, just blotchy brown islands on his scalp map. But you don't say this, because you are ten. You just go back to Spotting the Clue with Zip Nolan. Easy. The robber couldn't have forced his way in because the broken glass is outside the window, so it must have been an inside job. Turn to page 24 for the answer. Flick, flick. Correct.

Finally it's my turn and I climb into the chair of doom. Ted roughly tucks me in with an itchy cloth and carries on talking about horse racing while he sets about my hair with a no-nonsense attitude towards contemporary styling. There are two haircuts on offer. "Trim" and "short back and sides" – three if you include the ones in the window, but no-one I know has ever had those hairstyles, they only exist in photographs in barber's shop windows. I ask for "trim" in the hope that I might preserve my forward-combed fringe and the cute wisp of sideburn that is creeping down towards my earlobe, but Ted gives me a short back and sides anyway and sends me on my way with a side-parting plastered in hair oil I didn't ask for. Every six weeks in that chair I surrender any vain hope I might have of looking like the uncropped pop stars I watch on *Top of the Pops*. Staring straight ahead into the mirror I have no choice but to witness the ritual dismantling of my pop dreams. High above my head, mounted in a glass case, sits a stuffed three-foot pike. Directly in front of me on the shelf next to the Vitalis and Brylcreem bottles is a framed portrait of the Ivel River Boys, a six-piece beat group that features Ted's son Dave on guitar. In my mind's eye most of the sextet are cradling saxophones, relics from a time when every beat group seemed to be modelled on Johnny and the Hurricanes. More recently I discover that they only had one sax player (who doubled on clarinet). I also learn belatedly that they played the revolving stages of the Mecca ballroom circuit, supported Monty Sunshine's jazz band, and appeared on the *625* TV show hosted by Jimmy Young. Such was, and probably still is, the nature of small-town fame. Every six weeks or so I stare at the stuffed pike and at that framed portrait of the Ivel River Boys, publicity poised, styled with a glamour I can only imagine as Ted Weston takes me in a headlock and sets about unfashioning me.

One day in the school playground Andrew Hartley, Gerald Jarvis and I decided we would all get a Beatles cut. Despite our trepidation and the subtle connivance involved in getting three Mums to agree to a haircut on the same day Ted seemed remarkably complicit when the time came. He gave us pudding-basin Beatle cuts of a kind and sent us happily on our way, grinning at our sheer luck. What Ted knew full well was that our Mums would send us straight back for a proper cut, which is exactly what happened. I might have got away with it if my knowing Aunt Janice hadn't been there when I got home.
– Oh, look. He's got it in the Beatles style.

I'm not sure Mum would have noticed if Janice hadn't opened her big mouth, or perhaps I do her a disservice. Either way I was sent straight back to Ted's for an immediate de-Beatling. Andrew was already there when I got to the barber's, flicking through the comics, waiting his turn. Only Gerald Jarvis got away with it. The boy least likely. Fatty Jarvis with hair which resembled that worn by Friar Tuck and sat like an abandoned bird nest atop his head. Beatle Jarvis flaunted his Beatle cut for six whole weeks until his next short back and sides.

Help! was on at Waden Regal and all the boys from my road went. When they threw darts at the screen at the beginning of the film I thought someone in the cinema was doing it and there was that brief heart-rate-increasing moment where I thought the cinema was being vandalised. Afterwards we spilled out into the streets, vibed up on sugar, being the Beatles: "You scream and I'll run down here." Only a couple of years earlier we would have shouted our way down the fire escape as we fled Saturday Morning Pictures, acting out our cowboy-film fantasies, but pop stars were the new cowboys now. "Look at me. I'm Mick Jagger!", went Gary. He pouted his lips, clapped at the side of his head, and sang *Little Red Rooster* as the Barron Knights would.

My parents never had enough money to afford proper holidays, but we went out on regular day trips. London was the allure, an hour away on the train. The Science and Natural History Museums, Madame Tussaud's, the Commonwealth Institute, Regent's Park Zoo. I remember Dad pointing out the newly built Snowdon aviary. Although it was mocked by the architectural cognoscenti, Dad admired its architectural ingenuity and spent ages describing it in terms I didn't understand. He never talked down to you when he went into mechanical engineering mode. He expected you to level up. While the Snowdon Aviary was going up, much of the rest of London was coming down. All my memories of those early visits to the capital are dominated by bulldozers, cranes and wrecking balls. The demolition seemed to be occurring the moment we stepped outside of Kings Cross, and for many years I conflated several separate memories into one grand image of the station itself being demolished. I realised much later that what I actually saw was Euston and its splendid Doric arch being reduced to rubble. Amid the new structures of concrete, glass and steel, several bomb sites were pointed out to us from the top decks of buses. Half a house with the rafters showing and the wallpaper peeling. Terrace rows with fenced-off gaps. Spinneys sprouting on wasteland.

Once a year Dad took me to Westminster Hall to the Royal Chrysanthemum Show. Mum sent a note to school excusing my absence, and Dad and I went up on the train and looked at flowers. He was a member of the Royal Chrysanthemum Society then. He rarely exhibited but was keen to go and view the displays of those who had. We would walk round low tables looking at all the flowers, prizes were awarded, rosettes were pinned. And if Dad went and spoke to other men about chrysanthemum stuff I wandered around on my own, or sat on the stairs bored, flicking through chrysanthemum catalogues until he had finished his conversation. A small conference room was set aside for a question-and-answer session with a panel of experts seated behind a long table. There was frequent laughter at jokes I didn't get. At one point, Dad stood up and asked a question, speaking with a formality I didn't recognise. He clasped his hands tightly and said: "If I may call myself a gentleman." Not talking like Dad. The men laughed again at yet another joke I didn't understand.

Afterwards, as we walked the streets, Dad pointed out the people who didn't have a home to go to. It might seem an odd thing to say to your ten-year old son on a day trip to London, but Dad could be like that. He was occasionally sentimental but he was not given to illusion. One time when one of us was being a tell-tale-tit he snapped at us not to be so sneaky. "That's how the Hitler Youth got started," he said. Another time London Uncle was visiting, and while I sat in quiet-behaving boredom the brothers discussed their 1930s childhood. "I remember the rickets and kids going to school with no shoes on their feet," said Dad. "There was none of that," maintained London Uncle. That was the difference between them. One remembered the rickets. One chose not to.

Dad and I walked through a long narrow alley, half in shade, half in light. A flight of stone steps led down to a cellar. An unlit neon sign above said "Discotheque", and I asked Dad what a "Discotheque" was. He said it was a place where people went to drink and dance to music all night. Quiet now in the afternoon. No-one in the alley but us. Shafts of sunlight magnifying the dust. Looking down the steps to where the light doesn't reach and a door is bolted shut. Wondering what goes on in there.

SPREAD IT. SPREAD IT.

I stood behind Sammy Sampson in morning prayers and watched the hair grow down his neck. It spread in spirals and curls, arcing towards his collar. Nine weeks, ten weeks, eleven weeks, I tried to keep count. The longest I'd ever managed was six weeks and five days. As soon as my hair crept over my ears I was sent to Ted Weston's, but Sammy Sampson's continued to circle and loop into a 14th week until finally one morning he came in freshly shaven and shorn.

If I looked over Sammy Sampson's left shoulder I could see the new headmaster, Mr Chubb. Red-veined. Puffy cheeks. He stood in front of the commemorative plaque that said "We Will Remember Them" and said "Let us pray" and we all went: "The pa and the glory, forever and ever, are men."

If I looked over Sammy Sampson's right shoulder I could see the new girl. Two started on the same day. Wendy Hale was tall and ginger-haired. She had a giraffe-like neck and walked with her nose in the air. I immediately connected her with the opening line of that Ivy League song, *Funny How Love Can Be*. The other girl came from the Children's Home and was dark-skinned and made of mystery. "Have you seen the new girl?", everyone asked, and I said "Yes". "Then you must fancy her." "No, you do. You do." And I did. Watching her pout and sing and looking like a gypsy who lived with the witches. Her mouth opened and out poured hymns.

When we returned to school after the summer holidays we were in Mr Garrett's class. On the first day back he took the mickey out of the Byrds. "And who was that one with the ridiculous glasses on *Top of The Pops*?", he said. If I could travel back in time to anywhere in this book, this is the page on which I would land, just to look at the ten-year old me, the boy who stood up, defiant in the face of ridicule, and earnestly defended Roger McGuinn and his cool glasses. Over the years the memory has become dislodged from the song I defended. I always assumed it was *Mr Tambourine Man*, but when I consult the oracle Johnny Rogan I see that *Mr Tambourine Man* was accompanied on *Top of The Pops* by a promotional film. The performance I defended was of *I'll Feel a Whole Lot Better*, which was the Byrds debut *TOTP* appearance in the flesh. I don't think I even knew the singer's name at the time. I just thought his rectangular glasses were the most happening thing I had ever seen.

As a child I used to doodle obsessively. Cowboys in neckerchiefs wearing sheriff and deputy badges. Dick Turpin and Squire Trelawney in tricorn hats with the chunk bitten out Desperate Dan style, and a sign that said "Gone". Sailors in crow's nests and pirates with hooped shirts, eye patch and cutlass. In the front of the football annuals I got for Christmas I drew goalkeepers diving across stripy nets with the crowd going "Saved!". Fascinated, watching Dad shaving on a Saturday morning I went through a phase of drawing men growing beards. Filling faces with dots and more dots until the dots made a beard. But from August 1965 I began to draw pop-star faces, all wearing Roger McGuinn glasses.

Mr Chubb introduced classical music into morning prayers. When we walked into Assembly, music would be playing and a coloured piece of card sellotaped to the wall would tell you the name of the composition. Arranged neatly on a display table outside the Staff Room was a set of books called *Lives of the Composers*. Silhouetted busts adorned the covers. The books were junior introductory guides to the life and work, but I don't remember reading any of them. I preferred them as silhouettes, and shaded their lives in as I pleased. I liked the shapes their names made. Mendelssohn and Haydn and Schubert and Schumann. A family of Strausses and a couple of Bachs. Handel had the longest hair. He could have been in the Pretty Things.

My only previous encounters with classical music had been the light orchestral fare that *Children's Favourites* played, and the Wagner *Tannhäuser* 78 that sat neglected and unplayed among my parents' randomly average record collection. I think I put the needle on it once and barely recognised it as music. It sounded more like people grieving, and I never repeated the exercise. But I liked the music that Mr Chubb chose, and took a keen interest in his explanations. He suggested that Handel's *Water Music* sounded like water. He explained Haydn's major works to us, pointing out the metronome beat of the *Clock Symphony*. He alerted us the musical joke in the *Surprise Symphony* and the toy instruments of the *Toy Symphony*. I owe my initial interest in classical music entirely to Mr Chubb and those morning lectures. I learned how music could be divided into symphonies, suites and concertos, and how with their funny little Köchels and Kirkpatricks, Mozart and Scarlatti had a classificatory system all of their own.

What went in was piecemeal and impressionistic, but it went in all the same. Sometimes the music suggested the composer's name – a mild form of synaesthesia, perhaps, or more than likely just a keen, active imagination. Sibelius sounded like shields clashing, and the opening to his *Symphony Number Two* sounded like the theme to *Dr Finlay's Casebook*. Ravel sounded like the music they used on *Survival,* the nature programme on Anglia TV, whenever a barge drifted through reeds, and sunlight played upon the ripples. Sometimes the music gave off something mournful, but the music on *Noggin the Nog* and *Ivor the Engine* did that too. Vernon Elliott's sombre bursts of bassoon on the Oliver Postgate animations were, I later realised, my introduction to musical melancholia. After Mr Chubb's classical initiation, I began to hear music differently. My palate expanded, and a yearning quality entered my vocabulary which hadn't been there before. I began to hear the same mournful undertow in pop. And all the time I thought about these new things I looked at the new girl till she was the music too.

In the winter of 1965 they opened a new library in the High Street. Eager classmates joined at lunchtime, and I remember feeling envious as they showed me brand-new library cards, wishing that I'd had the initiative to do that. I rushed up there the moment school ended and breathed in the new-place smell of plastic, paint and underlay glue. A children's library section was set off in a side room with tiny chairs and age-appropriate books, but I immediately made for the corner farthest from the counter where the sports section was. Here the shelves were lined with names known mostly to my parent's generation. Jack Brabham. Gordon Richards. Jim Laker. Sam Snead. Lew Hoad.

I was hungry for knowledge, but didn't really know what to do with all that inquisitiveness. The only books we had in the house were seed catalogues and engineering manuals, and I didn't know how to read. That is to say, I knew HOW to read and read very well – what I wasn't familiar with was the rules, patterns and procedures of reading. None of this had ever been set before me. I borrowed books from that newly opened library almost as a novelty and raced through them inattentively, just so I could rush back within a day or two to borrow another one. This was a habit the stern librarian cottoned onto fairly quickly and she began to admonish me whenever I returned one with undue haste. "You can't have read this already," she would say, as I headed once more for the sports section. I worked my way along the shelf of biographies, devouring meaningless facts about age-old endeavours before concluding fairly rapidly that books about sportsmen, even my sporting heroes, were in the main rather dull.

Next to the Library they paved over a meadow and built a row of offices and shops, each of which had live-in flats above the premises. Where the annual fairground had set down the previous summer there was now a babywear shop, a Commissioner for Oaths, a toy shop, a bank – and at the end of the row Hartstone's newsagents, which soon became my alternative library. Mr Hartstone wore a moustache and a shiny blazer, and had something of the yachting club about him. By rural standards he was debonair, and had his moustache been a little longer he would no doubt have waxed and twirled it. All I can remember about Mrs Hartstone is that she had blue stuff on her gums. The liquid oozed through cracks in her teeth and made me feel sick if I stared too long, which I often did, fascinated as I was by whatever dental abnormalities must be going on in her mouth. Hartstone's stocked the latest American comics, DC mostly, with a smattering of Marvel. *Batman. Superman. Justice League of America. Teen Titans. World's Finest. Strange Tales. Captain America. Spiderman. Thor.* They were placed outside on the pavement in a swivel rack, tight by the corner wall, obscured by the window display and conveniently out of sight of the main counter, which stood at the back of the shop. It was dark by half past four, and on winter evenings with the shop lights all on you could see in but they couldn't see out...

mon-el

mxyzptlk   green arrow

brainiac 5   batman   superman

flash   green lantern   captain america   atom   lightning lad

We were hymn-singing in morning prayers when there was a noise two rows in front of me. A stumble, a fall, then a hastily convened huddle of adults and children. When the huddle parted I could see that the witch-eyed girl of mystery had fainted. A couple of teachers helped her from the hall and we continued with our prayers to "the pa and the glory". Afterwards I asked some boys in my class if she was all right. "I don't know and I don't care," one of them said. "She had fleas and if you stood near her she smelled."

– But you all said on the first day that she was a smasher and everyone fancied her.
– Not her, you clot. We meant Wendy Hale.

The giraffe-neck girl. The "there she goes with her nose in the air" girl. A reckoning silence. A penny dropping.

– Eeurgh, you fancy the flea girl. He fancies the flea girl. You must have the fleas. Spread it, spread it. He fancies the flea girl everybody. He fancies the flea girl.

The flea girl never came back.

BOSS RADIO

On a warm June evening at the top of the sand hills, with the big sky spread out before us and the sun slowly sinking in the west, "Judge" Jeffries sat me down beside him and initiated me into the ways of the ether world. I was hanging about on the fringes of the older boys, the much older boys, the ones you rarely spoke to unless spoken to. The ones who only directly addressed you if they wanted you to fetch their ball. I must have shown a precociously eager interest in what was pouring out of Judge's Grundig radio and asked what he was listening to, so he sat me down and explained. Working his way along the medium wave dial from left to right he said "That's Caroline North on 199. Radio Essex is normally there on 222 metres but you can't hear it at night because the signal is too weak. That's Radio England on 227. That's just started up. There's Radio Scotland on 242. You can only get that at night. Caroline South on 259. London on 266. That's Radio 270. Can you hear that? It's very faint. It comes from Yorkshire. Then Radio City. The Tower of Power on 299. That's what I was listening to just now. There's a couple more. Britain Radio on 355. That's a new one too. It's on the same ship as Radio England. And Radio 390. But I don't listen to either of those. They play old-fashioned music like what you hear on the Light Programme."

Judge explained to me that the top of the sand hills was a good spot to pick up radio signals. He told me that medium waves bounced better across water than they did across land and that the reception changed at night because of interference from foreign stations. "Listen to Radio London," he said. Something I would later learn to describe as a heterodyne whistle all but obliterated the Big L signal. "That's coming from Radio Prague, that is." Judge explained how Bedfordshire was a great place to receive the pirate stations – "probably the best spot in the country" – because of its geographical centrality and the flatness of the land.

The morning after my sand hills initiation I went to our Bush Radiogram in the corner of the living-room, and there they all were, just as Judge had described them. There was Radio Essex, where it wasn't the night before. And there on 242 metres, where Radio Scotland had been, was – not quite silence, there was rarely such a thing as silence on the medium wave – but an absence nevertheless, a hush, a marker of where something would grow louder later on. There was something else there too, something that Judge had half-described in technicalities but which I would only grasp later on. It had something to do with the atmospherics, the way certain stations sounded compressed, or echoey, or faint and far away. A kind of ethereal wow and flutter which I later realised was the unique property of the electromagnetic spectrum itself. It seemed to leak into the music and leave its watermark adhered to the melodies.

I must have heard the pirates before 1966, probably several times unknowingly, but at that time I wasn't attuned to the source of things in an acquisitive way. Television still provided my primary music input. *Top of the Pops. Ready Steady Go. Thank Your Lucky Stars.* The usual shows. But then one teatime in January 1966 I was watching the local news and they showed footage of the Radio Caroline South ship, which had run aground in stormy weather and was now sitting beached and breached on the Frinton-On-Sea sands. Anglia TV had a reporter live on the scene commenting on what had happened.

As he sat having his tea, weary after a hard day's work, I bombarded Dad with questions, and then bombarded him with supplementary questions, "What's a pirate station Dad?" "How do they play the records on a ship?" "Are they real pirates?" "And there are more of them too?" "How many?" Etc. Etc. As I recall I managed to annoy the fuck out of him. His answers grew ever more terse and impatient. I might even have been sent to bed early, or at the very least was banished from the room, but not before I had all the information I needed. "You mean they play records all day long?" "And all night long too?" "On a ship?" "Non-stop?" "How many of them are there again?" A spell had been cast. Like the discotheque sign I saw that time in London, with Dad explaining what a discotheque was, describing it as you would a sorcery sect or a coven. And now there were ships at sea playing pop records. I went to bed that night utterly sold on the dream, already wrapped up in the romanticism of it all. You mean that as I lie here they are playing records right now? And while I'm asleep they will still be…zzzz…

At school during craft lesson I constructed a crude balsa wood model of a pirate station. I fixed a rectangular wooden block to a flat base. Then I glued a long wooden stick next to the block, attached a triangle of nylon thread either side and pinned it from stern to bow to make it look like a mast. I painted the words "Radio England" on the side, proudly took it home and placed it in my bedroom window. It was the kind of thing a boy with special needs might have made under suitable supervision. It put the "dial" in "remedial" and it was my pirate-radio dream ship. Other boys executed steeply banked turns with their self-assembled Airfix Hurricanes. I sat and stared at my balsawood blocks and sang jingles in my head.

"Swinging" Radio England (SRE) sounded like a pop art explosion going off in our radiogram. It was the most overtly American (rather than mid-Atlantic) of the offshore stations and it only had the briefest of life spans – May to November 1966 – before its owners realised that the offshore gold-rush was over and they weren't going to make a zillion bucks. For the entire six months of its existence I was spellbound. SRE called its DJs "boss jocks". They had names like Bruce Wayne, the Boss Cat Bruce, Bill "Boss" Berry, Boom Boom Brannigan. The names seemed to be infinitely interchangeable. One week the Bruce Wayne I heard had a brash American accent. A few weeks later "Bruce Wayne" metamorphosed into something unmistakably southern English. Several of the DJs took their names from the jingle package they were given. That's how Birmingham-born Peter Dingley became Johnnie Walker when he joined the station as a rookie announcer. Radio England aired state-of-the-art space-age jingles (which Kenny Everett over on Radio London immediately pirated and customized for Big L because they sounded so good). Even the music bed for SRE's news broadcast sounded like it had been constructed by NASA rather than a commercial production company. The boss jocks frequently added heavy studio reverb and echo to their voices and to the music they played. To this day I still can't listen to *Getaway* by Georgie Fame and the Blue Flames without hearing the horn figure doubled up with echo, the way Radio England used to play it.

First thing in the morning, before Mum commenced her hoovering regime, I used to switch on the radiogram to listen to Radio England's breakfast DJ Larry Dean. At nine o'clock he handed over to Ron "on the radio" O'Quinn. They sparred and joshed with each other in a way that was ultra-familiar to

American listeners but completely alien to British ears. They traded mock insults. They called each other "losers" and "finks'. Like all the other boss jocks they were LOUD. Announcers on the BBC Light Programme were formal and polite. Radio England DJs seemed to shout all the time. By far the loudest was GARY STEVENS! Stevens didn't actually broadcast from the ship. His one-hour show was syndicated from WMCA New York, although from the sheer volume of his delivery it might have been just as easy for Stevens to open his studio window and shout to us from America. His show went out in the late afternoon and I used to rush to the radio to listen to it as soon as I got home from school. GARY STEVENS was brash to the maximum. His impeccably timed intros and outros were all delivered with the same unmoderated fairground barker pitch, regardless of mood and tempo. "*RAIN ON THE ROOF* BY THE LOVIN' SPOONFUL! BEAUTIFUL RECORD!", he would rasp. "*96 TEARS* BY QUESTION MARK AND THE MYSTERIANS. GONNA BE A NUMBER ONE!", he would bellow. On one memorable occasion he introduced *Summer Time* by Billy Stewart by shouting: "HEY, FAT BOY, GET IN HERE AND SING!"

As Stevens was gainfully employed by WMCA, he even managed to avoid the BBC embargo on pirate disc jockeys and appeared on *Juke Box Jury* at the height of his offshore fame. I was surprised to be greeted by the kind of regular news-guy visage that wouldn't have looked out of place reporting to camera as Lee Harvey Oswald was being shot by Jack Ruby. Because of his frenetic on-air delivery, I had expected something a little zanier. Not the full Dr Crackpot, perhaps, but certainly something akin to the more outré pop stars of the time. I soon learned that there was a considerable discrepancy between image and actuality. Pirate presenters might have had hip, slick he-god names like Rick Dane and Mark Roman, names that looked and sounded phonetically cool when you saw them in the newspaper listings, but most of them looked like the man who tried to sell you a TV set in Radio Rentals, or the bespectacled drummer who sat at the back of some of Britain's less rebellious beat groups.

I didn't care either way. They delivered pop music on tap, and that was enough for me. During the summer of 1966 the offshore phenomenon was at its peak, and the medium wave was as full of pirates as it ever would be. The listening habits of me and my mates were simple and utilitarian. Whoever was in charge of station choice worked his way up and down the dial, only changing channels when a pirate played a bad record or when the ad break went on too long. Caroline, London, England and City were our favoured stations, but everything got a hearing at some point. It was all effortlessly, unconsciously democratic and immediate and inspiring, and little did I know it at the time but it would never be that good again.

Come the autumn I knew what I would be getting for my 12th birthday. I had dropped enough hints, and sure enough a small brown package duly appeared on top of the wardrobe in Mum and Dad's bedroom. It was heavily sellotaped but I could tell what it was. I shook the box for clues and it rattled. I thought better of doing that again in case I'd broken something inside, but every day I went and sneaked a peak. Maybe if I just peel the corner a little, just fingernail some of this sellotape away...

...After a couple of weeks it looked like rats had been gnawing at the box. I continued to scratch away with my nails until I made a hole in one corner and could see shiny red plastic through the packaging. Mum must have noticed because one morning she came into my bedroom to wake me for school and said: "Here, you might as well have this even though it's not your birthday yet."

A transistor radio made my culture mobile. It was barely as big as my hand and had a tiny, tinny little speaker no bigger than a button, but it put a quantum spring in my step and revolutionised my listening habits. It brought me closer to the pulse beat of what was going on. I was now the captain of my own balsa-wood ship, the master of my fate.

CLASS

– 'Ang on a minute?
Mr Chubb stood at the front of the class with a pained expression on his face.
– 'Ang on a minute?

He flushed with anger as he repeated the words emphatically. It was raining heavily outside and we were confined to indoor break, and now Mr Chubb was angry. Everyone turned around from their circle of conversation and watched as his face went puce. Our new headmaster had introduced Chess Club, Drama Club and classical music. He had changed the house team names from Swallows, Swifts, Eagles and Robins to Drake, Scott, Nelson and Cooke. And if we walked past his office and heard the phone ringing we were allowed to go in and answer it if his secretary wasn't there. He said it was to teach us adult responsibility. But now Mr Chubb was standing at the front of the class glowering. "Ang on a minute?", he said again, rising to a crescendo of outrage.

– 'ANG ON A MINUTE? Who answered the phone just now?

I had. "Albion Sands County Primary School," I said, as required. A grown-up voice asked, "Could I speak to Mr Chubb, please?", and I replied: "Yeah, 'ang on a minute. I'll go and fetch him." Mr Chubb said I wasn't to answer the phone again.

At 11 I had no notion of class distinction or how demarcation might manifest itself in speech patterns. At that age you think everyone else is like you until proven otherwise. I had little idea what the parents of any of my classmates did for a living and I didn't ask. They were just people who answered the door. You glanced through the triangle of their arm as your mate sat grinning at the foot of the stairs, hurriedly putting his shoes on. I had no idea that there were council houses and private houses or indeed that there was such a thing as a private school. I assumed that Winker Watson and Billy Bunter were as fictional as Secret Squirrel and Quick Draw McGraw. I had never questioned the segregation of my Junior School classes into A and B, the bright and the not-so-bright. "'Ang on a minute" was the first real indication that I didn't sound right, that there were those who could speak proper and those who couldn't. Or coont as I would have said at that time.

Dad's workmate Harry gave me a tin of coins to start a collection with. He told me that coin collectors were called numismatists, a word that tingled on your lips when you said it, like playing a tune on a comb and tracing paper. My classmate Frankie was a coin collector. He even read a specialist magazine that his mum bought from Hartstone's. I deferred to Frankie's superior knowledge and began checking my change more regularly. Frankie showed me what to look out for. Young Queen Victoria had her hair in a bun. Old Queen Victoria looked like Ena Sharples. 1912 pennies had a small H in the bottom left-hand corner which stood for Heaton. 1918 pennies had a KN in the corner which stood for Kings Norton. A 1933 penny was as rare as a Penny Black stamp. I washed my coins in soap and water and kept them in an old Bournvita tin in the pantry. One day I dug up a 1773 penny in the garden, or it might have been 1778. The last number had worn away. When I told Johnny Craig in 4B that I collected coins he said: "Did you know that if you put a New Zealand two-bob bit in the cigarette machine you can get ten fags for free?"

I had a few Commonwealth coins in my collection, so we tried one in the cigarette machine that stood on the wall outside Mr Atkin's garage. Sure enough, Johnny was right. The trick worked with other Commonwealth coins too, as we soon discovered. There was a machine outside Mr White's newsagent which stocked exotic brands like Richmond and Buckingham in twenties and not tens, but that was a more prominent and busy location there on the Market Square and we feared someone might see us, so we stuck with Mr Atkin and his packets of ten. We used to take our fags to the abandoned cottage at the bottom of our road and smoke them in a falling-down shed stacked full of furniture and old newspapers. Johnny could do the bandito voice on the John Cotton Cigarillos advert off the telly. "Join the smoking revolution," he would say in mock Mexican as we puffed away. I didn't particularly like the smoking that much. It made me light-headed, and I spent as much time spitting as I did smoking. I think it was the stealing and getting away with it that appealed, and the sheer ingenuity with which we got something for nothing. And all because Helpful Harry had started me off on a coin collection.

Everybody smoked then: Harry smoked, Dad smoked, a lot of the Mums smoked too. The young Mums in the road would give you two bob to go and fetch ten Embassy for them and let you keep the change. Dad smoked Guards, but we smoked whatever we could nick. The wrong money going in the right slot, the expectant pause as it tumbled through the machine, the tray never failing to open.

Player's Weights

Woodbine   Senior Service

Embassy   Kensitas   No. 6

Navy Cut   Capstan   Park Drive   Guards   Pall Mall

One day, bored with smoking, we decided to set fire to the shed. We stuffed a load of the old newspapers into a wardrobe, put a match to the lot and went up the Rec. When we came back later the fire had been put out. We never did discover whether the Fire Brigade had been called or if neighbours had hurried round with buckets of water, nor did we enquire. In the aftermath of what had clearly been a fair old blaze, we went in the shed and had a cursory poke around. The newspapers were bricks of black ash, the walls were blackened, and the wardrobe had blistered with melted tar. A lightning-bolt crack ran across the mirror.

Another time someone dumped an old mattress in Feltwell's field, so we set fire to that too. It was a fog-bound day and you could barely distinguish the smoke from the gloom. Later when I got home Mum said that she'd been having her hair done at Mrs Elder's house – the policeman's wife who ran a hairdressing business out of the police-house parlour. While she was having her shampoo and set, some boys from the Empire Road gang came to the door to tell PC Elder that there was a mattress ablaze in Feltwell's. "I bet they started it themselves," said Mum. Give a dog a bad name and send it to live up Empire Road.

Eleven is a transitional age. The slow drip-drip-drip of disillusion kicks in. There comes a time when you're watching *Torchy the Battery Boy* or *Supercar* and you can see the strings. You always could see the strings, of course, but previously suspension of disbelief had overridden the unavoidably crude mechanism of clunky puppetry. Suddenly, though, those strings become an object of derision. You reach a point where you begin to see all kinds of other strings too. The cheap, tawdry connivance of all that is put to you begins to reveal itself, as a con, a swizz, a let-down, a sham. They sit you in the round when the school magician does his annual show, and from where you are positioned you can see how he does his tricks, the hidden props and playing cards, the rabbits falling from the false bottom of a black hat, all of it exposed as sleight of hand. The bun penny drops and you realise that Gary Rose's conker wasn't a ninety-niner that time, and Frankie doesn't get 14 Valentines. You've never even seen him kiss a girl.

You watch *Blue Peter* all the way through, even though you hate *Blue Peter*, just because you once saw the presenter introduce that funny group called the *Bonzo Dog Doo Dah Band*. You watch *Crackerjack* hoping for the Merseybeats or Mindbenders but it's always George Chisholm or one of those loud Americans like Stubby Kaye. You apply to join U.N.C.L.E. thinking you are going to be in Espionage with a Luger and a silencer but they merely send you a yellow card that says you are in Section 1 – Policy and Operations, and that you are on 12 hours notice for hazardous duties. It's just a crummy card that you put away in a drawer. (I still have that card.) You design a *Dr Who* villain for *Blue Peter* but it doesn't win because only

Look and Learners win those prizes. You send off to the Daily Express for a free Dalek, and instead of the child-size silver model that you are hoping for you receive a small cardboard square and some instructions. With the same level of competence that you previously applied to your one and only attempt to make an Airfix model, you stick the pieces together and they come unstuck straight away. You try again and still your Dalek doesn't stand up properly. You go and stare at your balsawood pirate radio vessel instead.

The culmination of this pre-teen disillusion arrives with the televising of *Batman*. The build-up is unbearable. The publicity trailers scream their way into your thoughts. You have dreams about them. The DC comics are dark and Batman moves in sinister ink through shadowy nightscapes. He encounters super-villains like the Scarecrow that actually give you nightmares. But the moment they put it on the telly they made Batman look stupid, and Robin just dumb. The theme tune was great and sounded as good as anything in the charts, but the TV show we immediately condemned with the ultimate 11-year-old's putdown. It was "childish". When Batman took out the Bat Shield he didn't fold it up and put it back in his utility belt afterwards. He just left it there leaning against a wall. In the playground next day. All us experts. Arms folded, bristling with indignation at the implausibility of it all. The jury think it's a "Miss". Within a matter of weeks we were in on the joke and began choreographing our play fights with the necessary quota of Zap! Blam! Pow! The comics were still there if we wanted darkness and intrigue. The TV show was hilarious.

In *Cider with Rosie*, Laurie Lee, writing in the 1950s about his childhood in the 1920s, reflected that had his behaviour and that of his rustic peers occurred in more modern times it would have landed them in reform school. Writing in the 21st Century about growing up in the 1960s I have no doubt that my antics, particularly in my final year of Junior School, would nowadays result in expulsion and a thick case-file of social-worker reports. I was mischievous more than malicious, but I was also a habitual shoplifter, arsonist and purchaser of cigarettes with counterfeit money. And in the middle of all this I was preparing for, or notionally at least, being prepared for the 11+ exam.

Some time around Easter 1966, my class was divided into two groups. There were 12 in Group A. The rest of us were put in Group B. Our teacher spent most of his time with the A Group. They worked to a different syllabus and were given homework. It never dawned on me that they were being coached with the 11+ exam in mind. Much has been written about the pros and cons of selective exams at such an early age, and about how children were effectively divided into successes or failures before they hit their teens. Educational apartheid was pernicious and ruthless, and I was to become both its beneficiary and victim. At my Junior School we had kids who were weeded out at the mock-exam stage and who didn't even sit the 11+ itself. Several of the less able children from 4B were nowhere to be seen come examination day. Some parents actively prevented their children from sitting the 11+. Like those 19th century households who saw the introduction of compulsory schooling as a threat to their income, such parents viewed the threat of Grammar School as a way of protracting their child's education when they could be more usefully employed bringing home a wage packet. When the 11+ results were announced, the number of passes in my school class matched exactly the number allocated to Group A and its extra tuition. Only two from that group failed the exam, and only two from Group B passed. I have no evidence but little doubt whatsoever that rural schools like my own were allocated a strict number of places regardless of intelligence. By the age of 11 we had already been sifted. A quota for the privileged. A quota for the also-rans.

Whenever I took a freshly thieved DC comic home Mum said, "That's a new one, where did you get the money for that?" My stock response was, "Frankie lent it to me," even though I no longer hung about with Frankie. "Oh," said Mum one day. "Frankie's Mum said you haven't been round there for weeks." The High Street grapevine. The beginning of my undoing. It all unravelled pretty quickly after that. One day Mr Atkin must have emptied the takings from his cigarette machine and seen all the Commonwealth coins. All he had to do was keep watch and wait. I was sitting in class one morning when Mr Chubb's secretary walked in. I was summoned to the headmaster's office. I knocked and waited. Mr Chubb came to the door. He said a big word. The big word was embezzling.

– Wait there a minute.

He left me standing in the empty corridor, fetched a cane, raised it high, and hit me five times on each open palm. Then he took me back to my classroom, still snivelling snot down my face, and in front of my classmates said: "Let that be a lesson."

The 11+ results came in the post on a Saturday morning. Mum, in the hall, slowly opened an envelope with fumbling fingers. "Oh, well, boy, you can only have done your best," she said apologetically as she read the letter that said I'd passed.

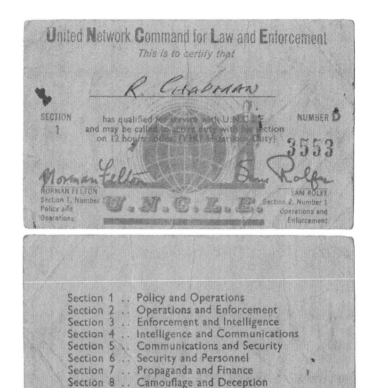

SWITHUNTIME AND TIDE

I walked to the edge of the greensand ridge and the world fell away into sky and space. There below, bordered by fields, was all that I knew – with me high above it. I gazed into a bright blue morning, down the bracken-scrubbed incline of the sand hills to the silver arrows of the railway tracks glinting in all their familiarity. That way leads to London. That way goes to Scotland. Over there lies the sandpit quarry and the woods that conceal the abandoned brickworks which hides Hawkesbury Meadows which slides to a coppice which sinks to a vale. And there, curving in a westerly arc, is the Cambridge to Oxford branch line that links all the villages. I watch a steam train haul its empty trucks across the open terrain of flat fields. The minutiae of my entire world is framed within this vastness. Everything set within a pyramid of main roads, the eternal geometry of my childhood, my everyday tread.

Stick people go slow motion about their business down at the shops. The cream white pillars of the Victory cinema proud and voluptuous. Firs and pines make a boulevard of Bedford Road. There's Albion Place, the Secondary Modern school, resplendent in acres of green. There's the Scout hut made of rust. There's the tiny black dot of a school cap pegged to the high branches of a sycamore. Dew-soaked and heady in the heat, I take in streets, houses and haulage yards; spinneys, rivers and pastures. There goes everyone and everything, all the way to the end of it. The A1 skims the horizon, cars glide in faraway silence, edging slowly out of my orbit. And there stands St Swithun's church. Its clock sounds a four-note chime.

Tar peeling from the roads – soft, black and sticky, blacker still on the underside. Fingernailing unset putty from the windows of the cricket pavilion. It comes away in oily edible strips. The Rec is perfumed with the smell of freshly mown grass and linseed-scented bats. Summer was beginning and ending and standing still all at the same time. We lay in the shade of the sand dunes, gazing up into the endless blue. A warm breeze ruffles the stillness then drops again. All you can hear is the nearby faraway hum of a buzz saw droning in a woodyard. The dazzle of an unrelenting sun glints from greenhouse windows. The A1 traffic crawls silently from finger to finger, horizon contained in a hand span. Somewhere in Albion Sands creosote is slowly soaking into a panel fence, grain by knotty grain. The chimes of the ice cream vans are all sounding at once: *Greensleeves, Popeye* and *Clementine*, all warped and distorted and going round on a forever loop.

Grummar pours Tizer while Grandad feeds grunsil to his aviary birds. Grummar just back from the beaning fields, Grandad from tidying riverbanks for the Water Board. The sun scorches in through a west-facing window. The afternoon never seems to end and the sun hangs there indefinitely, suspending its orbit before plunging into Harvey's haulage yard. Misty, Grandma's plump blue pedigree Persian, sleeps away her cat years in the shade of the backyard. A fly dozily bashes its brains out on the glass as I slurp my gassy Tizer. A Wubbse's lorry goes by. Runner beans in boxes wrapped in waxy brown paper, stapled down and stacked high. A leaning tower of straw bales sits on a trailer, secured by little more than a twine belt. A tractor passes, ploughshares dipped down, scuffing chunks from the road. A steamroller rumbles slowly down St Neots Road and the window frames rattle. A four-thirty procession of farm machinery grates and screeches and goes home. Done for the day. Silence comes soon enough. The fly resumes its kamikaze mission.

A white sun shrouded in a veil of haze. The air thick with harvesting. A long-time-ago memory smell acrid on the breeze as the stubble-burning begins. I sit on our front doorstep and watch the rats scuttle across the road from field right to field left as the threshing machine fetches them out. They run to Feltwell's empty sheds and seek refuge among the rubble. The weeds grow high and the desire paths cross-pollinate in a maze of intersections and thwarted routes.

Days spent up the sand hills or the station. The smell of soot and kippered wood on Platform 4 as we watch the last of steam and lounge on luggage trolleys, playing shove-ha'penny in the slots. Silver glinting from the rails, a quivering mirage off up the tracks, in dips in roads, in blistered tarmac. The August heat makes the music melt and the black plastic casing of Spooner's radio too hot to touch. Going back in time on the Sound of the Nation, it's a Caroline flashback. A summer measured out in pirate jingles and groovy theme tunes and *Summer in the City*. And although the song is about the city, the summer sounds like that in my town too. And although most of the songs had the summer stuck to them like a wrapper sticks to a frozen lolly, I liked the ones that came wrapped in autumn melancholy and winter clothing as well.

Walking down West Road in the evening in heat as thick as Bisto. All the tellies tuned to ITV. Hughie Green or *Weavers Green* blaring through every open window. Jimmy Dunn says Percy Sledge is the best record ever, even better than Roy C. Brian Dylan said, "No, *Sorrow* by the Merseys is." Brian left school in July and started courting Trudy. Courting was what they called it then.

Endless drowsy days spent on the alley bridge listening to the creak of signals going up and their clatter coming down. It's so quiet by mid-afternoon that you can hear the points switch. Vision is so microscopically fixed you see them move too, rails flicking from left to right, eyes picking out the lizards and sand frogs that dart from hot shale to shade. Sometimes a goods train on the slow line stops, sits and waits so long for a signal that you forget it's there. It shuts down its engine and becomes part of the scenery. When it jerks into life again your head does too. Couplings ricochet from truck to truck, that chain link sound, metal grabbing at metal, disappearing to an echo, away up the track.

We identify diesels by their distant rumble. Brush Two. Brush Four. Sulzer. Deltic. Hymek. A gift I had then and retained for years. Calling them out when they're barely in earshot, just a murmur on the breeze. Legs dangling from the buffers of a disused goods line, sleepers rotted, rails rusted to copper, weeds thrusting through concrete. Pencil scribbles and penknife carvings adorn a white picket fence with its paint all flaking. "I died here waiting for D5902. D. Jones. 28.4.65." The sign on the empty derelict goods shed says: "No Entry. Keep Out." Bored one day, we shouldered the door open and squeezed our way in. There was nothing in there but pigeon shit and a bird's nest that had fallen from the rafters. Dead chicks all shrivelled, purply pink and featherless. In the stinking station toilet that whiffs all the way to the footbridge it says: "What becomes of the broken hearted. Paid a penny and only farted."

I tethered myself to the gates of the Junior School like a servile dog that wasn't allowed in. They built a new swimming pool behind the dinner hut just weeks before I left. It remained open all summer to those who still attended the school but not to those of us who had just departed. Lingering like a lost cause, hugging the railings, listening to the splashes and shouts coming from behind the fence, crippled with an envy stitch. And I didn't understand why I got a gripey stomach when *God Only Knows* came on the radio. The music made me think of the swimming pool with Louise Muir in it. Louise was a girl in the third year I'd noticed just before the end of term and now it was too late, now she too was out of bounds. Counting down the days of that golden summer with the glow still on it. Hating those afternoons when I walked past the pool, knowing she was in there, splashing, shouting. Having to go home and push the clock hands round again until it was tomorrow. And all that time *God Only Knows* was like the hymns we sang and the symphonies we heard and the stubble-burning smell that made me ache with memories I'd never had and emotions that didn't have names yet. I still hear that yearning in *God Only Knows*, even now, its memory essence rolling out in waves across space and time to reach me.

You had to fill in a form that said, "Which school do you want to go to?". Dad, with misplaced optimism, put Bedford Modern, the public school, but they sent me to Waden Grammar instead. There was an advert on the telly, "Back to school in Bairnswear", that reminded you in the middle of your favourite programme that summer would be over soon enough. Off we trotted to Denny's School Outfitters to get kitted out in the hot, itchy garments of uniformity. Mum said you had to buy everything on the list. And everything on the list came to £100, said Dad, which was four weeks' wages. And they told me, not for the first time, that when I was 18 I would be able to draw out an insurance policy they had been paying into since I was three which would enable me to buy all the books that I would need for Cambridge. I had no idea why I would need books in Cambridge, and it was never adequately explained to me, but high hopes they must have had as I stood there in my size six-and-seven-eighths school cap, my brown leather satchel and my heavy, itchy blazer.

A sticky lolly drips from a stick. A riddle-me-ree is revealed backwards as a Skyrocket melts.

A Rainbow   What Bow Can't Tie?

Window pavilion putty in fingernails. Scrumping from hand to mouth. Tell-tale earth stains on trousers when we nicked carrots from the field by the alley bridge and polished them gritty clean on our thighs while we took down the engine numbers. Playing Waddington's Whot! on the embankment while Spooner told me and John Waller all about Waden Grammar. About prefects, about the house system, about rugby union, and the headmaster who was known as "the beak".

All the old farmhands wearily pushing their bikes homeward, a string bag of onions balancing on handlebars. Baby bonnets and freckles and the bare red arms of the mothers. Our lives measured out in Swithuntime. Mum sent off coupons for the music from the Summer County Margarine commercial. Brian sat Trudy on the saddle of his bike and pushed her down the road very fast until she squealed with fear and delight.

STOP TALKING!

The head boy walked up five steep steps that led onto the stage. He paused, surveyed the room and with eyes fixed on the clock at the back of the hall bellowed: "STOP TALKING!" Eight hundred children stopped talking. A phalanx of teachers sat in chairs on opposite sides of the hall and looked along the rows, girls seated to the left, boys to the right, to make sure everybody had indeed stopped talking. Through an entry door, stage right, the headmaster – the beak – bustled in, black cloak flapping. He welcomed us with a series of edicts. "Here at Waden Grammar we strive for success." "Here at Waden Grammar we pride ourselves on our high pass marks." "Here at Waden Grammar we encourage mixed clapping, not regimented and rhythmic clapping." When we clapped, which we had to do pretty much every time someone went up on stage, we were instructed that we couldn't clap as if we were at a football match. We had to learn the rules of clapping. I didn't know there were rules for clapping. It turned out that there were rules for everything.

There were rules regarding walking and running in the corridors. There were rules about which side of the corridor you were supposed to walk on and which staircase you were supposed to go up or down. There were rules about lining up outside classrooms, and lining up in the dinner queue, and lining up for the school buses that took you home at ten past four. There were rules about etiquette during school dinners. There were rules about addressing female teachers as "Ma'am" not "Miss". There were also rules about not combing your hair in the corridor. I learned this very early on one day after gym while attending to my own freshly showered mop. A ferocious teacher, short of stature but furious of mien, pressed his face close to mine and told me what I was for, combing my wet hair in public. I was a common little boy. What was I? "A common little boy, sir." I think there was something about juvenile delinquents in there too.

The deputy headmaster, Gummy Channon, was given to similar outbursts of ferocity. A regular sight in those first few weeks was a couple of love-struck Sixth Formers mooching about the corridors, mooching as only love-struck Sixth Formers can, dream drifting, hand-in-hand, wrapped up in their thoughts and each other. One day, affronted by these blatant displays of affection, Gummy walked up to them, put his face close up to theirs and screamed: "PERHAPS YOU WOULD LIKE JOINT LOCKERS AS WELL!" It seemed such a strange thing to say. It still seems weird now. The emphasis on lockers and not love or love letters, or French letters. I'd seen the girl walking across the forecourt one morning as I got off the school bus. She caught my eye because she was carrying a John Mayall's Bluesbreakers LP under her arm. I only knew the name John Mayall from the LP chart in my New Musical Express. I had no idea what his music sounded like, but I soon learned to hold great store by the artefacts that older kids carried under their arms. And now I watched Gummy Channon, as his ugly gummy orifice contorted and distorted as he spat his venom and contempt, and the lovers reluctantly parted at his command. The boy, a prefect, did so with practiced disdain, she – a hip girl who carried John Mayall LPs under her arm – likewise. No one was immune from the neurotic prejudice of the prohibitionists who patrolled the corridors. They were everywhere. Always ready to take you aside and remind you that you didn't belong.

The morning we started school it was as hot as it had been for weeks. The golden days of that glorious summer extended well into September. My new school jacket hung heavy on my shoulders and I itched all the way to John Waller's house. "Don't they look lovely in their uniforms?", said two women at their gates as we shuffled past.

Day after day. The same routine. The head boy shouts "STOP TALKING!" You stop talking. When he read out the weekend rugby results at the end of Assembly he spoke in the third person. "After a closely fought contest, the First XV scored a narrow victory thanks to late tries by Winterson R., Winterson G., and Peel R.," he would say. He being Peel R. He couldn't go: "And I got the winner. Yippee for me." I had never encountered such formality. There are numerous ways in which a middle-class grammar school with public-school pretensions can alienate a working-class boy who has slipped through the 11+ vetting process, the unfathomable formality of language being merely one of them.

There are many others. There's the sheer size of the place for starters. You go from being one of 200 pupils at Junior School, the majority of whom you know, to one of 800, only 11 of whom you know. You go from boisterous busy fish in a familiar shoal to insignificant minnow way out of his shallows. The alien environment encompasses everything from dress to address. By accident or design you quickly transgress. Even if you keep your head down and your mouth shut they soon sniff you out. Each morning in Assembly we were ordered to stop talking and eventually I did. That is to say I never knowingly shut up when out of class, never knowingly shut up for the first half of my teens in fact, whether at home or play. In school, however, once I'd worked out that little of what I said or did or knew had any value, I soon adopted the sullen disruptive attitude of the recalcitrant and the school refuser. The bright inquisitive kid of 11 went into abeyance. He didn't re-emerge for several years.

There's a lot they don't tell you. They don't mention that there will be streaming. They don't tell you that there will be a 1A, a 1B and a 1C, but you find out soon enough. You even discover that there is a Top C, Middle C and Bottom C.

– What class are you in?
I was in 1/30.

– That's Bottom C.

In educational parlance it's called "hidden streaming". In some schools, the hierarchy is disguised with pretty noun laden class names. One Elm. One Beech. One Oak. At Waden Grammar they were a little more utilitarian about the exercise and allocated classroom numbers instead. Everyone cottoned on quickly enough and pretty soon we all knew our place.

They don't tell you that you won't be playing football either. Or perhaps they did and I just wasn't listening. When I first gazed out across the vast school playing fields all I could see was rugby posts and hockey nets. I didn't get it at first. I thought maybe we played rugby one week and football the next. I even thought my rugby shirt would double as my football shirt. Riddle-me-ree. Where were the football nets? Answer: there weren't any football nets. Ever. Or football matches either. Association Football was for common boys to tussle over in playgrounds and parks.

Of all the ways in which working-class refusers and rejects learned to develop an alternative school culture, pop music was by far the most effective. Pop was the one thing that crossed those streaming boundaries, the one fail-safe dependable mechanism that transgressed all that 1A, 1B, Bottom C shit. In an environment where much of what was on offer rapidly became alien to me, music was a life-saver. I instinctively gravitated towards like minds.
– Have you seen the boy with really long hair in 1/32?
– How long?

Really long. Girl long. Dave Davies long. Phil May of the Pretty Things long. We peeked in through a window during one of their lessons.
– There he is in the corner. His name is Dickie Dangerfield."

Girly pout. Hair almost shoulder-length.

During break time I would see him seeking refuge behind the gymnasium with other delicate boys who gathered there in fear. Wild dogs went prowling at break time, picking out the runts of the litter, the weaklings, the cissies, the ripe for bullying. Someone kicked a ball at them, more in jest than anger. Dickie Dangerfield flinched and covered his genitals.

It was a while before I got to talk to him. We were discussing the unlikely grooviness of our art teacher Miss King. She wore long flowery dresses and fell down often. Walking between the Art Room rows observing our work and whoops there she goes again. She just gets up as if nothing has happened and continues her way down the narrow aisle between easels. She had straw-blonde hair and carried unfamiliar LPs under her arm. She also carried the promise of something altogether more exotic way beyond our understanding. In the first year she illustrated the techniques of light-shows to us. This is 1966/67, and she is showing us what's going on in the Underground. Pours a dab of liquid oil into a dish and projects it onto a screen. By the third year she was showing us how to tie-dye clothes. Take a shirt or dress, scrunch it up with rocks and string and plunge it into a tub full of colour. Ungrateful little twats that we were, we repaid Miss King for her insight by taking the big tin tubs when they were empty and pushing each other round the room in them. If she nipped out for a moment we arranged the desks and easels into a race course. We called it the Francis Chichester Olympics, in honour of the sexagenarian who sailed his ketch Gipsy Moth IV round the world. Miss King would re-enter the room and look upon us in quiet dismay as we rounded the chicane in our big tin tubs.

It was Dickie Dangerfield who pointed out that she was carrying a Ravi Shankar LP under her arm. At the time I had no idea who Ravi Shankar was, but Dickie Dangerfield knew. It was quite a while before I got to know him well. He spent most of his time hiding behind his defences and bringing in notes to get out of games. The first time I had anything like a civil conversation with him he was carrying a copy of Paul Oliver's *Story of the Blues* LP under his arm. "I like compilations," I said. "It's not a compilation," he sneered. "It's an anthology." He told me he had got an A for cribbing an entire English essay on Stagger Lee from the sleeve notes of the *Story of The Blues* LP and the accompanying book of the same name. Eventually he let me borrow both.

In History they favoured the "dream and draw" approach. "Imagine you are a Roman Centurion." "Imagine you are a Viking settler." It divides educationalists to this day. Those inclined towards a more fact-based pedagogy argue that History isn't English and should steer clear of the imaginative and interpretive. But "dream and draw" is what we got. In English, where I did want to dream and draw, we sucked the very soul out of the subject with endless comprehension exercises, while our teacher spent most of his time picking his nose, marking homework and staring wistfully out of the window. Knowing what I know now I recognise his type, a young teacher, possibly in his first post, prematurely disenchanted with his surroundings and his vulgar little charges. Would rather be prepping public-school kids, a role for which he thinks he is eminently more qualified. I tried to do what was required of me for a while but soon slipped into the habit of handing in a cursory paragraph of homework in exchange for an equally cursory mark. After a term or two it ceased to matter very much what kind of mark I got.

Educational development is predicated on progress. There is an assumption of gradual evolution, of constantly aspiring upwards. None of these tick-box criteria take regression into account. Academically I was far brighter and more inquisitive at ten or 11 than I was at 13 or 14. Many boys are. Hormones and base instincts kick in and you spiral off into immaturity, capable of conversing earnestly about your passions one minute, drawing pricks on each other's exercise books the next. You bond through refusal and resentment. Low expectations become self-fulfilling. Peer approval rapidly leads to actions that go against your inclinations. The first thing I learned to do in Music lessons was not get in the school choir. Someone said, "Sing flat, then you won't get in," so I sang flat and didn't get in. I had a really sweet voice at Junior School, sang in the school choir, sang in inter-school competitions, sang the solo verse from *Once in Royal David's City* in the Christmas concert, but once I got to Grammar School I kicked against the pricks and in doing so rapidly became one. Mr Budd, the deputy music teacher, walked up and down the rows listening as we went through the motions of auditioning. I sang like a tone-deaf idiot, as if melody and key were unfamiliar to me. "Good bass voice when you get older," Mr Budd said charitably. School didn't throw me many lifelines in that first year, but the choir was one of them. Instead I chose to wallow in self-inflicted peer-approved ignorance. It wasn't all the school's fault.

Mr Sherwood was head of music. He played the organ in Assembly and filled the school hall with his pedals and swells. In class he played us a piece of music by Debussy called La Mer, and we were asked to write a story about it. Finally given an opportunity to dream and draw, I wrote a domestic vignette about a man who has a dentist appointment. Thanks to a diet that largely consisted of chocolate-spread sandwiches and Spanish Gold sweet tobacco, I'd started having fillings myself by this stage. In my music-class composition, the man goes to the dentist thinking that it's going to hurt but they play him the *La Mer* music which soothes him and he forgets about his pain. Quite a charming tale when I think about it now, but I got the Impressionist question wrong. The right answer had something to do with waves crashing against cliffs and sea spray and gulls circling overhead. It hadn't occurred to me that there were correct ways of appreciating orchestral music, and the exercise killed my interest stone dead. I didn't come back to the classical repertoire for years.

– Come here! You, boy!

A prefect caught me running in the corridor and gave me lines. On a piece of paper he wrote: "If I persist in this tonifoolery I will be severely punished," and ordered me to copy it out 100 times. The following morning I had to go and find him in the Sixth Form Common Room. There he was with all the other prefects, sitting with their feet up on desks, casually chatting. I handed him my scrappy sheets of rough-book paper. He didn't even remember giving me the lines, and had to ask my name and the offence I had committed. Glancing at the pages he started laughing. He showed them to another prefect and he started laughing too. "It's not 'tonifoolery'," he said. "It's 'tomfoolery'. Run along now, Toni Foolery."

OVERSPILL

All through the winter of 1966 the thermostat clicked on and the thermostat clicked off. It sat directly above my head in the small front bedroom that I had to myself until my sister was considered old enough to require the privacy of her own room. Meanwhile she slept in the back bedroom with my brothers while I basked in the one-bar glow of the heater that Dad fixed to the wall to lessen the winter chill. Clicking on. Clicking off. A soft red light casting its reflection on the curvature of the silver plating, slowly getting brighter, slowly fading dim. If I woke up in the night and the heater was on I'd reach under the bed, attach the earpiece of my radio and tune in to Radio Caroline South. I listened to "TV on the Radio" (Tommy Vance) or the *Night Owl Prowl* with the "curly headed kid" Steve Young, and experienced for the first time that peculiar intimacy that comes in the small hours, that feeling that no one else is listening, that you and the disc jockey might just be the only two people awake on the planet right now. I frequently dozed off again with the ear piece still attached and the PP3 batteries draining away, the music continuing to seep in like the ocean through a seashell.

On a dull, dry January morning we go trainspotting. We take the two-car multi that shuttles between Oxford and Cambridge, through Blunham,

Willington and Bedford St Johns, on through the brickwork villages –
Stewartby, Millbrook, Ridgmont, Aspley Guise – to Bletchley, where the
electrified line runs up from Euston to the north. We've eaten our
sandwiches on the train before we get there. The morning remains murky
and never really brightens. After an hour of huddling in the waiting-room
with the heater spluttering out minimal warmth, Spooner says: "This is
boring. Let's go to Rugby." In an instant my mates have decided to take the
next train out of Bletchley. As he hangs out of the window waiting to depart,
Spooner says: "It's only four bob return. Come on. I'll lend you the money."

I barely had enough for the journey to Bletchley, and as I have no visible
means of support other than a meagre pocket-money allowance I can't ever
imagine being able to pay Spooner back, so I wave off my mates and trudge
begrudgingly back to the waiting-room. After not very long at all I'm as
bored as Spooner was before they all left me here on my own. The day
grows colder and after a while I can't even be bothered to take my hands
out of warm pockets to write down the numbers. Pretty soon I can't even
be bothered to leave the waiting-room to watch the electrics flash by, and
soon after that I board the next train home. By the time I reach Bedford St
Johns the morning edition of the *London Evening Standard* has arrived. I
glance out of the window at the billboard on the newspaper stand. It reads:
"Bluebird crash. Donald Campbell killed."

I have always associated that dismal, dull day with Campbell's death. It was
just before 9am when Bluebird flipped up out of the water. I was probably
larking about on the outbound train at the time. Shaking my bottle of fizzy
pop and threatening to release the contents. They showed the grainy
footage on the evening news. "Grainy footage" is a cliché, right up there
with tapes that "languish" in "dusty vaults", but the newsreel was grainy,
even at the time. I've just watched the Pathé clips on YouTube to remind
myself. For some reason Campbell's warm-up run is captured in pristine
35-mil, but by the time he turns for another ill-fated go the film stock has
deteriorated, the camera is hand-held rather than mounted, and Bluebird's
final moments are a blur. "I can't see anything. I've got the bows out. I'm
going," are Campbell's last frantic words. There is also, if you listen carefully,
a final impact-induced "Uh!". The murk of the lake and the hazy woodland
backdrop matches my memory of the weather that day. Curiously, as soon
as the fateful moment has occurred the quality of the footage reverts to
pristine. It shows the emergency vehicles arriving, skeletal trees with stark
bare branches, police cars waxed and gleaming, women in grey coats and
headscarves, a boatman in Shetland white weave. There are gradations of

silvery black on the gentle waves that lap the shoreline. There is clarity in all but those few fatal frames where Bluebird's bow goes sky-bound. In the final seconds of Campbell's life, as if anticipating the terrible moment, the footage goes smeary, dream-lensed.

Brian Dylan was courting. I didn't see him much anymore, certainly not to talk to. Sixteen-year-olds don't want to associate with 12-year-olds, especially when they've just acquired a motorbike and have a steady girlfriend. In the mornings I usually called for Jimmy Dunn and we walked to school. I got on my bus in the High Street. He was in his final year at the Secondary Modern. Usually we waited for his friend Woody at the corner of Laburnham Road by the Junior School, but on this particular morning Woody was already waiting for us because we were late. I'd called round to Jimmy's at 8.30 but he'd taken a long time to get ready. He told his Mum that he didn't want to go to school, and she said: "You have to." Yeah, we all have to. You don't have any say in the matter.

He took so long getting ready I thought I was going to miss my bus. The Dunns' kitchen always smelled of cabbage and lard, and I hated waiting there for long, but Jimmy lingered, not wanting to leave. I kept expecting his Mum to shout at him, but she just said, "Come on, Jimmy," in a quietly cajoling voice. Eventually he relented and we made our way to the High Street. He'd hardly spoken two words to his Mum that morning and as we walked through the alley he didn't talk much to me either. I might have said, "Did you see *The Girl from U.N.C.L.E* on the telly?," and he might have answered "Yeah," but that was about it. When we met up with Woody the mood didn't alter. The three of us walked in silence. Then Jimmy said something like, "BTV 774." Woody didn't respond, so he had to repeat it. "BTV 774. Gone." Woody still didn't get it, but I got it. "That's Brian's number plate," I said. Jimmy ignored me and made halting attempts to continue the conversation over my head, but I was Zip Nolan and I had cracked the clue. "That's Brian's number," I said again. Then Jimmy had to tell me. He'd been trying not to, he was trying to shield me from the truth.

Brian had ridden his motorbike down village B roads and side roads and slip roads, and out onto the A1, where he went straight under a lorry. Gary Rose said they found his hand in a glove a hundred yards further up the road, but someone always said something like that. When they found a German parachutist hanging from a tree during the Second World War, he was handless too. It's what everyone said. You had to have a dismembered limb somewhere in the story, otherwise it wasn't a proper death.

Radio Caroline ran a sponsored show called Caroline Cash Casino which offered big cash prizes if you guessed the answer to a quiz question from a series of clues that were updated daily. Each time an incorrect answer was read out the prize money increased by £10. I couldn't crack the clues in the first three Cash Casinos, but soon worked out that the answer to game Number four was "Ears". The show's main sponsors were Findus Foods, Weetabix, Galaxy Chocolate, VP Wines, Nabisco Shredded Wheat, Libby's tinned foods and Alberto VO5 shampoo. At regular intervals during the show the genial host Bill Hearne invited listeners to send in the label from one of those, or what he called "a reasonable facsimile," in order to be entered for the prize. I used to ponder what this reasonable facsimile was, and even when it was explained to me I was little wiser. Perhaps you had to draw a Shredded Wheat box or something. I can't remember if it was a Libby's peaches label or a Findus Fish Fingers box that I sent off in the end, but for several winter weeks I waited as the cash prize mounted and still no one had guessed that the correct answer was "Ears". I was walking over the footbridge by the old mill when the winning entry was read out and Mrs Muriel Berry of London won £2,490. I've often thought of a room somewhere in Caroline House and all those unopened envelopes reeking of fish fingers. One envelope in particular.

The first group I ever appeared on stage with was the Troggs. They gave a concert in the school hall and when they did *Any Way that You Want Me*, they invited me up on stage to sing with them. Louise Muir was there in the front row, even though she was still in the fourth year at Juniors and hadn't sat the 11+ yet. She was utterly entranced by my performance and I could tell she fancied me now that I was in the Troggs. Technically I wasn't strictly a member of the group, as I had just been invited to give this one performance with them and technically she didn't fancy me either as this was all a dream. The dream didn't wear off for ages. That's where all my desires went now, and for the next few years. Into my "dream and draw" pop world.

As I got bolder I edged my way nearer to the back of the school bus. When you first start Senior School there is a kind of unwritten ranking system and you sit at the front. After a while, though, realising that no one was that bothered where you sat, I slipped further and further back down the aisle. I liked to get as near as I could to the girls who monopolised the back seat. The hard girls, the girls who got on smelling of nicotine and womanly scents, the girls adorned in unpermitted make-up. I sat as near to them as I dared and earwigged away as inconspicuously as possible. Boys. Fags. Netball.

Hockey. Music. Clothes. Boys. Fags. Netball. Hockey. Music. Clothes. And package tours that came to Bedford Granada.

– Who did you think was best last night?
– I didn't like the Walker Brothers, did you?
– No, Scott was really moody, wasn't he? He's getting too big for his boots, I reckon.
– He didn't smile once.
– No.
– Nor did Cat Stevens.
– Yes, he did.
– No, he didn't.
– He smiled at me.
– That Jimi Hendrix looked like he could do with a wash.
– So does Steve Snell.
– Graaah.
– What? Smelly Snelly?"
– Do you still fancy him?
– Nah.
– That hair. Bet it harbours fleas.
– And his group was too loud.
– They were. I thought my eardrums had burst.
– Mine are still ringing.
– I liked Engelbert best.
– Ooh, me too, he looked right at me when he sang Please Release Me. He was staring straight into my eyes.
– What did you think Mandy?
– Mandy! Stop dreaming about Smelly Snelly.
– Who's got a fag? I had mine confiscated yesterday.
– What are you staring at, squirt?

The overspill was coming. London was getting so big that it was going to spill all the way to Albion Sands. In the barber's shop and the paper shop and no doubt in all the other shops the men all mumbled and moaned.

– They're going to build houses for them down the rubbish dump.
– That's what I heard. All on that old Ministry of Defence land down Low Field.
– What? Where the tip is now?
– Don't talk sorft.
– They are.

– Too right, an aarl. Just put them on the rubbish dump. Don't bother building the houses. Eh, did you hear that? I said to him. I said don't bother building the houses, just put them on the...

Mr White, newsagent, said that they would breed like rabbits and spread disease. To illustrate this theory he placed a huge display of self-drawn cartoons in his shop window illustrated with provocative speech bubbles. Among other things they depicted white girls being chased through the streets by black men. Mr White's tapestry of small-town hate clearly contravened the Race Relations Act and they made him take the pictures down. The story made Anglia News. There was Mr White, proudly unrepentant on the telly, standing in front of his hand-drawn display of bigotry and ignorance.

On the last day of the summer term we sat on the grass and watched Steve Middles and Smelly Snelly heading over to the far side of the playing field. About half an hour later they were swiftly escorted back by two teachers. They'd been caught trying to have it off with two town girls behind the bushes by the perimeter fence and were expelled. "Getting expelled on their last day," chortled everyone. "That takes some doing." "It will ruin their careers," tutted Andrew Hartley, he of the failed Beatles haircut plot from Junior School days. "It will ruin their careers," repeated our form master when we got back to class.

Everyone got out their school reports on the bus going home, some showing them off and waving them about, others expressing fake modesty at their achievements. I opened mine slowly. Number of pupils in class, 27. Class position: "27th." Exams: "27th." Sammy Sampson said, "Here, let's have a look," and snatched my report from my hand. He pulled a smug face and showed it to his fellow Look and Learners. Dad read it at the tea table. "Bottom of the bloody heap," he said and went back to his tea.

The white wall of Potato Castle was soon breached by the gravy river and the peas-and-carrot army rushed in.

– Stop playing with your bloody food. Eat it. Don't play with it.

A few days later Mum patiently explained that as I wouldn't be going to Cambridge University now and wouldn't need to be buying all those books they thought they might as well draw that policy out. I never did get to have the Varsity life they'd dreamed of when they saw promise in me. We got our first car instead, a two-tone cream-coloured Sunbeam Rapier Mark 1 with leather upholstery. The seats were really comfortable. You sank into them and they smelt great on hot summer days.

BLACKBERRY WAY

The man was hanging from a tree. You couldn't see if anything was supporting his weight – perhaps he was suspended from a branch just above his head. Or maybe he had been standing on something, but you couldn't see his feet either. The photo we were studying in the gymnasium changing rooms couldn't squeeze everything within the frame. The hanging man had been topped and tailed. All you could really tell was that he was in a wooded area somewhere and that he was dangling from a tree. Someone said, "Better put it away. Hardman is coming," but Mr Hardman the Games master was in his office next to the showers and his door was closed. Had he suddenly opened his door we would have had plenty of time to disperse. And anyway, Jonesy, whose photo it was, would have detected the slightest turn of that handle, the merest creak of a hinge. Hardman didn't like Jonesy so he kept a nervous eye on the office while the rest of us scrutinised the photo. Everyone was fascinated. Some boys were disgusted, but they were still queueing up to have a look. None of us had ever seen anything like it. The photo hadn't been cut out of a magazine. It was real, someone had taken it as a permanent memento of what had occurred in those anonymous woods, and now Jonesy had it. Instamatic stamped on the back.

The man's body was taut and oddly angled. He seemed to be gazing downwards but you couldn't really tell. You could only see half of his head in profile. Your eyes followed his sight-line to where he would have been looking, down past the blurry woodland backdrop, down past his shirt hanging out, down to his beltless trousers which were open at the fly, and where a blonde woman, side on to the camera, face partially hidden by hair, was sucking his cock.

You go back saying: "I'm going to be different this year. I'm not going to be the same person that I was last year. I'm going to reinvent myself." This only lasts a few days. Make that one day. Make that until break on the first day. Make that until Louise Muir gets on the school bus and you do a

Muskrat out of *Deputy Dawg* impression as she goes past. Louise Muir looks at you like you are shit. For reasons best known to your hormones you decide to follow this up with a series of armpit farts.

Mr Walters the Geography teacher pinned a map of the world up on the wall. He went round the class in turn asking us where we'd all been for our summer holiday. We then had to go out front and pin a flag to our holiday destination. I'd never been on holiday. I'd been on a couple of day trips to Skegness but excursions didn't count. As Mr Walters walked up and down the rows and flags began to dot the map I looked at my school atlas in panic. When it came to my turn I said County Clare and pinned my little flag to the appropriate part of Ireland. I chose Clare because it was a girl's name and sounded nicer than Kerry which was also a butter. Mr Walters nodded approval and moved on to the next person, who was Ian Donaldson, the new boy. Donaldson, to much ridicule, had turned up on his first day in shorts. He came from a large Catholic family, supported Dunfermline Athletic and soon began to give me serious competition for bottom of the class. "Where do you go on holiday?" asked Mr Walters. "I've never been on holiday," replied Donaldson. Everyone laughed. Including me. I conspired.

The other new arrival in our class, Howard Connolly, had been demoted from the A stream. We bonded immediately over music and our obsessive repository of useless knowledge about sport. One day he turned to me in class and said: "Do you live in a council house or in your own house?" I didn't understand the question. Of course I lived in my own house. I didn't go home at night and to find gypsies or burglars living there. "Yeah, but do you pay rent or do you pay a mortgage?", he persisted. I had no idea what a mortgage was, but I knew who the rent man was. He was just one of the many people who came to collect. One day it might be the milkman, another day the insurance man, the Betterware man, the Spastics coupon man, and all the others who came calling. When we first moved to our brand-new house Mum referred to a letter from the council that required all tenants to keep a tidy, well-manicured garden. Other than that, all I knew about the council was that if you snapped a branch off a sapling out in the road, or dug out a section of the turf with a penknife, someone would say: "I'm telling the council on you." That's what the council was to me. A threat, a sanction, a building in Bedford Road. Inasmuch as I thought about it at all I assumed all houses were the council's houses.

Hardman really had it in for Jonesy. I don't think he ever saw the sucking-off photo but sometimes it seemed as if he had, or at least suspected that

Jonesy might be capable of having something like that about his person. He often shouted at Jonesy for being useless at games. "Pick the ball up, boy. Grip that rope properly. Throw this. Kick that." None of which Jonesy could do with any degree of competence. One day he started having a go at Jonesy in the changing rooms after rugby. It was the afternoon double Games period and the whole of the Second Year was there. We were towelling ourselves half dry and putting clothes onto damp skin when Hardman started the shouting. Extra angry. Extra loud. Jonesy stood there petrified. Eventually the haranguing stopped and Hardman went into his office. In a rash moment of defiance Jonesy blurted out: "If he does that again I shall report him. I'm not a cissy. He's just a bully. I'm going to report him." Almost immediately, the door flew open and Hardman shot back out of his office. He tore into Jonesy, pushing him into the wall, slapping and punching him till he cowered and crouched and covered his face with his hands. All the boys went quiet, even the ones who hated Jonesy, even the first XV A-streamers who played for the school team. Looking at Hardman. Mouths agape. Astonished.

I attended Grammar School during the last golden years of corporal punishment. For those of you unfamiliar with the term, corporal punishment was a legal sanction that allowed someone who wasn't your Dad to hit you with a strap, a slipper, a stick or anything else that came to hand. This was a time when teachers still routinely did their talking with their fists or whatever weaponry was available. Children were routinely clouted on the head, assaulted by flying board rubbers, thwacked with three-foot board rulers, knocked clean off their laboratory stools with a well-aimed kick towards the lower spine. On any given day for any given transgression you could be punched, hair-tugged and otherwise assaulted by sadists who were free to bludgeon as they pleased. Those masters who only had a limited capacity for reasoned discourse or empathy or cutting a little slack, kicked, cudgelled and ear-flicked with impunity, and when they had exhausted their repertoire of physical abuse they fell back on their considerable reserves of finely honed verbal abuse. There was always someone ready to call you out, to tell you were inadequate, to remind you that you didn't belong, and that you didn't have to come to this school, even though this last statement was palpably untrue.

In November 1967 I turned 13 and was old enough for a paper round. Mr Sutton, one of the three newsagents in the town, gave me the one they always gave to the new boy – the longest route with the furthest to go. A four-mile round trip to a distant hamlet along the busy dual carriageway on dark winter mornings. Up every morning up at six. A quickly guzzled beaker of weak diluted orange juice and a piss. Pedal to the shop. Breathe in the ink smell of the freshly printed papers and put on a heavy bag that cuts deep into your shoulder. Belting down Ivel Hill on Mum's bike because I still didn't have one of my own. Over a narrow footbridge and on through the mill walk. Open pastures to the left of me, a wet willow meadow to the right. The roar of the sluice gates getting louder and nearer. A crest of riverbank hedging, clipped to look like hawk heads, looming up as terror shapes in the river mist. On into the quietness of a cratered lane, bone-shaking all the way to the A1 where haulage trucks thunder past me in the rain spray. My paper-round years coincided almost exactly with the experiment to suspend Daylight Saving Time. For four years I delivered more papers in darkness than daylight. Until the spring came, dawn was just a sickly yellow rumour in the eastern sky, the sun only rising as I headed home. You submit to all this in the same way that you submit to school. You do it because you have to, and because you need the money.

One winter's night. December. Howling a gale. Sitting in the front room trying to do my Geography homework. Curtains moving in the draught. Soot dislodging itself from the chimney and landing in the grate. Though the wall I can hear the telly and everyone laughing in the living-room. Here in the front room, which will remain unheated until the North Sea Gas arrives in 1969, it is freezing. Hunched at a small table in the corner of the room, the lamplight casting shadows on the wall. Staring at a page full of map references and contours. Find a corrie. Find a tarn. Find a hydro-electric power station. In Junior School I knew every capital of every country and recognised most of their flags too. Now I barely understand any of it. Geography has become a mixture of Spot the Clue and Maths. Then there's the actual Maths. In Junior School I learned my four rules and was as sharp as a tack with my times tables, still am. Now I leave left-handed ink smears on Venn diagrams and ponder imponderable quadratic equations. If rhombus over parallelogram equals x squared tangent and y over cosine equals pi what is the square root of ignorance? You boy. You are. They're all laughing again at the telly. I can hear them. A huge hydro-electric-powered dam burst of shared laughter. I make a decision. I can't be bothered with any of this. I put on Robbie Dale's Diary on Radio Caroline and listen to that instead.

On winter mornings the back-door shakes on its hinges. Wind whistles through the keyhole and rattles the latch. I sit in the kitchen, swigging my orange juice. Everyone in the house is still asleep. I have to go out there. I have no choice. In the ill-lit darkness you can't even read the papers and there isn't really time, anyway. After Christmas I started to take my transistor radio with me for company, for emotional succour. I listened to the final months of Radio Caroline, and then because there was suddenly no other pop radio to listen to I tuned to Tony Blackburn on Radio One. There are records from those winter months of 1968 and 1969 that I associate entirely with my early-morning deliveries in the dark. *Marjorine* by Joe Cocker. *Gimme Little Sign* by Brenton Wood. *Dear Delilah* by Grapefruit. *Pictures of Matchstick Men* by Status Quo. *Race with The Devil* by Gun. I can still hear my bicycle wheels cracking through dirt-track frost whenever I listen to *Blackberry Way* by the Move. Roy Wood's mournful dirge evokes those mill rides through the mist, the ghost shapes of those hawk-headed shrouds, and the spectre of a dawn sun that never seems to come. My own Blackberry Way was paved with frozen tyre tracks, postage-stamp squares of ice embedded in tractor tread, pothole puddles in cratered lanes, my reflection flashing by.

No one was allowed to see Jonesy's photo again. He took it home and wouldn't show it to anyone. Some people who hadn't seen it didn't believe you when you described it to them. We were walking past the Masters' Common Room just before the end of term. Andrew Hartley was coming in the opposite direction. I didn't really see him much now he had moved up into the B stream. I described the photo to him in great detail. "She couldn't have been doing that, because that's where the waste comes out," he said.

RAINBOW CHASER

It was Connolly who sniffed it. The corridor smell that lingered. An unfamiliar scent.
– What's that?
Connolly knew.
– It's joss sticks. They get you high.

I'd never heard either of those phrases before, but here they were, both arriving in the same school corridor on the same school morning as we shuffled from assembly to registration. Josticks. I thought it was one word. They get you high.

I told Connolly that I liked the Ultimate Spinach.
– There's no such group.
– And Iron Butterfly. And the Electric Prunes.
– You're making these up.
– Come off it. You must have heard the Electric Prunes.
– You made that up.
– And the Elastic Goose.

Connolly started hitting me. Not in a play-fight way. In a shut-up way. "I'm going to punch you on the arm until you stop making these groups up."

We were walking from the Prefabs to the main building. We'd just had English. You couldn't mention any of these groups in English.

– And Captain Beefheart and his Magic Band.

Everyone joined in the laughing. But Connolly went: "Oh, yeah. I've heard of them. Are they your favourite group?"

– One of them.

I was getting a taste for the Underground. Unless I saw a picture of them in the *New Musical Express* I didn't know what any of these groups looked like. Mostly I just heard them on John Peel's *Top Gear* on Sunday afternoons. Otherwise they were as alien to me as the DC comic superheroes I read. There was as much chance of seeing them on TV as there was of me encountering Mon-El or Brainiac 5 in the street, but I liked the names that groups were getting now and I willingly embraced the strangeness of their music.

For the best part of 1967 I remained ignorant of the drug references in songs. I spent most of the Summer of Love saving up for a bike. "Getting high with a little help from my friends" I took to be chumminess, just a handy phrase that rhymed with "getting by". I assumed *Strange Brew* by Cream to be some sort of reference to a witches' cauldron, out of the same steaming hot pot as Manfred Mann's *Hubble Bubble Toil and Trouble*, a record I had liked three years earlier, and which I always associate with Gary Rose, my pop-chart oracle. Three years is a lifetime in child years. At nine pop is all one huge sugar-rush of sound, the noise is thrilling but all nuance is obliterated. But by the age of 12 a boy on the threshold of his teens, a pop-obsessed kid in retreat from formal education, is slowly beginning to build a cultural vocabulary, an image repertoire, a lexicon of postures and possibilities. He is becoming increasingly attuned to the peculiar patterns that sounds can make, and lyrics are beginning to etch-a-sketch a landscape into his brain. Words are only a rudimentary matrix, abstract and at times unintelligible, but they are beginning to signify something other than the sum of their parts. They are beginning to shimmer and shine.

In your early teens you retain a trace element of everything you have ever heard. Memory is as yet untroubled by clutter, abundance or overlay. In my mind there was still a direct unimpeded lineage line between Strange Brew and Hubble Bubble Toil and Trouble. The connectivity between the two was all part of life's rich hubbub of playground chants and nursery-rhyme noise, and had nothing to do with drugs. *Purple Haze* by the Jimi Hendrix Experience evoked the Purple Cloud, one of my favourite comic-book stories from the *Dandy*, which featured sinister arch-criminal the Purple Mask, who spent each strip zapping his enemies with lethal purple-cloud gas. He travelled in a saucer-shaped spacecraft and was very cool indeed. The Purple Mask was pursued each week by good guys Dandy Jim Brewster and his brother Brody. You were supposed to root for the good guys, lantern-jawed Dandy Jim and sidekick Brody in their check shirts and neckerchiefs, but I always wanted the Mask to win, and spent a great deal of my junior doodling years sketching the arch-criminal and his purple ray gun. Plumes of deadly gas spray began to dominate my drawings and my thoughts. All adversaries, real and imaginary, could be zapped with a lethal dose of purple. The strip originally ran from March to December 1961, and was reprinted between October 1968 and August 1969. That first run coincides with my earliest comic-reading years. The reruns I saw when my younger brothers read the same comic a few years later. The cool Purple overlord was an essential component of my fantasy life, and now here was Jimi Hendrix singing *Purple Haze*. 'Scuse me while I zap the sky.

Around the time that Track Records released *Purple Haze*, the *News of the World* ran its lurid three-part expose of drug use in the pop world. There are many reasons why I would eventually succumb to the compelling allure of acid. If only Terrytoons and Hanna Barbera hadn't shown me so many trippy cartoons at an impressionable age. Perhaps if 1965-66 hadn't been such a golden age of satirical kiddie-show spooferama (Pete and Dud's *Superthunderstingcar, The Munsters, The Addams Family, Get Smart, F Troop, Hogan's Heroes, Batman, Bewitched, The Monkees*). Maybe if DC comics hadn't lured me into the inky scent of the superheroes. But mostly it's the *News of the World*'s fault. It was their weekly accounts of drug-fuelled degradation that first alerted me to the idea that there might be more to some of these songs than met the untutored ear. The exposé mentioned *My Friend Jack* by the Smoke, a song that I'd heard on the pirates and initially assumed to be about a horse. The *News of the World* suggested that more subliminal readings might be ventured. I still didn't see what sugar-lumps had to do with drugs, but thanks to these weekly briefings I soon got up to speed, as it were. As a result, my cultural barometer overheated to such an extent that for the rest of the 1960s my divining rod and radar began to detect drug connotations in even the most innocent of paisley patterned pop songs.

Rainbow Chaser by Nirvana was the one that finally confirmed everything. Trampling across the clouds like the giant in Jack and the Beanstalk, stalking the strawberry fields of my imagination like the electricity pylons that strode across Hawkesbury Meadows at the back of the greensand ridge. Between the arch-criminal nerve gas of *Purple Haze* and the hubble bubble of *Strange Brew* in 1967 and the release of *Rainbow Chaser* in March 1968, I built a rickety thought bridge out of rice paper and windmills and sandcastles and trelliswork and switch points and alphabet blocks that got me from know-nothing Point A to know-at-least-a-little Point B. After that it was all Jelly Jungles of Orange Marmalade-lade-lade-lade and a constant diet of pretty pastoral pop tunes all crammed in a jar full of "Eat Me" and washed down with sweets that hadn't been invented yet. Before those *News of the World* exposés I was ignorant, not even blissfully ignorant, just bereft of knowledge, lacking two dimensions to knock together. It was only a matter of time before I was all dressed up and laughing loud.

A couple of years earlier, when I was still at Junior School, we'd attended a wedding reception. My cousin Geraldine was getting married. A fellow guest at our table, wearing a black velvet jacket and with longer hair than I'd ever seen on a man, offered Mum a cigarette. Like many mums in those days she was a social smoker – weddings, dinners and dances. She politely declined, but it was what she said next that intrigued me. She turned to Dad and quietly muttered: "You never know what they've put in them." This stayed with me for ages. What could she mean?

Around the time that the velveteen-clad stranger proffered his strange cigarette it was reported that Donovan had jumped naked onto a policeman's back when the forces of straight society attempted to arrest him. This brought forth on my part merriment beyond compare, sustained hilarity that exceeded my reaction to the crudest, rudest schoolboy joke I'd ever heard. When older friends first alerted me to the Donovan story I was so poleaxed with laughter I tried to eat my own face. My hysteria proved infectious, and my friends fell about too. The story, the details of which were aired explicitly in the *News of the World*, contained ingredients sufficiently combustible to endanger the continence of any 11-year-old. There is nothing funnier to a pre-teen, barely out of short trousers, than the previously unimagined burlesque of a bare-arsed beatnik folk singer clambering enthusiastically onto the back of a member of Her Majesty's constabulary for a piggy-back ride. I couldn't shake off the mental picture for weeks. Indeed, a part of me still routinely pictures the Mellow Yellow bard, proudly protuberant, flushed and untrussed, gaily venturing forth on his helmeted steed, inhibitions shed to the four winds, resplendent in his birthday suit, going "Giddy up, copper, giddy up!".

Holding my little box of confetti at the wedding where Mum refused a stranger's cigarette.

In the greater *Rainbow Chaser* scheme of things, Donovan rapidly became intriguing to me in the way that the long-haired wedding guest and his potently laced cigarettes became intriguing. Donovan's biggest hit mentioned Superman and Green Lantern, so we shared a DC Comics wavelength too. When *Hurdy Gurdy Man* was released in June 1968 I was still sufficiently naïve about studio technology to assume that he got that wavering vocal sound by patting his mouth as he sang. But by then of course I knew something else was going on too. *Rainbow Chaser* had got me started. That's when cognition kicked in. That's when my key finally turned smoothly in the lock. Many miles to go. How many bridges do you cross?

Meanwhile on the television news John Lennon floated around in white robes. The Beatles were in India and the news cameras couldn't get a close-up. This only added to the intrigue. Lennon was caught in long shot through the perimeter fence of a compound, briefly glimpsed in an exotic garden, smoking a cigarette, softly filtered, sunlight reflecting in the lens. Mark Barry brought his John Lennon books into school – *In His Own Write* and *A Spaniard in the Works* – and Mr Cox the drama teacher let the two of us act out selected extracts to the class. This was one of the few occasions when I can remember a school teacher not holding our culture at arm's length, or reacting as if someone had brought road-kill into the room. He did so, I suspect, more out of weary resignation than empathy, and his tolerance soon waned when our recitations of *Good Dog Nigel, I Remember Arnold* and *Mr Boris Morris* dissolved into spluttery giggles. Lennon's accompanying illustrations made us laugh until we cried. Much time was spent doodling reasonable facsimiles of *The Fat Growth on Eric Hearble* and *Cassandle* into our rough books.

One Saturday morning while waiting to be paid for my paper round I was leafing through a copy of *Record Mirror* that sat on the shelf in the stockroom awaiting collection. "You can have that if you like," said Mr Sutton, as he counted out my seventeen-and-six. "He was supposed to come in and collect it but I think he's gone on holiday and hasn't let us know." I took the "You can have that" to mean "You can have that for free," but when I got home I noticed he'd docked my pay by sixpence. The same scenario occurred the following week. Same hanging about in the back of the shop waiting to be paid. Same perusing of *Record Mirror*. "You might as well have that as well," said the boss. "I think he's moved house without telling us." He suggested that as I seemed to like *Record Mirror* so much perhaps I could have it delivered, to save him cancelling the order. "Do you want it instead of *New Musical Express*, or as well as?", Mum asked when I got home. Gift horse. As well as.

I liked *Record Mirror* because a) unlike the grey-and-white *New Musical Express* it had colour pics and b) it featured not only the UK Top 50 singles chart where the NME only carried the Top 30, but also the Billboard Top 50 singles. It was here in the lower reaches of the UK Hit Parade and in the "bubbling under" section that I discovered all those records that I thought "destined for the charts", as the NME review would have put it, residing instead at Number 42. *Mr Second Class* by the Spencer Davis Group. *Green Tambourine* by Sun Dragon. *Sky Pilot* by Eric Burdon. *Spooky* by Classics IV. *Up the Junction* by Manfred Mann. *I've Got You on My Mind* by Dorian Grey. *Marjorine* by Joe Cocker. *Rainbow Chaser* by Nirvana. Number 42 in the chart became by default a genre in its own right to me. Years later I would make entire compilation tapes for friends based on all those late sixties also-rans.

As well as virtually memorising the charts, I also devoured the review pages, poring over every last nondescript detail of records which more often than not I never heard at the time, such were the limited media outlets during the years of Radio One pop rationing. These were the years when my information input far exceeded what I actually had physical access to. As a result, those record reviews were as much of a forum for my fantasies and dream associations as any group photo, interview or TV appearance. Some of the discs reviewed became life-long (or fortnight-long) favourites. Some would be heard once before disappearing into the BBC monopolised ether. Others, I never heard at all at the time. I would gaze at names like Cherry Smash or Toby Twirl or the Web (featuring John L. Watson) and try to imagine from the group name and song title alone what they sounded like.

Those weekly new releases lists took on a typographical life of their own, and fed into my pop consciousness in ways which had little to do with taste or fandom. This ritual went on week in, week out for the best part of my school years – days of innocence before experience. This is how many of us pop kids consumed our culture in the days before media saturation dictated our every impulse. The best thing about these weekly bulletins, the very pop-art essence of them, was their inbuilt obsolescence. The here-this-week-gone-by-next nature of their display conveyed the beauty of transience, a feature that was and still is the very essence of the pop process. I don't remember hankering obsessively after any pop record during that period, or mourning its passing. I lived in an eternal now. There would always be another great song coming right up.

The thing I liked best about Grammar School by the second year was being ill. Sauntering up to the doctors at ten to nine while everyone was waiting outside the Red Lion pub for the school bus. Walking past them in their uniforms. Sitting in the waiting-room reading the Four Marys in *Bunty* until the receptionist called my name. Leaving the doctor's at twenty past nine, perhaps collecting some tablets for Mum from an unlocked cabinet that stood on the gravel path outside the surgery, rows of bottles all neatly labelled with name and address of the patient, utterly unattended and left to trust in those different far-off times. In the High Street the school bus had gone and the Market Square was half empty. Just a few women leaning on their bikes gossiping away. I walked slowly down Bedford Road reading my *New Musical Express*. An advert for the Equals' *Baby Come Back* on the front cover. Luxuriating in the knowledge that I'd got all day to be poorly.

GROCER BOY

– One tin vegetable soup. One tin oxtail soup. One tin tomato soup.

I slowly placed the tins on the table.

– One Golden Shred Marmalade. One Libby's Creamed Rice.

The old man's kitchen smelt of rancid fat and his curtains smelt of kitchen.

– One quarter luncheon meat. One quarter haslet. One quarter pork roll.
His clothes smelt of curtains and his breath smelt of whatever he had last ate, luncheon meat probably, or haslet, or pork roll. Or tongue which he normally had.

– Not having your tongue this week, Mr Crawford?

– Eh?

Or spit. I think he lived off his own spit.

– One small Findus frozen beans. Forty Woodbine Plain.
– I asked for untipped.
– They are untipped.
– Eh?
– One packet McVitie's Digestives. One Fray Bentos Steak and Kidney Pie. One Fray Bentos Steak and Kidney Pudding. What's the difference, Mr Crawford?
– Eh?

S'wot 'orses eat.

– One packet Peek Frean biscuits with a piece of dog's muck on the top.
– Pop? No, I didn't order pop. And don't go so fast. I'm counting.
– One Robertson Blackcurrant Jam. One...
– One and elevenpence! Bring me Hartley's next time. Where's my Bisto?
– It's not on the list, Mr Crawford. Perhaps you forgot to write it down.
– Eh?

Every week I brought Mr Crawford his groceries, and every week he made me take them out of the cardboard box and lay them in an orderly fashion on his plastic chequered tablecloth while he ticked off every item and moaned about the bill. He lived in a tumbledown bungalow at the bottom of West Road. A trail of broken fencing barred the way as you edged past a lean-to that had leaned too far and was being propped up by a forest of weeds. You knocked loud and forced your way in through a back door that was always stuck.
– You forgot my matches. Go back up Bamford's and get them.
– No, look here they are, Mr Crawford. Under your list.
– Eh?

I pedalled a heavy, cumbersome trades bike with a big wicker basket and a small wheel at the front. In the middle of the frame, painted in white on black metal plating, it said: "Bamford's Provisions. Market Square. Albion Sands." Brian Bamford was a genial man with a bald head and a flushed face the colour of the luncheon meat he sold. He was the oldest of the three brothers who ran the shop. Next in the family line was Terence, who was tall and nervous and went "Mmm, yes, mmm, mmm" when he answered you. I asked Mum what was up with him and it was the first time I heard the term "shell shock". Youngest brother Kevin had a day job as a postman and only worked afternoons, driving the delivery van when he finished his Post Office shift. Mrs Bamford served in the shop in her blue overall and dotted headscarf. Mum had been at school with her and knew her well. The completed orders were laid out neatly in rows in the stockroom that always smelt of spilled Daz. The boxes all smelt of Daz. The Bamfords smelt of Daz. Brian in his white coat with moon spots on his head. Terence in his brown coat with a pencil and a red Ready Reckoner in the top pocket. Mrs Bamford in her dotted headscarf. All of them dusted in Daz.

****

Linda Bell walks into vision – "Enter stage left, exit stage right," as Snagglepuss would say if he was here, but he isn't because he is a cartoon animation, and we are all inanimate. We are concentrating on Linda Bell's legs without appearing to be blinking or breathing at all. Clip clop stiletto walk. Bare white legs which begin at her shoes and end at a belt that might be a skirt.

It's nine o'clock, high summer, and all the shops are shut except the off-licence, where at the outer limits of our peripheral vision Linda Bell opens a door, ding-dong, customer, and her legs go in first and last. They re-emerge minutes later. In the meantime nothing has happened. Daylight turns slowly to dusk without any of us moving. You'll get nothing from us but spitting.

Linda Bell re-enters our orbit, framed in furrowed gaze. Her legs are flesh. Her walk is scissors. Her skirt is curvy violet swirls. She carries a bottle of Bulmer's and arrives at the dead centre of our vision. Nearly. Nearly. Now. Pretend it's *The Golden Shot*. Bernie the Bolt. Up a bit. Up a bit. Down a bit. Left a bit. Suddenly through slippery fingers she drops the bottle. Smash. The sound shatters the silence. Without breaking stride Linda Bell turns and walks back to the off-licence for another bottle. No expression on her face. Or ours. You'd never guess what we were thinking. Or if.

We are the boys you see from the bus, the ones who promenade their smirks and frowns and long elastic gobs of spit that take an age to reach the ground. We are the ones who lounge languidly on Market Square bog roofs and bus-shelter benches, staring right through you as you look up from your book, on your way to somewhere. There will be another identical bunch of us at another Market Square further along the way. You'll see them, but you won't see what they see. One will aim a not-so-playful punch. Another will accidentally on purpose fall from the back of the bench, just for comedic effect, just for something to do that might break the boredom. Another will shake a bottle of fizzy pop and spray his mates. They will barely react. Soon you'll be gone. They will still be there.

We fix our gaze on the caff, the bookies, the shoe mender, the insurance office, the off-licence. Everything can be taken in with one lazy sweep of the head. We are life-proof. All sprawled on the roof of the blue-tiled subterranean public convenience that stands at the centre of the Market Square. There used to be a market there, now there's just these half-sunken bogs. Every summer evening with nothing much that we can be bothered to do, we are on our elbows or haunches fixing our sights on just enough.

****

I pedalled by Louise Muir's house. She was down her passage and I hoped she couldn't see me lumbering along on my trades bike and not on a smart racer with Disraeli gears.

The only thing worse than Louise seeing me on my trades bike would be if she had a friend who also saw me. Say that friend had moved down from Scotland and was called Patty. Suppose she went and lived on the overspill estate and was just as pretty as Louise, not milky skin and Silvikrin pretty but freckle-faced and crop-cut pretty. Imagine that. That would be a nightmare. It would be even worse if I had to deliver groceries to Patty's Mum and Patty was there. The worst nightmare of all would be if Patty's Mum ordered so many groceries that the box bulged and expanded in the bike basket and stuck fast. No matter how much you tried, no matter how much you sweated and heaved, the box wouldn't budge. Instead you would have to knock on the door and it would be Patty who answered and you'd have to say: "Your groceries are stuck in my basket. I'm going to have to bring them all in, tin by tin." Try saying that, the words turning to dribble on your chin.

Even in the dream it would be awful, let alone if it actually happened, which it didn't. And say this was a recurring dream, and it happened every week. You would pedal your trades bike to Patty's house and you'd be praying that the box would slip out easily. You might even try loosening it as soon as you'd put it in at Bamford's yard, just as a precaution. Perhaps you would stop half-way down the High Street and adjust it again just to check that it wasn't wedged, but something in the motion and the bumpy roads and that moment you peddled impetuously off a kerb would cause it to swell every time. There was just one time when this didn't happen, when the box wasn't too big – in the dream, I mean. I nearly tore my arms out of their sockets but I did eventually manage to lift the box clean out and stagger red-faced and sweaty to the door. This was even worse in a way, stumbling clammy-browed up the front path, as Patty's Mum smiled a kind sympathetic smile and leaned against the door of her shiny new kitchen in her nice new house on the overspill estate. (Mrs Patty was gorgeous too but you weren't supposed to fancy someone's mum.) Usually it was Patty's mum who answered the door, but sometimes it was Patty. All on her own in the house. I don't know what would have been worse if any of this had really happened. I would probably have concentrated on something else. The music coming out of the cream-coloured transistor radio perhaps. The one on the draining board. Alan Black on *Midday Spin* playing Underground records. Something like that.

And all the time that this dream which wasn't real was never happening, Patty never once took the piss or went: "Wur, shy boy on his trades bike, glowy face and can't speak for mumbles boy, look at him blushing, he can't even deliver groceries properly." Instead she just opened the door, smiled, helped me lay the groceries on the kitchen table, and said: "My Mum orders far too much stuff, doesn't she?" In the dream that never really happened, I mean.

****

Dad hated taking us to Brampton races. He enjoyed the horse racing. He just didn't like the journey. Six of us crammed in the car. One long slow crawl in bank holiday traffic up the A1, mostly in first or second gear. "This is doing the car no good at all." He was worried about the Sunbeam Rapier. It was costing us money, he said. New parts. Maintenance. MOT. Grumble grumble. Crawl crawl. Are we there yet?

Whenever we went to Brampton races, which we did most bank holidays, I liked to go out into the country on my own. My favourite spot was the open ditch at the far side of the course where you could see the horses coming up the back straight from the two-and-a-half-mile starting post. The family rarely wanted to venture out with me. Mostly they would stay close to the car which Dad usually managed to park right by the rails just along from the grandstand. A bag of crisps, a bottle of pop, a wave, and off I went. See you at the end of the last race.

I took my spot by the open ditch near the St John's Ambulance man and his helper, a boy about my age, 13, 14. The First Aid man was friendly, asking me what I'd picked in the first race. I said Number 12. We watched the horses go by, hoofs thunderous, snorts audible, everything louder and larger than it is on the telly. "There goes yours, Number 12," said the ambulance man, nudging me. Then he asked me what I'd picked in the next race. I hadn't picked anything, so we sat down on the grass by the fence and opened the *Racing Post*. His helper went off to the ambulance. He seemed annoyed. Perhaps he didn't like me talking to his boss.

The St John's man spread the paper open and we looked at the horses in the next race. It was a bit blowy so he had to keep the paper steady. When his young helper came back he got up and went back to his duties, watching the horses and jockeys go by, hoping there would be no accidents but prepared for all eventualities. In the second race there was a faller at the fence before ours and the loose horse veered off the track and went stampeding by on our side of the rails. I'd seen the horse coming, but the ambulance man grabbed me out of the way in case I got hurt.

– There goes yours. Number Three.

When the second race was over we sat down again and picked a horse for the next one. This time he couldn't keep the paper still and had to put both his hands on it to flatten it out. His helper stood there making an annoyed face and getting agitated again.

– Come on, hurry up. The race starts in a minute.
– Plenty of time yet, Simon.

I thought about going off to get an ice cream, but the ambulance man said, "Simon will get them, won't you, Simon?" He wouldn't let me pay. While Simon was away he asked me about my family and where I lived.

After the third race we sat down to look at the horses again but this time he kept moving his hand about underneath the paper, even though the wind wasn't blowing. Simon hopped from one foot to another, saying "The horses are coming," but the other race had only just finished. There was nobody about but us. The St John's man asked me if I'd ever seen inside an ambulance, but Simon got even more annoyed and said: "He's not allowed."

After the fourth race we sat down and the St John's man spread the Racing Post again. It only took me a few seconds to pick a horse, but I couldn't get up straight away because the ambulance man had his leg stretched over mine pinning me down. He seemed to be moving about quite a lot and disturbed the paper more than the wind did. Then he went to attend to some medical matters in the ambulance. Simon turned to me and said: "I don't like him, do you?"

When it was time to pick a horse in the fifth race I didn't want to sit down any more. The St John's man said: "Come on, you want to pick a winner, don't you?" Simon said: "He's already told you, hasn't he? He doesn't want to."

At the end of the day's racing the St John's man offered to walk back to the car park with me. I said, "It's OK. My Mum and Dad will be over there by the rails."

– Let's just make sure they're there. If they aren't I'll give you a lift home.
– They'll be there. They won't go without me.

But he insisted. Just in case. He told Simon to pack everything away in the ambulance and walked all the way across the course with me, saying, "It's alright. I'll make sure you get home OK."

I scanned the faces in the emptying grandstand. Everybody is the person you are looking for until they aren't. Eventually I could see Mum and Dad waving. I waved back and turned to say goodbye to the St John's man but he was already on his way back across the open country to his ambulance and to Simon.

ROUGH BOOKS

– I'm growing tits. I'm sure I am.
– See, I told you.

Connolly was right. There was a definite swelling.

When we had a dog I loved to go into Jordan's Pet Shop and Corn Store where the grain smell rose from the sacks and everything smelt of scented dust and husks. You could stick your head right into the sacks and sniff. Pretending to get dog biscuits. Taking ages. There was always a box of Spiller's in the pantry. The yellow ones tasted best, but when our dog died there was no excuse to go into Jordan's any more. They had little time for inquisitive boys and would invariably throw you out, even if you said you were looking at the tropical fish. When we had Agriculture lessons on the school farm there were sacks there too. Burying our heads in the husks and dust. Some of us, not all of us. Not Trevor Beech, who always handed his homework in on time and knew a thing or two about science.

"They contain fertility drugs for the cattle" he said. "And hormones." We took no notice of him and continued to inhale, but the more I examined my breasts, side on in Mum's dressing table mirror, I just knew it must be the cattle feed that was doing it.
– You'll need a bra soon.
– Don't joke about it. They're growing. Look. They are! It's not funny.

You go back saying: "I'm going to be different this year. I'm going to be someone else." This lasts until the second day when you get detention for something you did or didn't do. Playing a paper-and-comb version of *Thank You Very Much for the Aintree Iron*, for example, while you're waiting for the Geography teacher to arrive and being the only person in the class not to see him walk in. That sort of thing.

We were supposed to do all our working out in our rough book, and were rarely issued new ones until we provided evidence that every last page of the old one had been filled. The occasional lackadaisical teacher handed out a fresh one on request, but most made you beg. The hard-liners insisted that you write your rough notes entirely in pencil, then rub them out when you got to the last page and start all over again. In your Maths book you were asked to do your working-out in the margin, but a rough book was all margin, and after a while that's where I lived. My entire alternative curriculum took shape in my rough books, that's where all my real working-out got done. The first thing you did with a new rough book was decorate the cover with the names of your favourite groups. If you went off a band you couldn't really rub them out, it would spoil the design and make the cover look shabby. You had to wait till your rough book was full before you could invent yourself all over again. At 13 I sometimes wanted to re-invent myself every week.

It was around this time that I discovered Tyrannosaurus Rex. It wasn't the music that initially attracted me, although that seduction came soon enough. It was the photograph of Marc Bolan and Steve Peregrin Took that accompanied a *New Musical Express* interview shortly after the release of the first Tyrannosaurus Rex LP, *My People Were Fair and Had Sky in their Hair but Now They're Content to Wear Stars on their Brows*. Seated beneath a tree by a border of wild grass, Marc wears a breastplate of child's armour, a long-sleeved canary-yellow T shirt, and washed-out tangerine flares. He is not at this point wearing Anello and Davide shoes, and is shod in what by his androgynous standards are regular purple pumps. Round his neck hangs a buttercup-and-daisy chain. He cradles a pine cone in his hands. Steve Peregrin Took wears bug-eyed sci-fi shades, a pink granny cardigan, and purple flares. On his feet are black-and-white baseball boots. Round his wrists are what look like leather gauntlets. The pair of them look impossibly cool. Bolan is elf-like, yet stern and aloof. Took looks sullen, almost malevolent.

I only saw the photo cropped and in black-and-white at the time, like I only saw most of the media sixties in black-and-white, but that moody noirish monochrome spoke of darker, more beguiling, mysteries. It was like peering into the Narnia wardrobe. If only I could walk into that world and wander about and see what they see. And dress like that. Tyrannosaurus Rex, sitting in an English garden, with flowers and pine cones and granny cardigans and breastplates. They were my most fey imaginings come to life and of a life to come and I hadn't even heard the music yet! When I did hear it, on John Peel's *Top Gear*, their strange pixie pop sounded exactly like the photo.

I barely skim-read the *NME* interview that accompanied the photo. The image and that extraordinary album title gave me all the information I needed. It was the earliest days of my enchantment with the Underground, and my perceptions were mostly superficial. I figured that a long album title must be indicative of music that lay way beyond my understanding, right? This was my quantifying period. In the same way that long titles could be combed for hidden truths, lengthy album tracks must surely equate with musical genius if it took that long to get it all across. That was my reasoning. I'd heard of, but not yet heard the 17-minute version of *In a Gadda da Vida* by Iron Butterfly. And hadn't Eric Burdon recorded tracks of a similar length with his psychedelic Animals? For a brief moment during 1968 and 1969 long song titles and long songs were my naïve benchmark for musical progression. I was gradually disabused of this notion by the sheer quantity of turgid blues jams I had to endure, but before disillusion and disenchantment kicked in, in the high summer of my innocence and awe came titles like *Scenescof, Strange Orchestras* and *Wind Q-Q-Quartets*, and mysteries the like of which I'd never known.

Connolly's mate Jimbo, a top-of-the-crop A streamer, brought that first album into school soon after it was released. It turned out that it was his older sister I'd seen carrying a John Mayall's Bluesbreakers LP across the school forecourt in the first year, and now the family mantle of hipness had been handed down to Jimbo. "You'll need the lyric sheet," he assured me when he handed the LP over. "You won't be able to understand what he's singing. Nobody can." I fronted it out like any 13-year old would. "Yeah, of course I could follow the lyrics," I lied when I returned the album, eager to be on the path this music was on. The truth was I could barely follow a word of it. Momentarily I would think I was up to speed as a lucid phrase burst through with sudden unexpected clarity, but by the time I recognised another one Bolan had already scampered on a full stanza ahead of me. It took me a while to become fully conversant in Bolanese, but I persevered, chasing him down that lyric sheet as Alice chased the white rabbit, hopelessly hoping that I was getting it, desperately desiring that the pursuit would eventually lead to understanding. I'm not sure I have pursued anything with the same degree of purposeful intensity since.

My initiation was made all the more difficult by the fact that we were currently a household without a record player. I borrowed a tiny portable from my neighbour's daughter Pauline, she of the regional vowels and the dog-licked behind. The LP was bigger than the equipment it played on and the speaker was minuscule. Even by my no-fi standards this was cranking it down to insect level. And yet, even within this shrunken audiosphere the magic still revealed itself and was utterly compelling. Marc Bolan's songs didn't seem to be about any of the things that anything else was about. They didn't appear to be about drugs, even though I had started to work out by then that some music was about drugs, might even have been made on drugs. *My People Were Fair* and its follow-up, *Prophets Seers and Sages the Angels of the Ages*, presented me with a different kind of weird, one that I was utterly unaccustomed to and for which I had no reference points. I barely understood what any of the songs were about, but it didn't seem to matter. I could invent my own meanings. And if it was all nonsense, as some suggested it was, a half-digested hodge-podge of ancient myths and general hocus pocus, then it chimed perfectly with my own nonsense world, which was full of those things too.

I shrank Marc Bolan's visions to the lowly horizons of my own drab landscape. *Knight* made me think of the Crusader hymns I sang at Junior School. *Trelawny Lawn* evoked the rolling expanse of greenery at the front of the Secondary Modern school, the steep gradient of which we used to love to roll down at the annual town sports day. Trelawny was obviously Squire Trelawney, the landowner and financier of the expedition in Robert Louis Stevenson's *Treasure Island*. I tethered association to association by the most tenuous of threads and embroidered my limited vocabulary with Travelling Tragitions and wind q-q-quartets and chateaus in Virginia Waters (a place that was as fictional to me as Narnia). Every word that Marc sang and Steve augmented sprung a trapdoor in my unconscious. And it all began with that black-and-white photograph, that portal into another world. Had I been born a few years earlier I might have been one of those jaded old hippie heads who preferred the Incredible String Band, and detected in Marc Bolan a scheming little mod on the make. But I was born at exactly the right time to appreciate Tyrannosaurus Rex. From the summer of 1968 through to the end of 1970 they were my teenage Arcady, my otherworld, my everything.

In the third year Mr Isaacs took us for art. There were no light shows, tie-dye demonstrations or Ravi Shankar LPs with him. He was a traditionalist, immersed in classicism. Despite myself I was good at art, but I spent very little of Mr Isaac's lessons observing the finer points of perspective while trying to locate the golden section or the vanishing point. Instead I devoted myself to my rough book, where I developed an extensive portfolio of pop stars in the nude. Each casually etched figure from the pop world was distinguished by their protuberance, a curly whirl of barbed-wire pubic hair and a Bishop's slit hat poking out of it. We were at that age. We drew pricks on everything. On toilet walls. On each other's homework just as it was about to be handed in (those of us who handed in homework). Connolly was good at guessing them.

– That must be the Dave Clark Five because the drummer is at the front.
– Correct.
– That's Brian Jones. I can tell by the shape of his guitar. And that's Roger McGuinn in his glasses.
– Who's that then?

Two men are on a bed doing it. One is face down in the bedsprings. The other one is sticking it up him.

– Don't know.
– It's David and Jonathan.
– Oh yeah, you've got the hair right. One frizzy, one straight.

Our new English teacher was Miss Hunt. She came from Liverpool, looked like Cilla Black's sister with slightly more overbite, and wore miniskirts. We imitated her Scouse accent and she didn't seem to mind. At first, I did as little work for her as I did for anyone else, but I soon began to enjoy her lessons immensely.

Dad started working seven days a week in order to earn enough money to feed four hungry kids, and to keep us in clothes. From Mondays to Fridays he worked at Silvertown Plating, five minutes walk from school. I liked to go there in the late afternoon and wait for him to finish work. I'd stand and watch molten metal ooze into a press and come out the shape of a car radiator grill, then he'd give me a lift home. On Saturdays he would supplement his wage with some extra work at a local garage, a small business in a yard off the Market Square with a Derv diesel pump and car parts strewn everywhere. On Sunday mornings he went back to Silvertown Plating to turn molten metal into grill shapes. There weren't any buses till the afternoon so he walked. It was only three miles.

He said, "Who's this, then?"

– Who's what?
– Which one of your teachers is this?

Dad had been to the parents' evening. He rarely bothered any more. They all told him the same thing.
– Go on. Have a guess.

I had to guess.

– Why does Robert hate me? He's a bright lad but he mucks about all the time and he never does me any homework.

– I dunno. Miss Hunt?

– What do you think of her?

– I dunno. She's not bad.

– She's an absolute pearl. You're lucky to have a teacher like that. Why do you give her such a hard time? Do some work for her.

I left my picture parade book of pop stars behind at the end of an art lesson. Panic. Connolly said: "You'll get expelled if Isaacs finds it." I fretted till dinner break and plotted how I might sneak into the Art Room and retrieve it. When I went in Mr Isaacs was sat at his desk and handed it back to me without comment. It fell open at Peter and Gordon. One blonde. One brunette.

Trudging the endless green of the playing field. A distant bell sounds calling us in after dinner break but we only walk more slowly. The school buildings seem to recede in the heat. My transistor radio plays *Wichita Lineman*. It symbolises the space between us and the school. The space. The us. And the radio playing *Wichita Lineman*. The medium-wave signal sways in synch with the movement of my body as I surf the electromagnetic contours. The lyrics magnify my ache and the wind sings softly. And it was all about the getting no nearer and the getting further away. The school building where it was. Rising as mirage. And us where we were not but where we wanted to be instead. Skimming dreams like pebbles across the hard tarmac of the netball courts.

And it was all about the moment and the space between moments. And it all connected. It was a perfect moment with everything in harmony and the radio playing *Wichita Lineman*. Or it could have been *Galveston*.

WATERING CANS WALKING DOWN
TAVISTOCK STREET

A late autumn afternoon. Damp grass littered with firework shells. The dead end of the year. Marc Bolan's voice ignites the gloom. Spells are cast. I am in my back garden but worlds away. Top Gear. Tyrannosaurus Rex in session. Underneath the living-room window a sink unit sits empty in a purpose-dug plot. I think the plan was to put fish in there some day but we never did. Shoulder to the door-frame, hunched against the brickwork. *Conesuala* and *The Evenings of Damask* play on the radio. Why am I outside and not indoors? Probably because it's a Sunday and I'm fleeing the creeping claustrophobia of another endless afternoon inside, captive and bored. I let those fireworks off yesterday when Mum and Dad were out. Leftovers from another aimless evening spent prowling dark streets in a predatory pack. The allure of throwing another desultory banger down another unlit passageway vanishes in the cold night air. The thrill is gone, along with the feeling in my fingers. My clownish and increasingly cuntish mates go: "Come on, don't go, give us your fireworks, fuck off then." So I do. I fuck off home to a warm house. And now I'm out here listening to *The Seal of Seasons* and *Misty Coast of Albany*. Both songs are news to me. There's an LP coming soon, John Peel mentioned it, perhaps the new ones will be on that. I want to be outside so I can dwell in the magic without distraction. Just me, my dream world, my transistor radio and Marc Bolan's tinny piercing voice and Steve Peregrin Took's skittering palm dance on the bongo skins. *The Misty Coast of Albany* fades to grey on yet another fogbound Bedfordshire day. Mystic realms await. Memories coalesce. The muffled sound those fireworks made. Fizzing squibs. Blue smoke rising in the breezeless air. The gunpowder smell soon gone. Nothing lingers in the emptiness of a small-town Sunday except silence. It's just me, *The Misty Coast of Albany* and the ennui of a November afternoon. Except it isn't November because *The Misty Coast of Albany* was on a different session altogether and John Peel was on in the evening by then, not the afternoon. My memory has compressed everything into one long autumn swirl with the ground all sticky with leaves, my fingers numb, and Marc Bolan's voice "making things for everything that run, run". I attach no significance to this memory, no sense of occasion. Why would I? My day is dead brown leaves pressed flat between the pages of an unread book.

When I consult Ken Garner's Peel sessionography to check the date of that earlier rendezvous – *The Friends. Conesuala. The Seal of Seasons. The Evenings of Damask* – I see that it was aired on November 10th 1968. My 14th birthday. Remembrance Sunday too. But there's no remembrance in my head, no memory of cards and presents, nothing except the shapes that sorcery makes when you're enthralled by a magician's spell. All extraneous detail has been jettisoned. Like those discarded fireworks, the memories spluttered and expired long ago. All that remains is the shimmering aura of that music.

If my time at Grammar School could be plotted as a graph, with the vertical axis measuring my levels of attainment from ten down to zero, and the horizontal axis registering my five years of attendance between September 1966 and July 1971, the line would form a perfect parabola, with the axis of symmetry falling exactly at the halfway mark during February 1969. In retrospect, this entire period of my life seems pre-ordained, determined by the fates. By summoning the immutable forces of destiny and the universal constant of nature I can pinpoint the axis moment of low attainment and maximum drudgery to the actual day, to the actual Tuesday afternoon, in fact. We were doing cross-country and the downpour was unrelenting. The wind agitated the cold rain into horizontal flurries and my flapping boot laces whipped the backs of my legs. My socks were down to my ankles but I was too weather-numbed to stop and pull them up or tie my laces properly. So I blundered blindly on until I trod on a lace, tripped, stumbled and fell. I hit the wet ground hard. Everyone around me carried on running, heads turning to glance briefly at the fallen, hurrying on towards the changing rooms and the warmth of the showers. That was my quadratic function moment. My xy squared.

Or perhaps it was earlier that same day. On the Tuesday morning when we were doing double Metalwork and double Tech Drawing. By then it was clear that I had inherited none of Dad's practical skills. As a small child my Meccano sat undisturbed in its box. One day, placing some misplaced blind faith in my abilities, Dad let me take a Stanley knife into Junior School for Craft lesson. I expertly selected a blade and then inexpertly sliced through some balsa wood and into the top of one of my fingers. Dad was politely requested not to provide me with blades again. In Woodwork lesson at Waden Grammar it took me two terms to make a sledge, which I eventually carried home on a warm May evening, missing my school coach and lugging the thing through town to the bus station. Town boys and old-timers alike mocked me. One old bloke asked if I was expecting snow. In Metalwork it took me three weeks to make the name tag you were supposed to finish by the end of Lesson One. By the time everyone else was constructing elaborate mechanical contraptions, I was still designing a spanner that upon completion had the unique property of not fitting any known nut or bolt size ever devised. Tech Drawing was merely the nightmare of Maths with bigger protractors. The only thing that made that double period even remotely bearable was that we could sometimes get the teacher to talk about his friendship with leading professional wrestlers of the day. Apart from such brief diversions it was an hour-and-a-half of drawing-board purgatory every week.

Connolly wasn't there one Tuesday morning. He strolled in at lunchtime and said, "Just get off your school bus at the Market Square. Tell the driver you've got a dentist's appointment." So I did. It was raining and we went and sat upstairs in the café opposite the bus station and watched the shoppers come and go. The windows steamed up. An hour vanished in a blur of pop gossip and girl talk. The rain eased off for a bit so we went and sat in the Rec, dangling from the swings, twisting and untwisting without making the world go round any faster. *The Jimmy Young Show* played on my transistor radio. We were that desperate for pop rations. "We're not any good at anything, are we?", said Connolly. "We aren't in any of the teams. We aren't any good at any of the subjects." Like me, Connolly had forsaken his prime football years for the egg-shaped ball and the braying derision of the lunkheads who threw it. We were good at pop music, that was about it. Even now whenever I hear *I'm Gonna Make You Love Me* by the Supremes and the Temptations it reminds me of those brief snatched moments of freedom, truanting down the Rec in miserable weather. I don't remember feeling cold at all, just grateful that I could escape for a bit and go and sit somewhere, anywhere that didn't involve double Metalwork or double Tech Drawing.

By the third year, school had become a vast irrelevancy to me and I to it. Once you realise that most of the teachers don't give a toss who you are or what little you will amount to you ease comfortably into anonymity and indifference. Any learning that I did during this period occurred despite, not because of, what school offered me. The only teacher I cared about, and who cared about me, was Miss Hunt. In my end of third-year report, when the total aggregate of all my marks added up to some people's average mark, when most teachers penned withering critiques of my inadequacies ("He puts nothing into the subject, he will get nothing out of it"), Miss Hunt wrote: "Robert is fluent and articulate in both written and spoken English." She could see something that none of the others could, and even then I continued to bite the hand that fed me. Sullen one week, excitable to the point of detention the next. It's what you do when you no longer trust any of the hands that offer the food.

Another week. Another Games lesson. I had been thrown out of P.E. for cheating at Pirates, this stupid game we were allowed to play once a term, whereby an intricate obstacle course was set out among the gymnasium equipment. Participants had to negotiate a succession of vaulting horses, mats, ropes and wall bars while being chased by a selection of press-ganged oafish "pirates". You had to do this without putting a foot in the water (i.e. the uncovered parts of the gymnasium floor), otherwise you were out of the game. I dipped an incriminating toe and thought I'd got away with it, but little or nothing escaped Hardman's unflinching eye and I was banished to the changing room.

Dickie Dangerfield was in there. Having handed in his regular sick note he was sitting reading his *Melody Maker* and barely noticed my presence. I got my *New Musical Express* out of my bag and sat on the bench beside him. Mister sick note reading his *Melody Maker*. Mister cheating at Pirates reading his *NME*.

– That looks good. John Rowles' new one. Do you like him then? John Rowles?
– No. I'm doing the crossword.

Moments pass.
– Inez and Charlie Foxx.
– You what?
– 11 Down. Inez and Charlie Foxx. If there's an X or a Z in it it's always Inez and Charlie Foxx.
– Oh, thanks.

The sound of stampeding feet and shouting boys in the gymnasium fails to interrupt our contemplations.
– What's John Rowles's favourite colour then?
– Fuck off, Dangerfield.
– How about Solomon King? He's good.

His sarcasm is relentless.
– Solomon King will probably be on the front cover next week. "Solomon King bound for the top", it will say.
– He's a bit square for me.
– He looks a bit round to me.

Quiet for a bit.

– That's a good word. Square. Do they still say that in *New Musical Express*?

That night when I get home.
– Mum, from next Thursday can I start having *Melody Maker* instead of *New Musical Express*?

Not as well as. Instead of.
So began another crucial phase of my musical education. *Melody Maker* became my biblical scroll and I read it from cover to cover. Not figuratively. Literally. I read the news coverage. I read Blind Date (where records were played to a major artist of the day without revealing the source). I read the lengthy and often very earnest interviews. I read the live reviews page Caught in the Act. I read Chris Welch's hilarious singles reviews and was overjoyed to discover that it was permissible to take the piss out of this stuff. I read the Raver's Weekly Tonic, *MM*'s hip gossip-column version of *NME*'s Alley Cat. I read the folk pages and jazz pages. I read Mailbag, the readers' letters page. I read the Any Questions section where fans wrote in to enquire as to the exact gauge of Jack Bruce's bass strings. I even scanned the Musicians Wanted ads (Shilling a word. "No bread heads or timewasters. Must have own PA and transport.") and the Engagements Wanted ads ("An Able Accordionist" always at the top of the list). And like a kid pressing his nose to the sweetshop window, I perused all those Music Shop box ads and day-dreamed about instruments I could never afford.

– Miss Hunt told us what was wrong.

Everyone was talking like I had the lurgy or something. They looked at me differently. Schoolmates were all being kind, even some of the teachers were. Not in a false way. In a caring way. Connolly said, "Miss Hunt stood at the front and told us about your Dad and why you were off school for so long."

For months Dad kept up his seven-day schedule and walked to work every Sunday morning at half past seven, sometimes in the pissing rain. He contracted yellow jaundice, which led to pleurisy, which led to pneumonia. I think there was a double dose of malaria in there for good measure, a legacy of his National Service days in Egypt. He was taken into Bedford North Wing, and in the evenings I sat on the edge of his bed in a bleak soulless ward and read the paper while he and Mum chatted. One night he woke up and a window was open. Dad indicated an empty bed opposite. One of the patients had climbed out after being told he had a terminal illness. They found him wandering down Kimbolton Road in his pyjamas.

I stayed off school and helped Mum with the shopping and washing. Grummar came round and helped keep the house tidy. At dinner-time I fetched my youngest brother from Infant School and whizzed him home on the child seat of Mum's bike. When Dad came out of hospital he looked tired and drawn and had boils all over his body. He said it was because of all the bad blood in his system. One morning Mum told us that late the previous evening while we were sleeping one of the boils burst and the pus hit the ceiling. It left a hole in his leg as big as a bullet. Dad was asleep upstairs when she told me. Sometimes he didn't wake up till the afternoon. The medicine they gave him was too strong and they had to change it. He began to hallucinate wildly and told us that one morning when we went into the bedroom to talk to him we all turned into watering cans walking down Tavistock Street. We all had arms, legs, spouts and handles.

– How did the story end?
– What story?

I didn't have a clue what Connolly was talking about. I'd been off school helping Mum. Went to Bedford on the bus and got her some tea towels from the Green Shield shop. Went into Harlequin Records by the bus station and browsed the racks, perusing the sleeves of Underground LPs I couldn't afford. In Miss Hunt's English class we'd been asked to write a composition, so I wrote a story about a pop group who recorded their masterpiece but the studio burnt down and they lost it forever. I'd read a news item in *New Musical Express* about Brian Wilson abandoning a Beach Boys album in similar circumstances.

– How did the fire start?
– Did they make another record?

Half the class bombarded me with questions. They wanted to know more of the story. Miss Hunt had read it out in English in my absence.
– Why didn't you finish it?

It was eight pages long but they still wanted more. In most lessons I didn't write eight lines.

Dad began a long period of convalescence. I'd never heard the word before. I thought it had something to do with where nuns lived. What it meant was going for leisurely walks by the river. Sometimes went with him. I'd never spent that kind of time with my Dad, just relaxing, chatting, watching stuff.

We didn't go far, just down to the ironstone bridge and along the riverbank.

– I'm sure I saw a buzzard round here yesterday.
We looked up at the trees but there was no sign of a buzzard. You didn't get them round our way.
– Do you get them round Leighton Buzzard? Is that why it's called Leighton Buzzard?

And other intelligent questions like that. My starter for ten as we ambled along the river bank.
– There it is!
Movement in the trees.
– There!
A dark shape. Head tilted. Stock still. Watching us. We saw it again the next day. I hoped it would be there the day after that too and was disappointed when it wasn't. A couple of weeks later there was a report in the local paper about a buzzard seen in the woods in a village near Leighton Buzzard and I wondered if it was the same one. The village was called Wing.

Dad was convalescing for ages. Silvertown Plating told him they would keep his old job open, but they didn't, so he had to sign on the dole. He held out for months, too proud to take state handouts, relying on the charity of his older brothers until Mum's housekeeping allowance dwindled to nothing and he had no choice but to go to the unemployment office and draw what he was entitled to. The illness changed him. He stopped doing the garden. He stopped smoking too, for a while. A keen sportsman in his youth, he now took up playing bowls. A lawn appeared in our garden where the chrysanthemums used to be. Mum developed green fingers, planted carnations in the front border and did the weeding on warm summer evenings.

After a while he got a job offer. New firm. New factory being built. Blueprints were spread out on the front room floor, weighted down on the dinner table, then rolled up in a funnel when it was mealtime. Dad was going to be works manager and not in the tool shop any more. He was given responsibility for helping lay out the design of the factory floor, plotting where all the machinery should go. It all came to nothing. Mum said that when the plans for the new factory fell through Dad went for a walk and was gone for a long time. I don't know what happened exactly. One minute he had a job, the next minute he didn't. The factory was never built. Mum said he went for a walk by the river. When he got back he told her that he'd felt like throwing himself in.

THE NARROW WAY

In the late 1960s there was talk of raising the school-leaving age from 15 to 16. Twice, in 1968 and again in1969, it was mooted and then postponed. Many of my older Secondary Modern mates escaped while they could, the last of their generation to do so at that age. Those with CSEs landed the kind of semi-skilled jobs that were still semi-plentiful then. Anyone with legible handwriting and a lack of recidivist tendencies could find work as junior clericals, and several of my friends did.

With the routine of work came newly routinised leisure hours. Where once everyone had gravitated towards the Market Square bench or the bog roof or the Rec or the sand hills, schedules were now newly mapped out in darts nights, snooker nights, quiet-night-in nights. Sunday was cinema night. Bedford Granada. Didn't matter what was on. It was what they did now. So, where we all would previously have solemnly convened to make the scene or just hang about and do nothing, suddenly there was only me. On my own. Free to roam. Up the Rec. Round town. Through the fields. In my head. Anywhere. All alone with my *Top Gear*. Projecting myself into everything that John Peel played between 7pm and 9pm as the evening light softened and I lived out my solitary routine.

Five years previously I couldn't tell the difference between a Top 6 cover version and the pop chart original. Now I'm on the weirdness trail. A little note bending and slurred slide work from John Fahey can turn my world upside down. Pink Floyd's pastoral clouds of sound seem a world away from the Syd Barrett songs they used to sing. A pre-*Ummagumma* version of *The Narrow Way* is intro'd and outro'd with a simple wind-machine effect, but to me it is abstraction beyond compare. *The Narrow Way* plays as I walk my desire path at the edge of Feltwell's field and lasts until I reach the High Street. I can plot an entire Sunday evening memory map from record to record, each piece of music tracking my route round town, up and down the sand hills, walking towards the setting sun and home again.

There should be a heritage trail, laid out with arrows and a guide book, appropriate music playing at points along the way. Regular Sunday re-creations of those warm August evenings in 1969 with the harvest breeze ruffling the hair of a boy aged 14 who is playing the part of me as I too was playing the part of me at the time. Away in my head. Living anywhere but in the here and now.

When my Secondary Modern mate Jack left school, I inherited his paper round. He worked for Mr White, the anti-overspill man, and advised me not to tell Mr Sutton where I was going when I packed in my other round. The rival newsagents had a gentlemen's agreement not to poach or employ each other's paper boys. It was like Rangers players going to Celtic or City to United. You just didn't do it. Mr White paid better, though, and the shorter round meant that I could set an alarm for 6.45 instead of 6.00. For 18 months I'd been getting up before anyone in my house, my street, the world. Now I could luxuriate in a lie-in until nearly seven o'clock. I no longer had to pedal through wet willow meadows before dawn or zig-zag past moon craters in unpaved roads. I was done with lugging that heavy bag to distant hamlets in the slip stream and rain spray of haulage lorries on the A1. Instead I could watch the morning unfurl like a flower. I got used to the easy-going routine, greeting the new day going about its business, the same people following familiar patterns. There was this one man I could set my watch by. Every morning he walked his young Alsatian dog and I usually passed him at ten to eight on my way home at the end of my round. He adhered strictly to his clockwork routine and I could detect precisely how far behind or ahead of schedule I was, according to where I met him on his walk.

Jimmy Dunn asked me if I fancied going to London to watch Blind Faith play live in Hyde Park. He earnestly explained to me that Blind Faith were going to be the biggest band ever and that the supergroups were now taking over. He had seen the future and it was supergroups. The next few months seemed to prove him right. Humble Pie. Crosby, Stills and Nash, Blind Faith and all the supergroups to come. This is how it would be from now on. I began inventing my own. Taking stray members from Iron Butterfly, the American Breed and the Ultimate Spinach and imagining what they might sound like. For a short while Jimmy became my new pop oracle. He'd started to dress a bit hippyish and paid attention to the smallest details. I took notice of everything he said. He went to youth-club dances in distant village halls and got off with nurses at parties in Bedford who gave him love bites in intimate places. One day he rolled down his trousers and showed me one just to prove that it wasn't all talk. I looked on in silent admiration, both thrilled and bewildered that you could get a girl to bite you there on your inside thigh, just inches from your groin.

One summer evening walking past the Rec he pronounced with great authority that all the village-hall groups who used to do covers of *Ride Your Pony* or *Midnight Hour* were now doing *Born to Be Wild* instead. The way he described Blind Faith to me, enthused with the newfound belief of the initiate, I assumed that they would go on forever. I told Mum I was going to Bedford for the afternoon to look round the record shops, just in case she thought anyone in a velvet jacket was going to offer me a tainted cigarette, and we got on the train and went to watch the Third Ear Band, Edgar Broughton, Richie Havens, Donovan and the new supergroup gods. It was only the second gig that I'd ever been to. Every time I see the concert footage of that bright summer's day I look for the boy with the bowl fringe, earnestly squinting in the sunlight, seated stage left about 30 yards from the front, too much Steve Winwood in the speakers, not enough Eric Clapton.

****

Louise and Patty weren't inseparable any more. Patty had a boyfriend and Louise was up the Rec on her own. I'd had a thing for her ever since I'd hung around the Junior School gates in the summer of 1966, hearing her laughing and splashing in the pool, hearing the aching strains of God Only Knows and aching even more because I associated the song with her. Dreaming I was in the Troggs and impressing her as I performed *Anyway that You Want Me* while locking eyes with her in the front row. All through my adolescence she was that girl waving from a car at the little boy too late to lift his head. Running one step ahead as I followed in her dance. Well, now we were finally alone. Just us two dangling on the playground swings and listening to *Pick of the Pops*.

– And it's a rise of three places for Joe Dolan and *Make Me an Island*.
"I hate this one," she said.
"So do I," I hastily agreed.
– And it's a fifth week in the Top 20 for the Four Tops and *What Is a Man*.
"My sister's got this."

Insert dream scenario here. Her older sister, Mod girl Mandy in her bedroom, the spitting image of Julie Driscoll, putting on make-up, stacking singles on a Dansette.

"*Dick-a-Dum-Dum* is the worst record ever."
– ....means a new entry for Robin Gibb and *Saved by the Bell*.
"No. This is!"
None of my older mates were there. No intrusions. Just me and Louise dangling from the swings small-talking about the charts until we reached

an unspoken understanding. And the understanding was this. I realised that even if I chatted her up all summer this is as far as I would ever get. I just needed to know. And then I knew. Once I knew the yearning went away. In a way it was a relief not to have to fancy her any more. In a way.

You know that bit about halfway through the summer holiday? That bit where you can't remember if it's Week Three or Week Four because you've lost count? For the first two weeks you're just glad to be free of school. All through the final week all you can think is "This time next week, this time next week", while trying not to think that at all. But in the dream haze and heat of the third or fourth week of the summer break, adrift from your moorings, miles from shore, as far away from timetables and lessons as you can ever be – that's the best bit.

AD LIB FILTH

When you say your prayers at Infant School you interlock tiny fingers tightly, hold them close to your mouth and whisper to Jesus. When you say prayers at Junior School you make a cat's cradle and say "the pa and the glory", but you look around the room more and study the backs of necks. By the time you reach Senior School you suspect that God is no longer listening, so you mutter to your friends instead. Year by year your clasped hands drift down until they are barely clasped at all, your shoulders slouch, you edge further back down the assembly rows towards the rear of the hall. You mumble the hymns, if you can be bothered.

You go back saying: "I'm going to be different this year. I'm going to be someone else." This lasts until you blow what little cool you have by writing the word "Cajun" on your rough book. Cajun is a word you've read in *Melody Maker*. You're not sure what it is, but it's been mentioned that Fairport Convention are it and possibly Creedence Clearwater Revival are too. Connolly says, "What's Cajun?", and you've been found out. If you're going to be any good at pretending, you have to be sure you understand exactly what it is that you're pretending about.

Paul Mason is one of the A streamers. Good at games and girls gather round. Word of mouth travels fast. Jimbo tells Loco who tells Dickie

Dangerfield who tells us hep cats in Bottom C.

– He what?
– He wrote Mantovani on his rough book. He thinks it's a rock group.

Eyes light up. Elephant memories are activated. He will never be allowed to live this down. Ever.

By far the most enticing words printed in *Melody Maker* each week were "LP Winner". The phrase appeared in bold black type underneath whichever reader's letter was deemed by the editor to be that week's most erudite and insightful. And so it was, in October 1969, that me and Dickie Dangerfield devised a plan whereby we might win the coveted LP prize. *Trout Mask Replica* had not long been released, and retailed at 69/11. Three and a half pounds was well out of my paper-round range, and for all his Paul Oliver anthology acquiring habits it seemed beyond Dickie's financial orbit too. We started to plan our letter. "You can't just write 'Lulu is fab', or 'Come on Manfreds', like you can in the other papers," insisted Dickie. Instead, he suggested, we should write some sort of manifesto, full of eye-catching, hippie-baiting buzzwords, slagging off our favourite singers and praising people that we didn't actually like. We set about our task with enthusiasm. "Let's call Captain Beefheart ad-lib filth," he suggested.

– What's ad-lib?
– It means you make it up as you go along.

It seemed fitting.
– Right, what shall we say about Bob Dylan?

The exercise got us through an entire double period without once having to attend to pipettes and Bunsen burners. And we think we're the ravers. Each week Sonya Keaton also sits reading her *Melody Maker* in class. Absently scratching her thigh, chewing her biro, filling in her annual Reader's Poll.
– Go and see what she's put.
– I bet it's "Best singer Andy Fairweather Low".
– Yeah, or Steve Ellis.

Snigger.

Sonya is six foot tall. Germaine Greer hair and wild eyes that gave you a

"What are you staring at, creep?" look when you met her gaze. I'm volunteered to brush past her.

Best group. World. Country Joe and the Fish.

Best singer. World. Country Joe.

Best guitarist. World. Barry Melton out of Country Joe and the Fish.

Miscellaneous instrument. Roland Kirk. (We thought we were clever putting Ian Anderson.)

Best group. UK. Fleetwood Mac.

Best guitarist. Jeff Beck.
"What about Peter Green?" I ask.
"Fuck off!" she hisses.

Back at the work bench I relay her hipper-than-us knowledge. In matter-of-fact tones Dickie says: "Oh yeah, she goes up to the Marquee in the week and gets off with rock stars. Have you noticed she's never in Art on Fridays?"

– If you knew that why didn't you go up and ask her?
– I was too scared.

We laugh. Sonya Keaton glances over and stares her icy contemptuous stare.

During the next couple of Biology lessons Dickie goes lukewarm on the idea of putting his name to such an outrageous letter, so I rewrite it, amending an opinion here, omitting a swearword there. I add Julie Driscoll to the "love" list and crowbar in a reference to *Sugar Sugar*, which by now is Number One and will be for the rest of the year, the rest of my life probably. I send the letter off to 161 Fleet Street more in hope than anticipation. During the Christmas holiday the very last *Melody Maker* of the decade drops through the letterbox. On the front page is a photograph of Fleetwood Mac. On the back page a banner headline reads "DID POP STAND STILL IN '69?" They've printed the letter. A photo sequence runs across the top of the page, captioned with quotes from our Double Science piss-take manifesto. "BEATLES standstill." "DYLAN disappointing." "BEEFHEART ad-lib." "DRISCOLL ignored." "DOORS ignored."

To this day I'm crushed that they didn't print "ad-lib filth" in the caption like it said in the letter. What disappointed me more at the time was that they got my name wrong. Because I was given to writing my initials, R.A., in a joined-up looping line, they printed my name as M. Chapman, which meant that none of the sneering Fifth Formers that I showed the letter to believed I had written it. Feigning indifference, they were happy to assume that there was another Chapman from the same town in Bedfordshire, who had a thing for Julie Driscoll and Captain Beefheart. "I'd regard that as a blessing in disguise," said Dickie at school when I fumed indignantly at the Fifth Formers' disdain. He thought my amendments to the original letter were crap and now regretted not putting his name to the uncut version. "We'd have probably won the LP if you'd sent that in," he said. The real ignominy, though, was that after all that effort I wasn't even crowned LP Winner. That honour went to the letter below mine from one Barry McGowan of Marlborough, Wiltshire, who defended reggae against the "knockers". My letter had included Dickie's original vitriolic comments about having "simple reggae stuffed down our throats", and made me seem a hippie snob in comparison. I loved reggae. Four months after that letter was printed I became a suedehead. But at least they printed Dickie's pearl of wisdom about Beefheart turning from "electronics to ad-lib filth". Dickie thought that the phased trickery on the *Strictly Personal* album was the ultimate in scientific advancement. He couldn't understand why Beefheart himself had slated the released version for its gimmickry. But still, eh? The lead letter on the back page of the very last *Melody Maker* of the 1960s. My entrée into the world of pop writing. Fitting that it should have been a piss-take.

My classmate Johnny Bull lends me his copy of *Here We Go Round the Mulberry Bush* with the promise that there are dirty bits in it. For my convenience he has earmarked these on well-thumbed dog-eared pages. I'd long since stopped going to the town library, and my reading habits by 1969 consisted largely of pop mags and pop annuals. Johnny Bull was right, there were some mildly mucky bits in *Here We Go Round the Mulberry Bush*, but there was much else besides and I was hooked by paragraph three. At the beginning of the book Jamie MacGregor, the central character, talks about going up town on a Saturday morning, knowing that nothing ever happens but feeling that something just might. By the end of the first page Jamie is smoothing his hair and trying to walk unselfconsciously at the sound of an approaching bus full of High School girls. When the bus goes by it is empty. How did the author know so much about my life? Me and Jamie had so much in common. He does a grocery round on an old-fashioned trades bike just like I did. The basket stands on the front of his bike keep dropping down while he's riding. Mine just rusted off at the hinges so I had to tie them with string and rest the bike against a hedge or a wall when I took the groceries out.

Jamie is also forced to wrestle with his mate, who thrusts his groin into him when they fight, just like Spooner used to do to me on rainy mornings when we were bored and stuck indoors. There's even a bit where a dog comes along and ruins one of Jamie's snogging sessions. The same thing had happened to me one summer's evening at the top end of the Rec when a randy mutt attached itself to me, and a pre-arranged liaison that had offered so much promise ended in farce with a girl walking off in glowering contempt like the whole dog thing had been my fault. The dirty bits in *Here We Go Round the Mulberry Bush* weren't actually that dirty. They were poignant and pathos-ridden, just like adolescence is. There was also stuff in there about the demarcation between town girls and Grammar School girls, which was starting to become very real to me. I dreamed myself into every page of that book, every scenario, every anti-climactic encounter, and it's funny how if you keep doing that your dreams eventually become reality.

It was the custom each week at school for a different form to choose the hymns and Bible readings in Assembly. When you are in the first year you pay no attention and never think it will fall upon you to perform such duties, but suddenly we are Form Four Bottom C and the God spot shines on us. Morning Assembly has become a bit more liberalised of late. Some classes have even been allowed to choose a piece of popular music rather than a hymn, and the reading no longer has to be from the Bible. I'd recently read a lengthy interview with John Lennon in Melody Maker where he talked about his beliefs and gave his thoughts on God so I said: "I'll do it." I had to submit the Melody Maker interview to our form teacher for approval.

– You can read this bit, but not this bit.
– Why not?
– Because it contains the word "genitals".

Not being entirely sure what the word "genitals" meant, I read it anyway. With the Beak seated stage left and me standing stage right, I was meant to start reading after the hymn had finished, but I was so nervous I began before everyone was fully seated. Despite this, I still got to spout the thoughts of Chairman John to a hall full of 800 people.

When the Lower Sixth organised the Assembly they played the Edgar Broughton Band's anti-Vietnam song *American Boy Soldier*. When the track ended the headmaster addressed us in his best sorrowful tones and said: "And I hope that never happens to any of you." Dickie Dangerfield was shaking with silent laughter as we prayed to the power and the glory, but I thought it was poignant when the Beak said that. He suddenly seemed more human. Afterwards I asked Dickie what song he would choose if his class got to do the Assembly.

– *Machine Gun* by Jimi Hendrix.

John Lennon has short hair now. The Plastic Ono Band perform *Instant Karma* on *Top of The Pops*. Yoko sits blindfold on a stool and holds up signs. Smile. Peace. Hope. Breathe. It's the greatest thing I've ever seen on Top of The Pops. I'm very taken with Lennon's newly shorn look. I'm also intrigued by the photos of the newly shorn Manson girls who are paraded on the front page of the newspapers looking cultish and not so much defiant as in a trance. It was those two factors as much as my desire not to get beaten up by gangs of marauding boot boys that made me decide to become a suedehead. Mum thinks my hair is getting too long anyway and is so pleased that I'm actually volunteering to get it cut she gives me the money to go to Bernard's in Waden after school. Bernard's is a proper barber where they offer to wash your hair before they cut it and there is more than one hairdresser on duty. It's a warm Monday evening at the beginning of May. When I get home the 6 o'clock news is on. In America the national guard are prowling the lawns of a university campus like they are searching for Vietcong. I can date the exact day I became a suedehead from what I saw on the news bulletin that evening. Four dead in Ohio.

We're lounging on the grassy mound of the roundabout in front of Bedford bus station: me and the gang of schoolmates who are going to see the Edgar Broughton Band at Watford Town Hall. Johnny Bull says: "You're really going to stand out with a suedehead." "Not as much as you're going to stand out in that ponce's pink shirt," I reply. It's May 28th. Whit Week. Two strangers get off a bus and walk across the road, laughing and pointing at us. They look just like Connolly and Loco would look if they had suedeheads instead of long hair. Then we realise they are Connolly and Loco. I've started a trend. As it turned out the gig was full of suedeheads. There were as many short hairs as long hairs in the audience. I begin to notice that the more often I go to see Edgar Broughton. His audience isn't just hippies in headbands. It's people who are prematurely predisposed towards Punk, recalcitrant kids who are ready for their own hometown MC5 or Stooges.

A few weeks after the Watford gig, there was a photograph of the Broughton Band in Melody Maker. Same looking crowd. Half hippies, half crop-heads. They became our Fourth Form house band of choice. By the end of 1970 I'd been to approximately 20 gigs and half of them featured the Edgar Broughton Band. Shortly after the Blind Faith gig I'd seen them at the ICA when it was still called Nash House. Went with Jimmy Dunn again, my supergroup oracle. I remember they performed a long song called *Old Grey Day* which never appeared on any of their records. At Watford we all got up on stage with the band when they did their encore *Out Demons Out*. One of Steve Broughton's splintered drum sticks landed right by me and I kept it for ages as a souvenir of that unforgettable night. Some damage was done to a grand piano and the Edgar Broughton Band were banned from playing Watford Town Hall ever again.

On July 18th the same crowd of us went to the Hyde Park free concert. Pink Floyd performed *Atom Heart Mother* with a small orchestra, but as grandiose as that was I chiefly remember the day for other reasons. It was there under a clear blue sky that I had my Kevin Ayers epiphany. I hadn't realised that lyrics could be that simple and that complex. They spoke to me in a way that song words had never spoken to me before, sending lightning bolts of clarity through the afternoon air to where I was sitting. It was a Gurdjieffian awakening that I was ready for, had probably been ready for for quite some time. I heard nothing eccentric or weird or illogical in any of what Kevin Ayers sang that day. It seemed to me a new kind of truth, which I grasped instinctively and have carried with me ever since. There's a reason you're drawn to this stuff, and if the reasons are sincere and the motives are pure there's a residual essence in that lightning-bolt moment of contact which never leaves you. What I heard that crystal-blue afternoon was mainlined live from the stage directly into to my readily attentive soul.

When we arrived at Hyde Park that sunny Saturday I thought it was going to be Underground central. I envisaged the park being packed with people who looked like they had walked in full psychedelic multicolour off the pages of *Oz* or *IT* magazine. That's how it had felt at the Blind Faith concert a year previously. What had changed in the meantime was not the crowd but me. This time round I noticed a lot more people who were just like us, pop kids up from the shires. The questing kids who read the same music papers and dug the same groups. All trying to assume the full lotus posture without getting cramp. All desperately attempting to deny our most basic uncool impulses and not make stupid school jokes. A vendor in a Stars and Stripes T shirt picked his way through the throng selling his wares from a wooden tray. Little blocks of hash all neatly labelled, cellophane-wrapped and priced. The Hell's Angels rode in through the crowd, parting bodies like the Red Sea. A girl got up and danced topless. We Fourth Form boys affected a blasé attitude as if we saw this kind of thing every day of the week while erections burned a hole in our trousers. From the stage, Roy Harper announced, "I'd like to dedicate this song to the Hell's Angels," and we assumed he was going to do his song called *Hell's Angels*.

– It's called *South Africa*.

At one point during the afternoon we heard screaming. Everyone stood up and turned around to try and locate the source of the distressing sound, but we couldn't see anything. In the papers the next day it said that a hot-dog stand tipped over and a girl was badly burned by scalding hot fat.

Two weeks before the Hyde Park show there had been a rock concert at Bedford Town's football ground. Quaintly billed as Blues at the Eyrie, it featured in order of appearance: Skin Alley, Principal Edwards Magic Theatre (without light show), Tyrannosaurus Rex, Medicine Head, Principal Edwards Magic Theatre (with light show), Chicken Shack and Deep Purple. We turned up without any intention of paying. During the early afternoon we mooched about in the scrub grass by the gasworks until we were moved on by the oppressive forces of old grey day. From there we moved to a wall next to the turnstiles where you could watch the action through a gap between the stands. It was while perching there that I got into a conversation with a Bedford head about those full-page CBS ads that had started to appear in the music papers. The rock machine we own you wholesale. The only band listed that I hadn't heard of was Santana. "They're in the *Woodstock* film. They're great," said the headband-wearer. This was the sum total of my knowledge of *Woodstock* in the summer of 1970. It was a film and it was coming to the Granada soon.

As we sat on the wall watching Principal Edwards Magic Theatre prance about in the afternoon sun we were all too aware that time was getting on and Tyrannosaurus Rex were next up on stage. We really wanted to be inside the ground for that. Our quest was made more urgent by the stewards, who with little ingenuity but great dedication eventually managed to hook up a tarpaulin between the stands, blocking our view of the bands. I was delegated to go and bribe the man on the turnstile. "Look, mate, we've come all the way from the Isle of Wight." I don't know why I chose the Isle of Wight. "And we've got 30 shillings between us. Now we can stay outside and listen for free anyway or... six bob each, eh? That seems fair." I figured that if he was a full-time gate man and not just a hired security goon, he probably did this most weeks anyway. The transaction was swiftly completed. We parted with our money and were inside just in time for Tyrannosaurus Rex.

At the end of their set Marc Bolan surveyed the scene.
– This is our last number so, like, if you cats wanna do your thing. I dunno, like play football or something.

I don't know who instigated it. Let's blame Jimbo. For reasons known only to ourselves we got up and pretended to kick an invisible football around. I doubt if any of us had seen Blow Up at that time. If we had, we might have stuck to our pretentious task with a little more conviction. It was meant to look Art but it quickly looked Wank. I'd hate to think anyone was watching us. Pretty soon we all got blushing guts and jelly legs. We sat down again.

– Nobody is to mention this at school on Monday.
– Or ever again.

AH-AH YAWA EM EKAT OT GNIMOC ER'YEHT

Jimmy Dunn stood up in the Market Square Library and his orange cord trousers melted away. They had been decaying for ages. Stitching unravelled. Hems frayed to ribbons. Seams split and spread to meet other rips and splits until it was no seam and all split. Jimmy had bleached them, dyed them, re-dyed them, tie-dyed them and then they died.

Jimmy had a new bunch of mates. Jimmy 2, Dazzle, Mitch and Roy. They sat in the Library. It was the thing they did. Sometimes I went and sat with them. You didn't see them around very often. They weren't to be found lounging about on the Market Square bog roof or dutifully observing darts night, snooker night, flicks night. Mitch even had a car. On the day that Jimmy's trousers died we sat whispering and waiting for Councillor Chisholm to finish reading Punch so we could look at the cartoons. Mr

Chisholm's face creased when he laughed, and his sideburns went back to the Queen Victoria days. *Punch* magazine was kept in a plastic folder that gave off agreeable fumes. I hadn't been in the Library much since I used to read the sport biographies. The place still smelt the way it did the first day I walked in there. The Library staff were still the same. They hushed us even when we didn't think we were making much noise. And when Jimmy stood up and shed the remnants of his cords they pointed to the door and said OUT.

Jimmy says, "Do you want to come for a ride?" It's Sunday morning. Mitch picks us up in his car and we drive to the old chalk quarry at Cople. Mitch and Roy in the front. Me and Jimmy in the back. We cruise slowly down a bumpy track and sit and watch the wading birds landing on the water. Everything is quiet and everyone is sleepy, all talking inconsequentially in near whispers. Soon I'm bored. A hand-rolled fag is shared but they don't pass it to me. Roy regards me warily in the rear-view mirror and says, "Is he OK?" The implication is, "Do we trust him?" Jimmy goes, "Yeah, don't worry about him." Everyone stares straight ahead. The wind ploughs furrows on the water.

In the summer holiday I work down the beaning fields with Grummar. Walking the shaded pyramid rows, picking runner beans for easy money. Grummar and the other grummars take long relaxing tea breaks and sit chatting till they hear the muffled slither of car tires coming over the dusty ridge. Then they make a great show of getting up, brushing crumbs off dirty pinafores and swilling out their flasks. Mr Blackwood, genial employer, catches them out every time but he knows they get the work done and stands laughing and joking with the women for a few minutes until everyone resumes their labour. I'm already back down the bean rows, dappled in green. There's an old caravan we sit in when it rains. It smells of axle grease and burlap. Weeds poke up through a hole in the floor. A hawthorn hedge presses tight against the window.

– You walk like you've shit your pants

Rose-Marie calls out from a Rec bench. She's with her friend Nelly Webster. I hope she doesn't mean me, but there's only me and my mate Jack walking past. I sneer at her. She smiles sweetly back.
– Dint mean it. I like your hair short.
– I'm growing it again now.

She's right though. I do walk like I've shit my pants. I'm crippled with *Here We Go Round the Mulberry Bush* self-consciousness whenever there's town girls like her about.

Days pass. Jack says: "Let's get up on the cricket pavilion roof and be the Beatles doing *Get Back*." He's been out of Secondary School for a year but he's not above miming to the Beatles soundtrack that plays in our heads. It's like we're back at Junior School, running out of Waden Regal after seeing *A Hard Day's Night*, or being chased around the Infant School playground in the Fab Three days. When we clamber down from the roof, Nelly and Rose-Marie are there. They make themselves available to us and we go either side of the tall hedge that shields the entrance to the toilets. Rose-Marie is 14, a year younger than me. Chubby not tubby. Sturdy pale white legs. Pink miniskirt. Blouse too tight and bra showing where the buttons don't quite meet. We wander into the girl's bogs which stink even more than the men's do. There is a graffiti grid felt-tipped on the wall in the first cubicle, all filled in. Name. Prick Size. Marks out of ten. All you get in the men's toilet is a drawing of a dripping knob and some barbed-wire pubes. Nothing as detailed as this. We stare and read and point and wonder who. Then we go outside and muck about on the grass. You'd call it kiss chase if we could be bothered to chase or kiss. Nelly and Jack have disappeared to the top end of the Rec. Some noisy little kids are playing by the water fountain. Rose Marie drags me behind the tall hedge again. Her breasts are warm, her knickers moist, and when I stick my fingers down there she doesn't try to stop me.

The cunt is underneath. It's not where it is in the drawings on the bog wall. I was so lacking in sexual awareness that when my fingers went down to where I thought they should go there was nothing but soft downy hair. Rose Marie eased herself forward and my fingers slid into the wetness. The noisy little water-fountain kids poked their heads round the corner of the hedge and went, "Oooh, you've been snogging. Spread it. Spread it."

The Daily Express carried a story on its news pages about a boy who had appeared in court after being found by his parents high on drugs. They discovered a diary in his room containing everything he'd written while under the influence of LSD. One of the diary entries was, "Here, have my head. It's not mine to keep anyway." What a thing to say. What a thing to think. I read it over and over again until I could imagine I was him. And if you dream about something for long enough...

Roy only had two records. *See Emily Play* and *They're Coming to Take Me Away Ha-Ha*. I'd gone round Roy's because no one else was in the Library. I'd gone to the Library because Rose-Marie was with Nelly and there was no parting them. Why are girls always chained at the waist like that? I mooched about for a bit, sulky boy, spare part, and when I said, "See yer then," and Rose-Marie shouted "When?", I didn't bother answering.

– Suit yerself!, she shouted.

I did. In cellophane armour, a helicopter hat, and a tangerine tie.

Roy said, "Have you taken this before? Only I'm not going to be responsible." He opened a small blue puncture-kit tin and tipped a piece of folded silver foil into the palm of his hand. He carefully unwrapped the foil and there sat two tiny pink tablets, the colour of Rose-Marie's skirt.

– Strawberry Fields. You have taken it before, haven't you? Only I'm not going to be responsible."

And nor am I. Here, have my head. It's not mine to keep anyway.

The B side of They're Coming to Take Me Away Ha-Ha was They're Coming to Take Me Away Ha-Ha played backwards. There was something about the way it sounded when Roy put it on. I was beginning to understand the words.

Roy said: "Let's go and sit by the river." We reached the end of his road and there was a wall. I pronounced that it was Hadrian's Wall and it was in the tick-tick seconds that followed that the person in my head who wasn't tripping knew that I was. It doesn't tell you that in the News of the World. The part of me that remained grounded rationalised that it wasn't Hadrian's Wall. It was Mr Pike's wall and he hadn't towed it back from Scotland, but as long as I irrationalised that it was, then it was. Soon enough you're in another country. Choose your own reality. Pow! It all explodes.

We sat by the river and the centuries flowed by. The meadows were never this green when Dad was convalescing and we went for our walks. I'm sure they weren't. After a while the water looked so peaceful that Georgie Fame felt compelled to write a song about it. The song flowed through my head. Perhaps it was only ever in my head and not even a real song. Perhaps that goes for everything. And went.

Although I'd lied to Roy – I hadn't taken this before – it felt in a way like I had. Roy didn't need to be responsible. I had irresponsibility to spare. I got up to explain the everything equation. A family went by on the ironstone bridge, just heads and shoulders showing.
– Look, they're marching like toy soldiers.
– They aren't that far away. Don't shout. They'll hear you.

Roy was laughing when he said it, cry-laughing. Seated the river bank he put his head between his legs and for a moment it looked like his head was going to shoot out across the water like a cannonball. I tried to tell him this. To the tin soldiers on the bridge we must have looked like writhing crustaceans burrowing into to the very core of the earth.

Later – whatever that is – I decided to walk across the water. I wasn't really going to do it, although afterwards – whatever that was – I realised that Roy thought I was. In the *News of the World* horror stories you either dived out of a window draped in your Mum's curtains which you took to be the apparel of a superhero, or you thought you were Jesus on the silky Sea of Galilee. I was in up to my ankles before Roy decided we'd better go somewhere else.

After we'd walked around the mill meadows for a bit we went to see Jimmy Dunn. A warm breeze dried me but I retained a leaky mind. My squelchy legs left a tell-tale watery trail. I was halfway up my toy road before I realised where I was, or who, the houses all askew, rainbows skimming off the skies, my polo mints a pocket full of halos. Kids were playing out. The little ones were chanting a nursery rhyme. It was the grooviest nursery rhyme ever invented and one day it will be Side Two Track Five on something magnificent that John Peel will play on *Top Gear*, or so I assured myself. I think I might have tried to tell the children this but Roy nudged me along. Safely ensconced in Jimmy Dunn's bedroom we watched the kiddie games continuing outside. An olden-day tapestry was glimpsed through lace curtains that were somewhat in need of a wash and made my dreams go smeary.

– How did he do that?

Jimmy beckoned at my damp legs as I dried in front of his two-bar. They were talking like I wasn't there but it was OK because in a way I wasn't. Jimmy laughed and I knew everything was fine. Looking out of Jimmy's southwest facing window. Watching the day drop.

Mum must have seen me because she called round and Jimmy's Mum came upstairs and asked if I was going in for my tea. I was concentrating hard on the glow bars of Jimmy's fire at the time. My trousers steaming and scorching.

– God, you've got it hot in here boys.
– Yeah, Rob fell in the river.
– Can you tell them I'll be back later?

"Just fly back," said Roy, and I wish he hadn't. I tried so hard not to laugh that I thought I'd peed my pants. Then Jimmy suggested we go downstairs and watch *Lost in Space*. I couldn't follow the plot. Dr Smith kept shouting all the time and the background music just never let up. I'd never previously noticed how noisy that programme was. Space is very loud.

Rose Marie writes a letter and gives it to a girl who lives in her street and goes to my school who gives it to me. The letter is written in pencil scrawl on exercise paper. Smudge marks and crossing out and littered with spelling mistakes. Starts off chatty. I'm in Housecraft thinking of you. Then it gets to when are we when will we why what smudge smear. It's a really nice letter. Better than any Valentine. All a Valentine's card says is "Guess who?" This one is basically saying: "Come and get me." So why am I looking at all the spelling mistakes and thinking the way I'm thinking? *Here We Go Round the Mulberry Bush* has a lot to answer for. Secondary Modern Girls. Grammar Girls. Town Girls. Cuntry Girls. When you turn into a book you can't just leave out the bad bits.

I burrow a blackberry trail. Circling the sand pit which has been hollowed bare by mechanical diggers until there's nothing left to excavate. I hack my way through trailing thorns on into the thicket, always stretching for one last berry just out of reach, then another, wading so far in that the brambles wrap themselves around me. No one would ever know I was here in the stillness with the late summer sun haze all softened, the harvest heaped up and gone, the fields blackened with stubble and the afternoon acrid with the smell of burning. There won't be many more days like these. You can feel it in the air. I'll fill a tub and take it home. Mum can make a pie. I prefer them raw and could eat myself purple, but Mum likes to bake on Sundays.

High above me a glider circles in silence, trapped in a whirlpool current.

PECULIAR

The River Ivel narrows at the sluice gates and the water oozes through. It quicksilvers under the footbridge, swirling into bubbles and whirlpool currents on the other side. Riverbank reeds sway to and fro with the flow. An undulating lily pad carpet rides the tide. We never called it the sluice gate, we called it the rush, because that's what the water does. It rushes through. At the point of most force, where the water runs clear and shallow, the stones are polished clean and flat.

You can see everything clearly if you look for long enough.

You go back saying, "I'm going to be different this year. I'm going to be someone else." And I was. I walked across the netball courts, picked up a goalpost and pretended to play it like a ten-foot guitar.

They don't bother you so much in the fifth year. You're leaving soon. The sweep of the parabola continues its upward curve as you edge closer to the end of your sentence. My careers talk lasted as long as the one in Kes.

– What do you want to do?
– Go to Tech college.
– What qualifications do you need?
– Two O levels.
– Better work hard then, hadn't you? Next.

At the end of the fourth year my English Literature teacher had taken me to one side to inform me that as I'd only got 48% in the mock exam and the pass rate was 50% I'd probably struggle next year.

– We are within our rights to prevent you from sitting the O level, but as you are sitting so few – five, isn't it? – we'll make an exception."

And so, on little more than a teacher's whim and a paucity of exams to sit I wriggled through to the fifth year. If you failed a mock O level, and I did fail some of mine abysmally, you sat CSEs. There wasn't a CSE in Agriculture, so after we'd failed the mock in that me, Dickie Dangerfield and his mate, the new kid Danny Hanson, were either given menial tasks to do around the school farm or we sat at the back of class and amused ourselves as quietly as we could. While the diligent applied themselves to soil tests and the history of the Wankel engine we stared at the bottle of Swarfega on the window ledge and made up songs about Swarfega. Swarfega has got me on the run. The world is just a great Swarfega. For example.

"Have you seen the *Crossroads* hippie?", said Dickie Dangerfield. I had. I'd been an enthusiastic *Crossroads* viewer from the day it started in 1964, when it was on at teatime. Mum loved it, and it rivalled *Compact, Dr Kildare* and *The Newcomers* in her affections. The parroted wisdom of bargain-basement pundits is that *Crossroads* was all shaky scenery and Amy Turtle picking up phones before they rang. In fact, it wasn't any better or worse than a lot of other one-take TV shows in the era when a stray boom mike or technician's shadow frequently hove into view.

Like most light-entertainment TV, *Crossroads* was both more banal and more bizarre than the received-wisdom merchants could ever contemplate. On one show in March 1966, Ken Dodd made a guest appearance. He rapidly departed from the script and the majority of his cameo consisted of him and Meg Richardson bouncing up and down on adjacent motel beds while Meg fed him lines about his forthcoming tour and he recited the itinerary. I am not making this up. I still pretty much remember all of the early cast from the black-and-white days. Meg, Jill and Sandy. Carlos the Chef and Josefina. Token tearaway Vince Parker. Suave Hugh Mortimer. Quiet Brian Jarvis who looked like Cat Stevens. Sexy Marilyn. I hadn't watched it so much of late, but recently a tall, dark, long-haired stranger had moved into Chalet Six. Diane the waitress took him his meals but he only wanted orange juice. One day, in an attempt to engage him in conversation, she asked him what groups he liked. "Crosby, Stills and Nash," he replied. Reading Diane's blank face, he added: "You know, like Nashville, Tennessee, man." We sneered ourselves stupid as we recited the line back and forth across the Ag Lab benches.

The *Crossroads* hippie started to act strangely. Several people acted strangely in *Crossroads*, but this was like Strangeville, Tennessee, man. Diane's noble efforts to reach out and understand him came to naught, and after a long reclusive period during which he refused to leave his chalet, he finally wrote the staff a long, rambling goodbye note and disappeared from our screens forever. It was impossible to make out what he'd written on the piece of paper, but from Meg Richardson's sorrowful homily it became clear that he had decided that his head was not his to keep and that he had fallen victim to the drug peril menace that was sweeping the land.

At the end of the first week back at school we went to another Hyde Park concert. I found a black felt hat on the train and thought I looked exceedingly groovy wearing it, especially when it started to rain, which it did halfway through Michael Chapman's set. I watched fascinated as Chapman conjured magic from his effects pedals, half expecting him to be electrocuted at any minute. Following his brief, curtailed performance, the afternoon's entertainment came to a halt. It pissed down relentlessly for a couple of hours, and a crowd of 50,000 dwindled to little more than 5,000 diehards. We sheltered under trees, tarpaulin, polythene – anything we could find. Eventually the music resumed with Eric Burdon and War.

Burdon came on stage, hair matted, water dripping down his face. He grinned at us all soaking wet like that, then stepped up to the mic. "You all must be crazy," he said. "But that's OK 'cos I'm crazy too." His band then proceeded to play the best live set I'd ever seen up to that point. War were followed by John Sebastian, and with a supreme gesture of stage direction, ordained from the gods on high, the sun came out the moment he launched into his first song. Top of the bill were Canned Heat, who finished their set with a version of *Refried Boogie* that would have gone on for the rest of 1970 if someone hadn't pulled the plugs. On the train going home, Connolly looked at me and said, "The colours have run," and I thought "Yeah, they have, haven't they? How true that is and how did he know about my acid trip? Could he tell just from looking at my eyes. Would everyone be able to tell from now on?"

– I mean your hat.

The non-fast dye in my headwear had dripped down, streaking my T shirt and ruining my maroon cords.
– Oh, shit.
– No, they look great now.

That's what Jimbo thought, and so did I, two weeks of bleaching and dying later.

During the autumn half-term break a classmate got us some work on the farm where his Dad worked. Beating.

– What's that?
– All you have to do is walk in front of the gunners, knocking on the trees with sticks. Scares the birds out.

And then they shoot them.

I biked eight miles on a grey November morning, strapped on a pair of rudimentary bin-bag leggings and walked through acres of rain-moistened yellow rapeseed. My inexpertly tied legwear rapidly worked its way loose and left me unprotected against the elements. After a while you don't get any wetter. Your legs warm up once the blood does.

We trooped across open fields into leafless spinneys where the partridges and hares thought they were safe. The first kill came to me. A hare broke loose, disturbed in its bunker. Disorientated by the noise it zig-zagged in open field for a few futile seconds until one of the farmers shot it. It staggered towards me.

– Kill it, boy.

I clunked it a hopeful one across the head but caught the eyes and mouth instead. The bagger scooped it up in front of me. Still twitching.
– Christ, boy, you made a mess of that!

I plodded on across heavy clay fields, the bagger in front of me, the hare, a cudgelled lifeless bulge at the bottom of his sack. For an hour I was at eye level with my kill, red stain spreading through the sackcloth with every fresh hare that was dumped on it. On we trudged like conscripts.
During a short lunchbreak Connolly told us he'd bought *Ride a White Swan*.
– Get it now and you get a picture sleeve.

One or two of the others had bought it as well. They were all turning into T Rex fans. Me first. Me. Me. Me. It was me who ordered *Warlock of Love* from the school Library and was amazed when it turned up and I had to pay for it. It was me who pretended I could understand every word Marc Bolan sang. It was me who heard them when they went on Radio One Club to promote *By the Light of a Magical Moon*. It was me who cut pictures of Marc and Steve Took out of New Musical Express and stuck them on my wall. Marc in his Roman breastplate. Steve in his granny cardigan. Me. Me. Me.

By late afternoon frost had begun to form in patches in the corners of meadows. Dusk was coming on. Nobody had shot anything for a while.
– All right, boys, go and get your wages.

Not bad for a dishonest day's slaughtering. More than I got for a week's paper round. Biked a million miles home on aching legs. Ate my tea by a warm fire.

– Mum, I'm thinking of becoming a vegetarian.

The last thing I can remember saying before falling asleep on the carpet with everybody walking over me.

The slow drip, drip, drip of disillusion begins. All through the winter of 1970 and into the spring of 1971. Cosy in the centrally heated warmth that North Sea Gas had finally brought to our front room, listening to LPs on our brand-new stereogram, records borrowed from mates in good faith, chasing every last fade to its echo. Willing to be persuaded by anything that might take me up away and out of here. Mark Barry lent me his Curved Air picture disc. It was the only record he had that wasn't by the Beatles. I liked some of it, especially Vivaldi and the mournful coda at the end of *It Happened Today*, but the record sounded like someone had sandpapered the surface.

Dickie Dangerfield lent me a compilation album on the Mercury label called *Blues Package '69*. It had melting blue baby dolls on the cover so it must be really far-out, right? But the record didn't sound like its cover. Hardly any of them did. I craved weirdness, but mostly what I got was dodgy blues groups doing their 12-bar boogie thing. Jimmy Dunn had this LP by Hard Meat. You got a free poster with it, which he gave to me. Silver and white. The poster was better than the music so I put it on my bedroom wall and stared at that instead. Roy played me Black Sabbath who he said were going to be big. The name sounded witchcraft good and graveyard dark, but once again the cover was scarier than the music. I tried to imagine what Black Sabbath might have sounded like if they had been as good as that sleeve. Then Jimmy told me about a group called Hawkwind. Imagine that. Just the name prepared me for sonic blast-off. The *Melody Maker* that came out the week we went back to school had featured an interview with them. They sounded really cool. They played for free and had this device called an audio generator which apparently could shatter the universe with one carefully calibrated vibration. But when I eventually heard their debut album they sounded like underpass buskers and not particularly stratospheric at all.

The music papers still called it "Underground", and most record shops had an Underground section in the racks, even Boots and W.H. Smiths. This was where I gravitated to now. As a starter kit I'd bought *Nice Enough to Eat* for 14/6 from the Underground racks of Carousel records next to Bedford Bus Station, and eagerly purchased all the other affordable samplers, too: *Picnic, Bumpers, Fill Your Head with Rock*, et al., hoping they might lead me to the technicolour pastures of transcendence. Meanwhile the first references to "Progressive Rock" were beginning to appear in the pop papers. In that *Melody Maker* interview, Hawkwind complained about promoters saying they were too Progressive for the Progressive clubs. I liked the idea of a progressive tendency in music, but was disappointed by much of what I heard. I over-invested emotionally and projected onto the music far more complexity than most of those 12-bar boogie merchants could bear. But, fairly rapidly, "Progressive" became the new thing. I preferred it when it was Underground.

My hatred of the term "Progressive Rock" was pathological from the start. I saw first-hand the effect this music was having on that first generation of Sixth Form Grammar School fans. Being a Fifth Former at the time I was therefore uniquely placed to comment on the onslaught of "clever" music, being one of the initial recipients and targets of its attendant snobberies. All those genre-defining records came out during my final year at school. *Time and a Word* by Yes, *Trespass* by Genesis, and the first Emerson, Lake and Palmer album were mainlined live and direct into the Sixth Form Common Room at school. I didn't dislike the music because it was Progressive – much of it quite evidently wasn't. I disliked it because of the way it was appropriated.

I can still remember the exact moment when we came to the conclusion that the Lower Sixth were wankers. We had been playing football against them at lunchtime. The 1:30 end-of-Break bell went. Loco had lent one of them his copy of *After the Goldrush* and wanted it back. Half a dozen of us tagged along with him to the Sixth Form Common Room. They had armchairs and a record player in there. *Time and a Word* was actually playing at the time. I recognised that busy bubbling bass and that irritating impulse to fill every space with complexity. The Sixth Former went to his locker to get Loco's LP and we stood around just inside the doorway, waiting. He came back with the record and saw us milling.

– Get out. You're not allowed in here.

Other voices joined in.
– Yeah, get out.

– This is a private room.
We'd just been playing football with them.

That was the day.

All that A Stream, B Stream, Upper C, Middle C, Lower C crap that they threw at us for five years, and not once do I remember any of us using that as a measure of our worth. None of my mates ever called me a dunce, a retard or a thicko. None of us ever called our more conscientious mates "swots" as they handed in their homework on time. Our culture and the music we loved cut across all snobbery and false demarcations. But the Sixth Form lovers of Progressive Rock felt otherwise. They made it clear that their music was better than ours and that they were better than us for liking it.

By 1970 all of my useful learning was taking place outside of the school curriculum. Pop-music culture was pretty much my culture, full stop. I was getting the majority of my information from my music papers and from the newly emerging Underground press – *Friends* magazine was a particular favourite. On the radio I was listening to John Peel, Pete Drummond, Bob Harris and Mike Raven, to the pirate stations Radio Veronica and Radio Northsea International (RNI), and to Radio Geronimo which broadcast after midnight on Saturdays. I had begun sending off for pirate radio magazines from the Free Radio Campaign and the Free Radio Association. I attended the RNI anti-jamming demonstration in Trafalgar Square in July 1970. Simon Dee and Ronan O'Rahilly brushed past me as they went to hand in our petition at 10 Downing Street. I had much of my Free Radio literature confiscated at school like so much samizdat, and it was only given back to me on the final day of the autumn term by a Deputy Head who held it between her pincered thumb and forefinger like it was a used Durex.

Brendan Brotherson started in our year. Tall and wiry, with a shock of silvery curly hair, he'd been thrown out of Bedford Modern for failing his mocks, so now he was free to come and fail with us. On his first day he said, "Hi, I'm Brendan," and I replied "'lo, I'm Dudeney Johnson."

– That's an unusual name.
– It's the name of a supermarket, you twot. Look, it's written on my lunch bag.

I showed him a blue-and-white striped bag with a squashed chocolate-spread sandwich inside, our local provisioner's name smudged by a brown smear.

– Oh yeah, I get it. Dudeney Johnson. What's your real name, then?
– Edgar Broughton.

Brendan was deep, earnest and learned. He also wrote poetry. He turned me on to *Howl* by Allen Ginsberg, and the Liverpool Poets on the Penguin label. I'd already seen the Liverpool Scene live several times, so we Basildon bonded immediately. Brendan could quote the band's lyrics and I could misquote them back. He lent me his copy of the Liverpool Poets Penguin anthology and a school exercise book full of his own efforts.

I lay on my bed/car lights circle the ceiling/dancing across my dreams/and my graveyard night fear.
Every thought/expression/walk by the river written down. Phrases/divided like/this/
w/out proper punctuation. W/out writing without.

– I've got four more books full at home, he said, offering to let me borrow those too.

He also lent me his copy of *Howl*.
– This is a City Lights original. First edition. If you lose this then don't ever come to school again, right?

I took *Howl* home, read it and reread it. I absorbed it through every pore. I dreamed freight yards full of junkies and street angels. After a while *Howl* disappeared into the debris of our house. It turned up in a basket full of Mum's ironing the day before we broke up for Christmas.

– Wow, Edgar you must really be into it. You've had it for weeks. I thought you'd lost it. I'll lend you some other ones of his. Do you like Frank Sinatra? I went to see him at the Albert Hall. That line in *I Will Drink the Wine* about gazing at the flowers for several hours. Do you like Gilbert O'Sullivan? That line about Napoleon brandy and apple pie. He's going to be better than John Lennon."

And on and on, through private study periods and playground lounging, through the recess, the chalk and numbers. While Johnny Bull applied a magnifying glass to ants and the cricket team had a lunchtime net practice, me and Brendan talked endlessly about poetry and song lyrics.

It was around this time that we formed a group. The group didn't have a name yet and we didn't have any instruments either. Nor had the eight or nine of us settled on a final line-up, but every lunchtime we gathered by the tennis courts and acted out, in 20-second bursts, an approximation of our desires as we dreamed of the fame that surely awaited us should we ever go pro. Having mimed in postures appropriate to our chosen instrument we would then resume our languid positions on the grass, content to fantasise about stardom till the bell went. Mark Barry pointed out that our lack of musical equipment, or indeed any discernible ability to play an instrument, might yet prove to be a handicap when it came to getting famous, but we knew this was just his jealousy speaking because he hadn't been invited to join the group.

Jimbo's new favourite word was "peculiar". He decreed that *Peculiar* was to be one of our first numbers. I agreed that I'd write the lyrics but first I needed the timing. The timing was very important. About 9.57 I'd say, with an extended guitar break. I offered another title.

– *We've Got an I on You*. Spelled with the letter I rather than e-y-e.
– Wow! That's really cool.

In my mind's I the song was going to be based on the Soft Machine's *We Know What You Mean*, which I'd heard on *Top Gear* in 1967 at a time when I thought every Underground record was weirder than it was.

– Yeah, thanks. It's about paranoia.
– You didn't know what that word meant till Black Sabbath came out.
– Yes, I did.
– Do they really sing "Esso Extra Really Works" in the second verse?
– Yeah, I read it in *Melody Maker*.
– Is it Cajun?
– Fuck off, Connolly.

THROUGH THE RECESS,
THE CHALK AND NUMBERS

It was a clear spring morning when Jordan's corn store burned to the ground. I'd walked to the High Street to get the school bus. I stood and watched the fire for a while and thought about how long it had been since I'd been in and inhaled the grainy scent from the sacks, probably not since Mum used to buy dog biscuits and I thought I was growing breasts. The fire hoses were gushing, but the building was already down to its char-blackened rafters. I got on the bus and went to school.

That same week there was a story in the *Chronicle* about a seven-year-old boy who was killed when a lorry ran out of control and crashed into the wall he was sitting on. It made me think of the wall I used to sit on when I was small. Stacking my milk crates, static in my universe, the cars and lorries a moving backdrop. I thought about my wall and the little boy who got killed. He lived at 122 London Road. I lived at 120. It was the same wall.

The head of History, Mr Avebury, looks like a kindly vicar. He doesn't waste his wisdom on plebs, and only teaches the A Stream. But now for some reason he's standing at the front of our class and speaking in his kindly vicar's voice, asking for volunteers to appear in the school concert. The Lower Sixth are going to perform a version of Country Joe's *I Feel Like I'm Fixin' to Die*. We disdainfully decline the invitation to join them. A couple of weeks later our History teacher Miss Lloyd asks again on his behalf. There's urgency in her voice. She's almost pleading with us. Why would we want to be in anything with the Lower Sixth?

– Because they are having trouble finding enough people who look the part.

Ah, why didn't you say so?

Every lunchbreak we get to sit in the History room and sneer at the Lower Sixth. They are trying to learn the song off the *Woodstock* live album, which is time-consuming because Country Joe keeps stopping to berate the audience for not joining in. I offer to lend them my single, which doesn't have all the pauses on it, but my kind gesture is rebutted. The Lower Sixth don't listen to singles, man.

– Singles are finished. LPs are the future.
– Bollocks. The singles charts are great.
– Yeah, went Connolly, Jimbo, Loco, all of us. Jethro Tull. Freda Payne.

Family. Chairmen of the Board. Kentucky Rain. Atomic Rooster. Plastic Ono Band. *My Brother Jake*.
– Teenyboppers!
– Plastic hippies!
– Nobody asked your opinion anyway. Fifth Form plebs.

One of the Sixth Formers, Lucas – Lunky we call him – tries to be placatory.
– Tony Blackburn wants shooting, doesn't he? Have you heard the way he takes the piss out of the *Sounds of the Seventies* trailers?
– We think he's really funny.
– Yeah, we think he's hilarious.

Ordinarily we would have bonded on our dislike of Tony Blackburn, but if the Lower Sixth were against it, we were for it. Blackburn was pretty much the Antichrist by then. When he ended his breakfast show and handed over to Johnnie Walker at nine o'clock, Walker could barely contain his indifference, and the between-show patter would regularly dwindle to silence before Walker played a record. Blackburn had a jingle that went, "Here's a time check, here's a time check, here's a time check now," then he would tell you that he was going to tell you the time and then he did. To us he was the personification of imbecility, even though he played some great records and loved all the Motown stuff we liked – and actually, come to think of it, it was really funny when he took the piss out of the *Sounds of the Seventies* trailers on the breakfast show. This guy called Michael Whale used to come on, and in a deeply portentous voice would announce: "Dando Shaft. Not so much a band. More a state of mind. Open yours. Be in tune with the times. *Sounds of the Seventies*. Six o'clock this evening. Be there." And all the time Blackburn would be going, "Yeah, groovy man, right on," in the background. Then he'd say, "The Supremes and the Four Tops are the Sounds of the Seventies," and play *Stoned Love*. What was even funnier was when Blackburn almost got kidnapped by the Hard Rock Society of Peterborough for crimes against music. It made the daily papers and turned out to be a rag week stunt that got out of hand, but nowhere near out of hand enough for our liking. We speculated that perhaps it was really the Lower Sixth who had tried to kidnap him.

– Yeah, I bet they write all those letters to *Melody Maker* too, the ones that go (adopt loud Gumby voice): "Dear Sir. Today I bought my first and last reggae record. Imagine my surprise when I flipped to the B side and it was just an instrumental version of the A side. PS I am a moron. PPS L.P. Winner."

– Someone should kill him.
– Who?
– Tony Blackburn.

We all laughed, but Dickie Dangerfield meant it.

We sang so atrociously on the first night of the school concert that Mr Avebury herded us into the school hall the following lunchtime for an extra rehearsal.
– And if you repeat that performance tonight I shall have no hesitation in taking this piece out of the programme!

We blamed the Sixth Form cheerleaders for screwing up the verses. A headband does not a hippie make. It wasn't our fault. You can't blame the supporting cast. All we had to do was stand at the back and go "1-2-3-whaddawefightingfor". We were much better on the second night, which was the night the local press came. The following week's Waden Chronicle reported that "there was no lack of topicality in the production, and a pointed message about Vietnam was performed with great feeling". To this day it remains my greatest review.

Jimbo pointed at an advert in the back of Melody Maker.
– That's where I got my greatcoat. Stevenage Old Town. Try and get one with bullet holes.

What is that smell in army surplus shops? Is it the dried blood? The man who served me said, "Yeah, bullet holes, no problem mate. We get loads with bullet holes. And blood. Especially from Russia." But he couldn't find me one, no matter how many times he sorted through the heap of greatcoats piled up high in his stock room.

– Do you want it in a bag? Only it's a bit big and I don't know if I have –
– It's OK. I'll wear it home.

I hadn't noticed how hot it was until I left the shop. Clammy sweat formed on my forehead. My shoulders began to ache. Fuck, how do the Russians wear these things with a back pack and a gun? No wonder they get shot. You can't move in them.

I had half an hour to kill before my train, so I went into a record shop. What is that smell in record shops, when the sun pours in and bleaches the window display and the polythene fumes rise from the plastic LP covers? It's one of the most seductive aromas known to humanity. It was a quiet weekday afternoon and in the shop two bored assistants were serving absolutely no customers. A third assistant, possibly the boss, emerged from a back room and dumped a batch of LPs into a crate on the counter, all wrapped in plain brown paper.

– How much are these, mate?
– 20p.

All I had left was 20p, so I bought *All of Us* by Nirvana. Just as I was about to leave, the boss came out from the back again with another batch, also wrapped in brown paper. I asked what they were.

– John and Yoko. *Two Virgins*. Can't give them away.
– I'll have one.
– 20p, mate.
– I haven't got any money left.
– 20p.
– You said you couldn't give them away.

He gave me the "Are you still here?" stare. It's probably ad-lib filth anyway. Who would want to listen to that?

I walked back to the railway station sweating cobs in my greatcoat. There was a timetable pasted on the wall outside the waiting-room, and on the bottom, in thick red capitals that went wavy across an air bubble, someone had felt-tipped HAVE IT UP. I studied it hard. Every up and down stroke. It sounded like an order rather than a suggestion. I had been sitting in the waiting-room, but it's amazing how oppressively hot it gets in there when the two-bar heater is on and a load of Stevenage New Town schoolkids come in and you're the only one in a hippie greatcoat studying the sleeve of a record that clearly isn't *Tighten Up Volume Two* or *Motown Chartbusters Volume Three*.

I wore the greatcoat twice and sold it to a mate. Screw that for a game of dead soldiers. As the weather got warmer I was in danger of being boiled alive.

A few weeks before we left school a shop called Disc-A-Day opened in Waden. Disc-A-Day was possibly the smallest record shop in the world. It should have been called King Tardis in Reverse. If we all squeezed in, in single file, and formed an L shape of bodies between the counter and the record racks you could get anywhere up to six of us in there. Five if Mac was in his corner. Mac was the "There's one in every town" resident hippie. Rarely in gainful employment on account of a bad back and a doctor's note he spent most of his days in Disc-A-Day listening to records and ogling the owner. It was hard not to. Early thirties. Voluptuous. Tolerant of hippie wasters and schoolkids who just want to listen to some Underground. Tight black dress and ruby-red lips. Long nails also varnished red and dark hair tumbling over her face and breasts and leaning forward now to point out which section the compilations are in. So close I could kiss her. Right there, just where her velvet choker meets the nape of her downy neck.

Mac was listening to the Incredible String Band when we walked in. We gumby-voiced and mock trilled the words to This Moment until we couldn't sing for giggles. "Take it off," said Mac. "They probably don't understand it."

Oh, but we did. We understood it all too well. "They probably don't understand it" would become my watchword in years to come, my early-warning signal that pseudery was afoot and that I was in the presence of those who wore their rock tastes as a badge of superiority. As I got older I discovered that the Sixth Form Common Room isn't a place. It's a state of mind.

– You're going to need O levels soon just to listen to this stuff.

That was Connolly's response to the Incredible String Band. Connolly had his soul-boy bullshit detector on full alert. He'd already secured a job on a building site and was told that he could leave school as soon as he'd sat his O levels. Next, our voluptuous host put on Slightly All the Time off Soft Machine: Third. My choice. After a fair bit of tape loop Connolly asked: "When does it start?"

– Oh, very good. When Does It Start? I get it. You should write a letter and send it to Sounds. They're bound to print it.

There's a free CND benefit at the old Alexandra Park racecourse. "Is that still going?" Dad asked. "No, it closed down last year," I replied. "I meant CND," he said. "Not the racecourse." I didn't know what CND was and had to ask. There were only a few hundred there, the usual gathering of London long-hairs and Home Counties heads. We divided our time between sitting in the old whitewashed grandstand and walking the inside rail past the furlong poles that separated the two main stages. The Liverpool Scene, Kevin Ayers, Bridget St John, and the Barrow Poets were playing. John Peel was the compère. All through the Liverpool Scene's set, this vision in white kept standing up and shouting about his mates who were in a group called Egg. He'd tell us to go and buy their record and then he'd sit down and play the bongos for a bit. Then he'd stand up again and shout some more about Egg. He was called Jesus, and I saw him everywhere after that. Every London gig I went to, outdoors or in. Sometimes he had a flute instead of bongos. After the Liverpool Scene's set I wandered around on my own for a bit, pretending I was stoned.

Alexandra Palace April 1971. Jesus top right by that blue rail standing in long dark coat.
We are sitting just in front of him.

And before you know it it's that time of year again. The Hyde Park free concert. Our annual tradition. Head Hands and Feet. Humble Pie. Grand Funk Railroad. The line-up doesn't look that appealing, but let's go anyway just to laugh at the Lower Sixth. You never know, one of them might try idiot dancing. The weather is all sun and no shade and we sit sweltering in the middle of a huge gathering that stretches from the Serpentine to Marble Arch. The Lower Sixth are in their headbands waiting for some prefect rock. There's this girl sitting with Lunky Lucas. I've never seen her before. She ever so politely smiles at their crap profundities, but she looks bored. And so am I. Think I'll get an ice cream. It's miles to the van but hopefully by the time I get back the concert will have ended.

– Does anyone want an ice cream?

Only the girl.
– I'm Cindy. I've just started at your school.

I took her for a Sixth Former.
– No, Fourth.

Younger than she looks. I buy two ice creams. Stepping through the multitudes, licking vanilla from my wrist. By the time I find our lot again I've eaten most of mine. "Sorry" I say. "Yours melted on the way back." It's the crummiest of lines. *Beano* bad, but Cindy looks up, squints into the sunlight and laughs a natural laugh. Greasy black hair, centre-parted, hazel eyes, a cheesecloth blouse, fabulous tits. For the few minutes that I can be bothered to sit among the mumbling headbands I'm prepared to talk any amount of bullshit just to hold her attention, just to be in her sight line. "Yes, I'm thinking of getting a guitar." "Oh yeah, electric definitely." "No, I don't go to gigs in Stevenage but I think I will now if you go." "Yeah, great yeah," to everything she says. Lucas has barely spoken two words to her since I got back with the ice creams. She sits there fussing with her hair, absently twirling locks in her fingers. She is way out of my league. I'm flattered that she should even speak to me. Halfway through Grand Funk Railroad we decide we've had enough. Me, Connolly, everyone from our year except Jimbo, who is getting to like that sort of thing.
– We can get the five o'clock train if we leave now. Are you coming?

Cindy thinks she had better stay. She did come with Lucas after all and it wouldn't be polite.

One afternoon me and Connolly bunked off lessons, just for old time's sake. Hadn't done it for ages, but we felt like an hour's respite so we said we had food poisoning. That's always a good one. The teachers are too scared there might have been something in the school dinners to question you. Or leakage from the science lab gas taps. That's another good one. Nobody is going to challenge you over that. The last thing they want is your parents up the school saying: "Why did you gas my child and give him the shits?" A Fourth Year called Mickey Stevens was in the sick bay when we got there. We'd obviously interrupted him doing something he shouldn't have, because when we walked in he hastily closed the drawer of the little desk that sat in the corner, set aside should any puking gas-choked child wish to carry on with their school work while they waited to die. Mickey wore a "caught in the act" expression on his face. We kept up the pretence of casual conversation for a while until Connolly popped the question.

– What did you put in the drawer?
– What drawer?
– We saw you. What's in the drawer?

The first joint I ever smoked, that's what. He'd rolled two. We let him keep one. It seemed only fair.
– We'll take this down the Blues Club tonight.

The Blues Club didn't play much blues. It was run by a bloke called Phil the Pill who took his record player and his LP collection down the Waden Scout Hut once a week. It was mostly attended by the members of the Lower Sixth whose Mums had sewn flares into their trousers, plus a few of the local Secondary Modern hippies and of course resident waster about town Mac. Hardly any girls. Six of us scrambled down the railway embankment next to the Scout Hut and huddled round the joint. "It's Lebanese Red," said Jimbo, who knew about these things. A good nine months after I dived in at the lysergic deep end I finally tried a bit of pot. It made me go quieter.

During Whitsun Week Sally Bowe is sitting on the Rec swings with her friend Anita Day, dangling in twos as girls do. I'd just been to Bedford and bought my first three-button grandad vest. I'd decided that most tie-dye looked rubbish but this one was maroony grey with faint lilac streaks and looked cool. I'd also just bought the second Chicago Transit Authority LP so I was all measured up for my adoration. I cycled by the Rec and there they were. Look at me in my tie-dye, with my Chicago Transit Authority LP under my arm. But they are facing the wrong way and have their backs to me. Be patient. It's only ten to twelve. Not quite dinner time yet. I slow wheel up to the High Street, turn around and cycle back down Bedford Road past the Rec again. This time they're facing the right way but studying their shoes. How many times can you ride by without looking like a twerp? OK. Just once more. Down to the traffic lights at the A1 and slowly back again. If they aren't looking this time I'm definitely going home for my dinner. Shit. OK. Just once more then. Shit again. Right. If I cycle down to the traffic lights and they change from red to green and back again three times I'll give up. OK, five times. How do you make a face that says I'm not doing this to attract your attention? I just happen to be cycling by. Oh, sod it, I give up. What a pointless exercise and anyway I think they may have been laughing at me that time even though I look so cool in my new three-button T shirt. Which I take off when I get home – and notice the big white price tag still dangling from the back. 99p.

Our English teacher Mr Shanks sucked the life out of Shakespeare by getting us to read by rote. Julius Caesar made little sense to me until shortly before the exam, when we were taken to see a film version at Waden Regal. I finally got to experience Shakespeare the way that Shakespeare should be experienced – on celluloid, in a fleapit cinema. The same cinema where I'd seen the Beatles' Help in 1965, and which looked like it hadn't been swept or hoovered since. It was the 1953 Joseph Mankiewicz production, with Marlon Brando as Mark Antony and James Mason as Brutus, the very movie which Roland Barthes analysed in his essay Romans in Films. I wasn't too hot on signifiers and mythologies at that point, but I picked up on the themes immediately: betrayal and loyalty. I did eventually pass the requisite two O Levels I needed to get into Tech College – History and English Literature – and owe the latter largely to that visit to the Regal. I remember the local Secondary Modern were there too but were all thrown out after half an hour for being disruptive.

– Hot Love is slipping down the charts. Bolan had better write another one quickly.
– Yeah, otherwise all his teenybopper fans will go off him.

Sharpening our claws in the cloakrooms. "Dear Marc, it's over. Here's your ring back. I'm taking your name off my rough book. I refuse to share you with little girls. PS bring back Steve Peregrin Took. PPS I didn't understand what you were singing anyway. I just pretended. L.P. Winner.

We stretched out on the cloakroom benches, malingering the last of our school days away, limbs dangling, limp-lifed. A trolley went wheeling by. Two First Year boys, as was the custom, had been excused all other duties in order to deliver a consignment of stationery from delivery van to stock cupboards.

– Step aside. We'll take those.

We helped ourselves to a significant portion of the spoils and sent the small boys on their way with what little remained. What were we going to do with all those rough books? It would take a lot of dreaming and a lifetime of thoughts to fill one, and what would you write about anyway? Somehow, I managed. I still have one left. Green cover. Lined paper. It sits next to me as I type this, a blank-paged reminder of a life etched in marginalia and rough-book scribbles.

The final week of school. Another dinner break ends and so few to go now. Counting down the days. The bell rings and we're drifting back to class. Jimbo nudges me.

– It's that girl who...

Cindy walks over shyly with a friend.
– You said you wanted to borrow this?
– Did I?
– You said you were learning to play the guitar.

Oh yeah, I did, didn't I?

She hands me *Dan Morgan's Guitar Book*. Revised edition.

I would have been better off with a beginner's guide to bullshitting.

On the last day of school Mickey Stevens said, "Lick your finger and have a dab of this." Me, Jimbo, Loco, Brendan, Danny, Dickie. Some dabbed. Some didn't.

– It's probably only crushed aspirin anyway.
Junior hippie placebo kit. Whatever it was it made me sleepy, tired and dry-mouthed, and gave me a headache. We had a couple of joints round the back of the gym and decided not to go in for the last Assembly. The

final grand gesture of the refusers. We sat outside on the stone steps just across from the Dinner Hall listening to the singing and praying and chair-scraping and the muffled sound of speeches, our heads lolloping lazily. That same noise your brain makes when you try not to drift off in class but you do anyway. The suddenly louder sound that jerks you back to life. Soft lamentations drift from the School Hall, the gentle lilt of the final chorale. It was curiously affecting and we were aware of the significance of the moment, the last time we would all be gathered like this. Miss Austin the Deputy Head opens a side door.

– I understand, boys. It's very moving, isn't it? A time to reflect.

No Miss. It's not that. We is just very, very stoned. Or pretending to be.

Joy of A Boy. Summer of 1971.
Trying to look deep and meaningful but just looking a bit of a mirthless twat.

ACT TWO.
REPEAT

Nos patriae fines et dulcia linquimus arva.
(I am leaving my native countryside with its delightful fields).
Virgil. *Eclogues i, 3*

O words are poor receipts for what time has stole away.
John Clare. *Remembrances.*

PAVILIONS OF THE SUN

It was a Friday morning in September 1977, shortly before I started the final year of my degree at Bristol Polytechnic. Kid Jensen was hosting the Radio One breakfast show and the record he was playing was *Get It On* by T Rex. This struck me as unusual. It was a little after half eight. Radio One adhered rigidly to format and always played a chart hit after the news, not an oldie. Then Kid Jensen made his sombre announcement and I realised why. "As you'll have just heard on the news, Marc Bolan…"

On hearing those words I did the strangest thing. I sat down at the breakfast table and cried. I hadn't cried for years. I was Punk-hardened, body-armoured and in my prime. But now I was blubbing into my cereal bowl. I rationalised fairly rapidly that I wasn't crying for Marc Bolan as such. I wasn't even that much of a fan any more and hadn't been for some time. Sure, he'd come through his bloated coke blimp years and was likeable once again, but as I watched him slyly/shyly mugging away on kids' telly ("Same Marc time same Marc channel"), I couldn't ever envisage him being the king of the rumbling spires again. What I was doing of course was shedding tears for my youth, a youth that wasn't even over yet. Other rock deaths hadn't provoked that response. I didn't blub when I woke a few weeks earlier to the news that Elvis Presley had died. But then I hadn't built a dream house around Elvis. My teenage serenade was *Salamanda Palaganda*, not Hound Dog. Elvis was a hand-me-down from another era. Marc Bolan was a signpost on my road to self-discovery. He was flickering fireflies illuminating the forests of the night, he was dawn's dancer in the crackling ether, princely Pan of the everglades. And now he was dead.

Within seconds I had snapped out of it. Briefly I felt a little foolish and thought, "Wow, where did that come from?" Then I dried my tears, composed myself and went about my day.

When you're a kid death doesn't impinge in the same way that it does later on. Death of a pet. Death of a distant relative. Death of a near neighbour. Death of a sporting hero. Sometimes the curtains stay closed for a morning, sometimes they remain open. You dwell for a moment and then you go back to being young.

Because my pop year zero occurred when it did, I had no idea that the rock'n'roll highway was already littered with corpses. When I heard him sing about Bo Diddley on *Children's Favourites* I assumed Buddy Holly was alive in the same way that I assumed everybody was alive. I didn't know about the Big Bopper and Richie Valens. I didn't know that Eddie Cochran had met his fate at a notorious accident black spot just outside Bath. The first rock'n'roll death that I was consciously aware of was Johnny Kidd, who died in a car crash in October 1966. Shakin' All Over was part of my pre-Beatles vocabulary, alphabet blocks that formed words that formed a world. I remember seeing Johnny Kidd and the Pirates on TV, fancy-dressed and hanging from makeshift studio rigging. At eight years old I was happy to see my pop stars wearing eye patches and wielding cutlasses. The distance from *Captain Pugwash* and *Treasure Island* to swashbuckling pop stars was not as great then as it was later.

My abiding Johnny Kidd memory is of Terry Beecher washing his legs in a Junior School cloakroom sink while singing *I'll Never Get Over You* in a voice that seemed manly beyond its years. As he posed balletically, one foot up on points, the other in the sink, soaping football practice mud from his bare legs he hit the baritone notes with confidence. I was spellbound. There was something vaguely homoerotic about the moment I suspect. Terry was a couple of years older than me, dark-skinned, brown-eyed and broody, one of the bad-boy stars of the good boys' school football team. In his teens he got caught and convicted for siphoning fuel from lorries. The last I heard of him in the mid-80s he was an established dealer of connoisseur Northern Soul. From sink serenades to siphoning petrol to Northern Soul dealer seems a not-altogether-unusual trajectory to me now, a career pattern and life path I've encountered numerous times since, in scoundrels I have known.

Unless you were ever in a newsagents' while the bundle strings were being cut, unless you've shivered and blown on your fingers in the dimly lit darkness, unless you have stood there kicking your heels at 6 am along with all the other sleep-deprived delivery boys and girls, you have never inhaled such sweet pungency as that which seeps from a freshly printed newspaper. The smell of newsprint was one of the great chemical aromas of my youth, right up there with a bubbling vat of builder's tar and a creosote-soaked fence on a hot summer's day. The fragrance of still-wet newsprint emitted the very essence of up-to-the-minute urgency. At the bottom of the back page, or sometimes in side-strip columns on the front, the news agencies – Reuters, PA, UPI – post-scripted the stop-press news. You could almost imagine the copy editors running alongside the delivery vans, making their last-minute adjustments, linotyping the late bulletin into each individual copy. The dog-racing results from Harringay. The test-match score from Sydney, Australia. The latest Vietcong insurgency. Lifeboat disaster. No survivors.

It's a warm summer morning and I'm a dozen deliveries into my round before I fold the first Daily Express of the day and catch the headline in the right-hand column of the front page. 2am. Brian Jones found dead in swim pool. It's the headline they still sometimes use on pop documentaries. Swim pool rather than swimming pool because you can't fit that into a stop-press headline. Tragedy set in galley type and trimmed by a compositor's hand.

Dad had gone off the Rolling Stones long before Brian Jones died. He didn't approve of the drugs, and I think he associated the decline in the music with the increase in narcotic intake. When *Honky Tonk Women* came on the radio I lingered in his vicinity, eager for an endorsement. "Sounds like their old style," he said, the barest hint of approval in his voice. But it was a last reprise and he never took much notice after that. Nor for that matter did I.

I was intrigued by the tabloid tittle-tattle that was printed in the wake of Jones's death. The *News of the World. The People. Reveille. Titbits. Weekend*. They all ran it. The penchant for Nazi regalia. How ill-suited he was to stardom. What an utter cunt he was to his women. But most fascinating to me was the revelation that he liked to re-enact explosive car crashes with his Dinky Toys. I borrowed Dad's lighter fluid when everyone was out and tried the same procedure in the back garden but I couldn't get them to ignite.

It's September 1970 and we've been back at school for two weeks. The summer warmth lingers. It's a little after five and I'm in the front room getting out of my school uniform and into looser less restrictive clothing when Jimmy Dunn walks slowly up the front path. He cuts a sombre figure in the late afternoon sunshine. I've just turned on the radio. Tommy Vance is playing *Voodoo Chile*. What is Jimmy Dunn doing walking up my front path? He rarely does that. He keeps a distance. Mum thinks he might be on drugs and that he might be trying to interest me in drugs. She'd be better off blaming the *News of the World* on that score. I open the front window and Jimmy closes another.

– Hendrix is dead.
Dad comes into the front room for something. Hears *Voodoo Chile* playing like a lament now.
– Never wrote a bloody note of music in his life.
Thanks, Dad.

It was Hendrix wearing military regalia and Mitch Mitchell wearing an RAF jacket. That's what did it. It wasn't Dad's hatred of Hendrix as such. It wasn't residual working-class racism either. He liked Little Richard, Ray Charles and Nat King Cole, so how could it be? If he was partial to Little Richard's outrageous screaming queenery, he wasn't about to come on all Alf Garnett when the Jimi Hendrix Experience appeared on *Top of The Pops*. No, it was the sight of pop stars in I Was Lord Kitchener's Valet uniforms. That was taking the piss.

Next morning at school we keepers of the faith gathered by the incoming buses, greeting fellow mourners with reassuring nods as they disembarked. We walked a slow funeral procession up the drive, hoping that cool girls might notice us from classroom windows. We deliberately missed Assembly as a mark of disrespect. "Well. There's no disputing who is Number One guitarist now," said Donaldson, who thought *Disraeli Gears* was the best LP ever made. "Yeah," said Simon Parr. "Peter Green." We wore our grief self-consciously. Bearing up gave us cachet, or would have done had anyone noticed. By the time Janis Joplin died a couple of weeks later we'd adjusted magnificently.
We were building a Dutch barn on the school farm. O Level rejects. Skivvy duty. Child labour.
Dickie Dangerfield said: "Who's going to be the next dead rock star?"

– Ian Anderson. He's really weird.

– Do you reckon? I think he's really straight.

– You must be joking. Did you see him on *Top of the...* er, *Disco 2*?

– That's all an act.

– Yeah. And they have orchestras on their records.

– Who else shall we put on the list?

– Canned Heat are all junkies.

– Yeah put them down. Canned Heat.

– What, all of them?

– Yeah. I bet they all die in a plane crash like Otis and the Bar-Kays.

– Wasn't it the Mar-Keys?

– He's got a warehouse full of records.

– Who? Otis?

– No. That singer in Canned Heat. Bob Hite. I read it in *Record...* er, *Melody Maker*.

– How many has he got then?

– About 18,000, says Dickie Dangerfield. Blues mostly.

– Imagine a warehouse full of records. A barn this size.

We gape. We dream.

– What about Wild Man Fischer?

– Yeah, he'll definitely be next. The spazz!

– Let's sing *Merry Go Round* really loud.

They sing *Merry Go Round* really loud as they build a Dutch Barn. Their farmhand supervisor Les makes inappropriate comments about 14-year-old girls walking across the school yard and asks his young charges if they've "been broken in yet".

****

By the summer of 1971 the music papers couldn't separate the myths from the facts. A fortnight before I left school the Melody Maker front-page headline was "Satchmo Is Dead". Inside on Page Three a short news item headlined "Morrison death rumour exaggerated" relayed an unfounded story that the Doors singer had died of a heart attack. "Elektra Records told the MM this was the third similar rumour in the past month," the piece concluded.

****

When Marc Bolan died it didn't even make the front page of the national newspapers. In London it did, in *Evening Standard* banner headlines, but not elsewhere. Maria Callas had died on the same day and the press had different priorities then.

Me and my mate Pete watched the final Marc TV show, the one they showed posthumously, with Bowie as the special guest doing Heroes. They had a little rockaboogie jam at the end, and the show's host toppled off the stage. The final shot is of Bowie looking down at Bolan, laughing his fangs off. Pete and I had front-row tickets for Iggy Pop at the Colston Hall that night. We watched Marc's last stand on children's TV and then, fortified by bathtub speed and rough cider, went and watched Iggy. Bowie sat at the back, check-shirted, anonymous on keyboards, while the main attraction wriggled and writhed and flashed his cock. He arched like a crab. He mickey-monkeyed. He contorted his way through a set drawn mostly from *The Idiot* and *Lust for Life*. The Colston Hall bouncers, as always, tolerated the barest minimum of dancing except during the encore when we were permitted a token frug. Pressed tight against the lip of the stage and penned in by the throng of 50 or so hardcore fans who could be bothered to get up out of their seats, I found myself within arm's reach of Iggy Pop's set list. Emboldened by speed blam I began picking away at the masking tape that held it down. Pretty soon I had half of it peeled and ready to go. A bouncer, seeing what I was doing, made to intervene. Iggy, alert to the bouncer's intentions, positioned his microphone stand between me and the hired goon and allowed me my million in prizes. The set list, written in bold black marker pen on a sheet of plain A4 sat proudly on my bedroom wall for a few weeks until I got bored with the sight of it, peeled it off and threw it away. It left a scar of bare plaster on the wall.

Shortly after that I joined a band.

****

When Hendrix died something happened that I was quick to recognise but slow to respond to. I sensed an immediate disconnect between the figurehead they were talking about on the telly and the music that I was drawn to as a kid. Alan Price was paying tribute on the news, I remember that. He must have been going into Broadcasting House or Television Centre to record a radio session or one of his TV shows. Intercepted by the roving mike and the grief-watch hacks, he was press-ganged into a comment. You're a light entertainment celebrity. You'll do. "Well, obviously it's a shame, like." It seemed odd at the time. It's the norm now.

In 1980 I turned on the Radio Four news to hear that John Lennon had been shot dead. When I got in to work, a co-worker – middle-aged, female – said: "It's the end of an era, isn't it?" I can't be certain, but I suspect this was the first time anybody had used that expression in my presence. I don't mean I'd never heard the term before. Commentators on this and that were always working the angles over some demise, finding significance that might define a decade, a lifespan, an absence. The public's critical consent was never sought, always assumed. And here once again my complicity was being taken for granted. A Beatle is dead. It's the end of an era. But I didn't feel that it was the end of an era. And in the days and weeks that followed, as a mawkish mood took hold and the sentimentalist's grip tightened and the candlelit vigils refused to disperse and Bryan Ferry crooned his way to Number One with *Jealous Guy* I began to feel something akin to nausea.

Lester Bangs spoke to me, spoke for me, when he wrote his "Thinking the Unthinkable about John Lennon" piece for the *Los Angeles Times*. Bangs came to praise Lennon, not to bury him, and justified Lennon's greatness in ways that didn't need to be articulated, but he also said this: "I don't know which is more pathetic, the people of my generation who refuse to let their 1960s adolescence die a natural death, or the younger ones who will snatch and gobble any shred, any scrap of a dream that someone declared over ten years ago." He railed against the "gut-curdling sanctimonies", and the people who gathered to sing *Hey Jude* (Paul's song) outside the Dakota apartment. "What do you think the real – cynical, sneeringly sarcastic, witheringly witty and iconoclastic – John Lennon would have said about that?", asked Bangs.

A new procedural orthodoxy kicked in the day John Lennon died, and it's been with us ever since. Some attribute that touchy-feely, weepy-waily collective grief thing to the death of Lady Di. I don't. I think it was there long before the Spencer girl was driven incautiously into that Parisian underpass. The disengagement between individual sorrow and public soul-baring began with Lennon. That's when the death sting began to say more about the mourners than the mourned. That's when the herd instinct took hold and rode rough-shod over the quiet dignity of tears shed at breakfast tables in memory of private passion. End of an era? No, the beginning of one. The pop afterlife. The grift that keeps on giving.

When John Lennon died, a wife lost a husband and two children lost a father. *#9 Dream* was the last thing of his that I liked. That was 1975. I always assumed he would pop up on the *Parkinson Show* several years down the line, thinning on top, that acerbic nature undiminished, agreeably grumpy about all the things a man of his bearing would be agreeably grumpy about. He would have been good value as a chat-show guest. But shit intervened, as shit does. As Paul McCartney put it, stunned, numbed and honest: "It's a drag, isn't it?"

McCartney was pilloried for that. The microphone thrust. The crass, hack enquiry question that carried impossible expectations. The magnitude of the music they made together compared unfairly to the banality of that stock response. But there are times when banality is the only available option. Those who detected the end of an era in John Lennon's death were articulating death in the abstract, and you can fill an abstract with anything. A void will allow you that indulgence.

But when death in the abstract ceases to be an option. What then?

BIG LOAD GOING SOMEWHERE

My driver spoke in broad Bedfordshire, so it came out "big lowde gooing smwerr". Slightly mournful. Hint of a sob in the somewhere. And he was right. I couldn't fault his observation. A big load was indeed gooing smwerr. We waited patiently on the A1 slip road as a long low loader and its heavy haulage took an eternity to pass in front of us. We had an eternity to spare that morning, so there was nothing else to do but watch the warning lights on the escort vehicle and the muddied caterpillar tracks of the construction-plant machinery as the big load crawled slowly northwards.

If this was a film I'd be a Midwestern cattle rancher with a cargo of bleating calves in the back of my truck. If this was a film I'd be a small-town scrap dealer towing a beat-up Chevvy to the breaker's yard. A railroad engine would be passing and I'd be waiting at the crossing gates, chewing a match as a flicker flash trail of wagons reflected in my mirror shades. I'd be wearing a ruminating expression. I'd have a "don't have to be anywhere anytime soon" attitude about me. If this was a film I'd be one of these things first. One of these things instead of. If this was a film.

"Big load going somewhere," agreed my driver's wife in the front passenger seat. Similar intonation, albeit more vacant and distracted. Her thoughts elsewhere. Her deadpan emptiness echoed in my head. Still echoes in my head. There is always a big load going somewhere.

****

That really was the strangest dream. I'm home from college going, "Ha-ha, he didn't, did he?" "Yes, he did," replies my sister. She shows me an item on page five of the *Waden Chronicle* which says that Andrew Hartley of Ivel Way, Albion Sands, wishes to make it clear that he is not the Andrew Hartley mentioned in last week's news about a man who was convicted of rape and serious assault and sentenced to three years imprisonment. That clears that up then. Grammar School-educated Look and Learner Andrew Fartley has not been violently abusing women and is not to be confused with another man of the same name. Thanks for drawing it to our attention, Andrew.

I'm in the kitchen wiping while Mum washes. The living-room door is slightly ajar, and in the gap between door and frame I can see Dad sitting in his favourite armchair, smoking, reading the paper. When he's not there he's down the bowling green. In 1973 he decided that he would rather pluck his own eyes out than play bowls for the Conservative Club, so he decided to start a club of his own. Not on his own. Some of his brothers and their mates chipped in, but his was the vision. He was the driving force. I remember him sitting in that armchair sketching a club badge, skylarks in a crest. In the early days when the club was just a dream, and the green was still an unseeded rectangle of barren brown earth, he was down there after work one evening when a lark took flight and burst into song. He tells me this as he sketches. He sees the easy poetry of it.

After I've had my tea I'll go for a walk and see the fruits of his labour for myself. The green was built on the edge of the overspill estate, next to where the Cambridge to Oxford branch line used to run. A slight elevation in the land, an embanked ridge overgrown with grass, is all that remains of the railway. The cricket club is down there as well, these days. Some houses got built at the back of the Rec. One of the new residents complained about cricket balls landing in his garden, and the danger this posed to his French windows. He petitioned the council and won. The cricket team now plays on what was formerly the rubbish dump. The smouldering mound where we used to scavenge for go-kart wheels is now part of the outfield, wide of mid-on. And the resident who complained about those well-struck sixes? He moved out a few months later.

The sand hills are still there. Can't flatten those. As long as there is an Albion Sands there will always be the sand hills. There will always be a town with a beach many miles from the sea. I climb once more to the summit and enjoy the elevation. An industrial estate has been spreading northwards alongside the mainline railway for several years now. Light industry mostly. "Tin-pot firms," Dad called them disdainfully, remembering the factories and prestige employers that were promised but never came. There are fewer fields now, and a lot more housing. Everything else is as familiar to me now as it was when I was a boy. The silent glide of the distant A1 traffic, a farm plough raking the stubble from straw blonde to black, sunlight gleaming off hot-house windows, stick figures going about their business in the Market Square, the cold concrete steps and swollen voluptuous pillars of the Victory Cinema, which no longer shows films and had surrendered to the bingo long before I went away. A poster advertising the last picture show is still pinned to the wall outside in a little glass display case. The lock has rusted away, but nobody has bothered to remove the poster or deface it. It sits there, slightly askew on its discoloured drawing pin. Washed-out Technicolor. Frank Sinatra in army uniform.

A funeral procession passes me in the High Street, heading for St Swithun's church. The mourners wear the same glazed faces you always see when you are this side of the glass, carefree and short-sleeved, and not their side, blank-eyed, suited and veiled. An old farmhand respectfully removes his cap. The shadow of the cortège soon passes in the bright August sunshine. Life resumes its sedate pace. Why wouldn't it?

Outside the paper shop the wording on the billboard reads "Stalwart Is Ousted". The story is about some old parish councillor who has been counselling since Domesday but has been ruthlessly swept aside by the new-broom brigade. The headline amuses me. It tickles my presumption. The Chronicle has definitely got more Chaucerian since I went away. Ye Olde Stalwart Stands and Delivers. Ye Jousting Stalwart Is Impaled Upon His Opponent's Pole. His head falls off. Ha-Ha Bonk.

Everything is agreeably in its place. Swithuntime. Swithuntide. Dependable down to the last mundane detail. But when you look closer, everything is not the same at all.

The old alley bridge with its rotting panels and wood knots, just the right height and diameter for a small boy to stick his prick through and piss on a passing train if he can time it right, that's all gone. It's been replaced by a concrete bridge with sides too high to peer over. The sandstone station bridge, that's been upgraded too. Now it's a line of ugly blue-grey panels, rivet-gunned into place. Walking over it now is like walking beside a battleship, or gazing at a big load going somewhere. The worn flagging where Mum used to carefully prop me at the end of an afternoon's shopping so I could wave at the steam trains, that's all gone.

The railway station has been modernised too. The booking office and the station master's house present a familiar façade, but everything else has been ripped out and replaced. Where Platform Four on the old Oxford to Cambridge line once stood, the spot where we whiled away those endless 1960s summers, they've constructed a Perspex shelter – you'd hesitate to call it a waiting-room. An "enduring-room" perhaps. Dad calls it a Matchbox station because it looks like it's made of the same off-white plastic as the Matchbox toy garage you'd get for Christmas when you were six. The enduring-room stinks. The red plastic chairs and dirty windows have been branded by lighter burns, the signature of the casually indolent. Those idle August memories of my childhood have been erased, along with the landmarks and the steadily crumbling ruination that went with them. The dead-bird empty shed, the old signal box and buffers, the flaking white panels of the picket fence, the wrought-iron foot bridge (how many times did Mum wriggle a pram or pushchair down those steps?), the sand buckets, the bogs, the shove-ha'penny trollies, the hanging baskets, the flower beds that used to spell out the name of our town, the smell of track oil and kippered wood. Nothing left of it.

The funeral service having ended, the hearse and procession makes the short slow haul from St Swithun's up to the top of the High Street and over the station bridge, before dipping into the gently banked hollow of the cemetery. It all looks so serene from where I am. The headstones file neatly, one fresh row a year, down to a tall hedgerow and a meadow where three horses suddenly break into a trot and run for the fun of it.

I stand at the roadside and watch respectfully as a snaking line of mourners park their cars on roadside verges and follow the coffin to the freshly dug grave. In the shade of a maple oak, a group of men have gathered. They let themselves in at the side gate. They don't look like they've been to the service, but they've come to pay their respects anyway. Stubbing out fags and tightening the knots in their ties.

I go home to where everything will be exactly as I left it.

****

That really was the strangest dream. The phone rings. My wife answers it and shakes me awake. A neighbour. Something about a neighbour. We'd only been asleep half an hour. Just nodded off. Around midnight.

A neighbour? None of our London neighbours have our phone number. And what would they be doing calling at this time of night anyway? Is the downstairs flat on fire?

No, not a London neighbour. Home neighbour. Jimmy Dunn's mum back in Albion Sands. She's calling from the phone box at the bottom the road. Why did she say it's a neighbour? Why didn't she just say –

By the time I'm handed the phone my youngest brother Geoff is on the line. "It's Dad."

Ambulance. Something about an ambulance. And oxygen.
I get through to the right ward at Bedford Hospital surprisingly quickly and am put on hold. In that brief moment of denial and self-deception, in those final precious seconds where everything is still exactly as I left it and an entire dream life can be lived in a micro flash, I surmise that there won't be any news yet, not till the morning, but in no time at all a woman comes to the phone and in clear measured tones says: "I'm sorry to have to tell you that your father has passed away."

"I'm putting you through to your mother." I'm told that. Then it's Mum's voice on the line. She sounds small and far away. I can hear the echo of an empty room as she speaks.

The next morning I'm heading up the A1, having thumbed a lift from Hendon, my favoured spot. "Don't hitch," says my wife, offering me the train fare. "Promise me you won't hitch." I promise her I won't but I do. I'm not spending an interminable hour on a train listening to other people's pleasantries and bullshit.

And so I head up the A1 once more, as I have so often in the past, a passenger in a comfortable car. Window down. Castle of high cloud. Cumulus battlements. A sunny morning. We talked about the cricket, my chauffeur and I.

– Do you think we'll level the series?

West Indies one up. Three drawn tests. One left to play.

– Can't see it, can you?

– Perhaps if we had Holding and Marshall.

– Two best bowlers I've ever seen.

This from a Yorkshireman.

– They never seem to pick the right players, do they? I mean what's Gatting done to justify his place in the side?

– Plays for the right county, though, doesn't he?

– Aye, you're not wrong there, lad. You're not wrong there.

A week ago, a week to the day in fact, we'd been to the second day's play of the fourth test at the Oval – wife, brother Geoff and I. Chasing a ball in the outfield, West Indian captain Clive Lloyd pulled a thigh muscle and crumpled to the turf, a tangle of uncoordinated bones. It was like someone had shot a gazelle. One minute gliding gracefully, the next posture all gone, limbs dangling useless. Still, I expect Richards will make a good skipper in his absence.

I didn't tell my driver about the drunken Australians who sat behind us. Who grew more boorish and belligerent as the afternoon wore on, who asked us if we were "white West Indians" whenever we clapped a four from Richards or Kallicharran. "Hey, fellas, we got a couple of white West Indians here. Did you hear me Doug? I said…"

I didn't tell him any of that. Kept it focused and polite.

– Do you think Botham is going to make a good captain?

– Not showing much sign yet, is he?

– Perhaps he'll come good in the winter.

Yes, you always have to consider the winter.

All the bollocks that men can talk when they talk about sport. All the way to Albion Sands. No other topic passed our lips. I was grateful for that.

– This where you live, is it?

– This is where I used to live. Just visiting my parents.

"They'll be pleased to see you," he said as I got out of the car.

They.

He didn't have a clue. He didn't have the faintest idea about the hollow cargo he was carrying. I'll always be grateful for that ride and for that time whiled away in his unsuspecting company, talking our small talk.

I'm home again dreaming another dream. Mum's voice seeps into my sleep and worries me awake. A faraway sound from nearby. She sounds weak and bewildered. Exhausted by grief by mid-afternoon we'd all fallen asleep in separate rooms. I'd crashed out on the front-room sofa. Indents from the cushion buttons ran up my left arm and reddened my cheek. Mum's thin frail voice calls out for her daughter, but it's only me that wakes. House like a train crash. Sister asleep on her bed. Brother Chris on his. Youngest brother Geoff on Mum and Dad's, where he had cradled Dad till the ambulance came, knowing already that he was dead in his arms.

"They wouldn't let me travel in the ambulance," said Mum. "I knew then."

On the death certificate it gave the deceased date as August 1st, but that's when the ambulance reached the hospital and the necessary paperwork was done. Mum knew he had gone before midnight. As I lay sleeping.

"He had to come off me," she explained in more detail than she'd ever shared with me before. "We hadn't made love for a while, and he stopped and…"

She makes a gesture towards the bedroom wall. "He went for his tablets… and he slumped against the wall there… and…"

It's two weeks later. Mum washes. I wipe. I'm looking through the gap in the living-room door for the shape that isn't there any more, sitting in his living-room armchair, among the living.

That absence. That gap. A portal. Peering into nothingness and the black shore beyond.

That night of the phone call, sleep was only fitful and the dreams came sick and fast. An undertaker's workshop full of coffins. Limbs poking out through rotted lids. They came thick like fever after that. Every night for weeks. Crunching my way across a gravel yard towards the Chapel of Rest. Passing a shed full of rigor mortis and forbeetoo. Thinking back to the summer of 1970. Me and my mate Jack phoning the undertakers for a laugh from the call-box in the Market Square. Ordering a coffin. Giggling as the undertaker played along and asking us if we wanted forbeetoo. Putting the phone down in hysterics then the guilt rebounding and phoning him back to cancel the order just in case he'd made a start. Just boys larking about in the springtime of their lives. That would have been August too. Who knows? It might have been ten years to the day. The fates do conspire like that.

The day of the funeral. Passing the newsagents. The banner board reads "Popular local man dies". What happened to the stalwart who was ousted? People are going in and out of shops, carefree and oblivious. A white-haired lady carefully props her bike against a wall. It clatters to the ground the moment she walks away. A farmhand doffs his cap and looks me in the eye. I meet his gaze, looking but not seeing. One day you are that side of the cortège glass, and then everything changes. Now you are this side, barely aware of who is driving you where and why.

St Swithun's church sings out. Psalm 23. *Jerusalem*. I organised the service. The vicar came to our house and asked which hymns we would like. He suggested *To Be a Pilgrim*. "That's usually very popular. Would you like that?" "No," I said. That was the Waden Grammar official school hymn. I'm not having that at my Dad's funeral. Mum and Dad were married in this church, but they've rarely been back since. "People sinning all week and going there on Sunday. Hypocrites." Mum's take.

"The Tory party at prayer." Dad's take.

"We are gathered here today to commemorate..." (Looks down at notes. Says name of deceased here and at regular intervals until the ceremony is over and we can go outside again into the sunshine.)

The skylarks are silent. A soul ascends. The harvest gathered in.

I choked upon seeing the church so full. Some people couldn't get in for the service so they went straight to the cemetery. As the procession snaked down the winding path to the long white row of headstones I noticed that the tyre on the right side rear wheel of the coffin trolley was flat. For a fleeting moment nothing seemed as reassuringly real as that flat tyre. It mesmerised me. The life-affirming banality of it. I fixated on the tyre all the way to the freshly dug grave. I looked up just once and noticed that a group of men had gathered in the shade of a maple oak, down by the roadside, three or four of them in their suits. Stubbing out fags and tightening the knots in their ties. I could see that they were trying to judge the appropriate moment to walk up the path and join the mourners. Too early and they would get to the graveside first. In their hesitant respectful steps I saw the dignity of man.

The wake is a carnival side-show of horror masks and distant close relatives. London Uncle proffers a manly handshake, and comments on the limpness of my grip. His youngest brother's in a box and he's asking me if I call that a handshake. An Auntie is dressed like a tart on the pull. She's wearing her best slinky number with a split up the side. London Uncle asks me and my wife where we live. There's been no contact since we moved to the city, but on this day of unavoidable proximity and small talk he enquires about our postcode. "Near Clapham North tube," I say. "Sort of bordering onto Brixton," adds my wife. "Ah, Brixton," says London Uncle. Then he makes a joke about monkey men swinging from de lamp posts in de old Brixton town. At his brother's funeral. In this dream I had that was far too sick to be true and far too real to be fiction. My wife and I exchange a look and go among the mourners.

Later in the afternoon, back at home, funeral clothes discarded, Chris gets the dartboard out of the barn. I nail it to the door and we all throw arrows. We get Mum to join in and in no time at all we are laughing on the outside. Warding off numbness. Mum says, "Nobody would ever guess we've just buried your father." Momentarily we see ourselves as others in adjoining backyards and gardens must see us, aiming for double top. The day goes quieter and the sky tries to rain.

That night we sit and watch *Coronation Street*. It's the episode where René Roberts gets killed. Alf is teaching her to drive and with mounting annoyance in a country lane he demands that they exchange seats. René gets out of the car and is knocked down by a passing lorry. Should we really be watching this? Mum doesn't seem to mind. "I used to think this was such a dreary programme," she says. I know. So did I. "Your Grummar used to have it on all the time. I never knew what she saw in it." I know. Nor did I. Sitting round there some nights. Watching those old ladies bickering in the smog of the snug. That mournful theme tune. Glad when it was over and Benny Hill came on. Laughing like drains. Grummar, Grandad and me. The ITV stuff in the early 1970s. Rurry great irriot. The years when Hill still had a twinkle, before he went with gentle irrelevance into his decline, like most of them do.

Mum came late to *Coronation Street*, too late to enjoy it with her Mum, who died in November. She's lost her Mum and her husband in the space of nine months. We all glance warily and think should we really be watching René and Alf, but Mum seems OK with a fictional death. There's none of the stress we'll face in a few months time when that fucking Grandma song is the Christmas Number One. Of all the tragic-farce that life can conjure, of all the ways in which Beelzebub can have a devil put aside, releasing a song called There's No One Quite Like Grandma, when your Mum has just lost her Mum and her husband, and is raw with grief this cold cruel winter, that's right up there. At the first sound of those introductory bars and that taunting refrain we children perfect the art of hurling ourselves bodily across the room in order to hit the off switch.

In the dreams Dad is still alive. Then he's not. Everything is OK, then it's not OK. Dreams embedded deep within dreams within other dreams that turn out not to be dreams at all. That's where the sickness is for a long time. It has to go somewhere. In the dreams I try to have a conversation but the words won't come and Dad doesn't speak. He just smiles his knowing smile, his fool-suffering, son-appeasing smile. And then one night I have a dream that finally makes it all right. A dream that makes the nightmares go away. We walk down the road together, Dad and I. Casually acquainted in the early evening sunshine. Chatting about nothing much. We pass the old people's bungalows at the bottom of Spring Grove and walk on past the crumbling outbuildings of Feltwell's. When we reach the cycle-path bollards at the end of Church Path I continue on towards Bedford Road, heading for the High Street. But Dad veers right and walks off down the narrow lane towards the A1. "I have to go this way now," he says. And in the dream I understand. He has to go that way now. Parting with glad tidings, we go our separate ways and there are no more bad dreams. I've never dreamed about him since. Mum many times, but Dad never. In the final dream, the one that brings resolution, he doesn't evaporate in a cliché puff of smoke, he just carries on walking, across the A1, and into the Elysian fields where Feltwell's relocated when they sold their Nursery plot. That's where the White Lodge is I'd imagine. That's his heaven. The final portal.

– Do you still go and watch the cricket, Grandad?
– They moved it. It's down where the rubbish dump used to be now.
– I know.

I went once. Just the once. Early September not long after Dad died. End of season. An old lady came over. I didn't know her but she said, "Your father was a good man. The Lord always takes the good ones first." The cricketers were flannelled white dots in the distance. There's no windbreak of trees. No shelter for the old men. Therefore no old men. They used to go to the Rec every week, come drizzle or dry, to sit on the mossy benches in the shade of the poplars. Now there's just a gaggle of cricketers girlfriends, random dog walkers, muffled handclaps. The players' shouts are carried away on the breeze. Bar the odd rimshot crack of willow it's mostly silence.

I watch for a while, lobbing memories, fumbling dolly catches, catching sight of Roy Harper's *12th Man at Silly Mid On*. Soon after tea the mist descends. Everything goes hazy at the edges. Autumn stops play.

The remainder of Dad's life is in the loft. I climb up there one day to take a look. There's an old brown suitcase, which hasn't closed properly for years. It's lined with yellowing newspaper – a Beds Courier headline reads "Stalwart Is Ousted". There's some mounted prints which Dad was going to hang in the hall but never did. Birds and wildflowers etched in watercolour. Let's see what else is here. Bundles of seed catalogues, gardening magazines, horticultural and chrysanthemum society membership cards. A boxful of scorecards. Mementos of all the games he played: snooker, billiards, bowls. And several years' worth of *World Bowls* magazines to which he had an annual subscription. In the middle of one of these mags I find a single sheet of A5 paper. Title underlined, <u>"The History of Bowls"</u>, and one neat paragraph written in blue ink, concerning the correct dimensions of a bowling green. That's all he's written. As far as he got. Half a page and put away in the attic, along with who knows how many other ambitions? In one of the magazines, January 1971 edition, I find an article he wrote called "Can Old Men Play Bowls?". I remember him writing it and his quiet pride when it was published. It always annoyed him that bowls had a crotchety image, and the article is an impassioned rallying cry against the stereotype. It's well written, philosophical, polemical and as cussedly pedantic as he could be sometimes. It's the only piece I ever remember him writing, and I wonder how much more of this he had in him. There is no pull quote because that wasn't house style, but if there had been I would have gone with: "A 75-year-old bowler has my respect and admiration. A 20-year-old spectator at any sport has my pity." He was anti-couch potato, anti-armchair spectator. He couldn't understand why you would want to sit and gawp at any sport when you could be playing it. He expected to still be playing it at 75.

In the final year of his life Dad got to play at the national championships at Worthing. The gods of sport reward their own, and he played on an adjacent rink to the then current world champion, David Bryant, his long-time hero. They chatted freely. Keen to prolong his bowling years for as long as possible, Dad asked his hero (four years his junior), "What goes first?" "The legs," Bryant replied. With snooker players, it's the eye. With tennis players and cricketers, it's the reflexes. With footballers, it's pace and precision. "The legs," said the 48-year-old to the 52-year-old. Wrong advice. It's the heart. Three hours before he died Dad won his final bowls match.

****

"Big lowde gooing smwerr," said Mr Smith the postman, as he sat waiting patiently with his foot on the clutch. We'd been to Bedford Police Station to collect Mum's death certificate. The kindness of neighbours. Mum had been at school with Mrs Smith. I had been at Junior School with their son Keith. "I was only thinking the other day, wasn't I?" she said to her husband. "It's coming up to a year since Bob died." We continued to watch the wall of heavy haulage slowly grinding by. Blocking out the day.

Mum had planned to put something in the paper. She showed me a commemoration verse she found in *The Sunday People* and asked me what I thought. It was inadequate in the way that all words are inadequate. Therefore it was fine.

At Bedford police station a Scottish officer with sympathetic demeanour and a rough brogue took me into a small interrogation room and explained that I could have full access to Mum's medical records if I wished, and if I didn't wish then they would be destroyed. "My Mum died of cancer too, if it's any consolation," he said. It was and it wasn't. I expressed some sort of numbed irritation that she'd been admitted to hospital on the Saturday and then sent home, then re-admitted again the very next day when she relapsed. "So, they sent her home to die, basically," I said. That's when the officer offered his consoling words. The phone call had come from my brother Chris this time. My wife wouldn't let me make the hospital call. Not again. Not twice in a year.

Back at the grave-side so soon. Raising a reflex arm to ward off a blow. A coward's flinch. That's how it felt the second time. Death found me wanting. That evening, newly orphaned, we sat on the brand-new three-piece suite that Mum had bought with the life insurance when Dad died, and tried to figure out how best to hold onto the three-bedroom council house where now only my two brothers remained. My sister's friend Sally popped round with her little dog which started to claw at the furniture. "Oh God, if your mum could see this she'd die," said Sally. She immediately looked mortified. We fell about laughing. The brothers got to stay in the council house. Not now they wouldn't. They would have been out on their arses before the tombstone was set.

Mum's cancer was only diagnosed when she died, although I wasn't oblivious to her sudden decline. In the final photos she has dark foreboding rings around her eyes and looks like she's had ECT. In the last few letters she wrote to me her tone alternates between making do and existential emptiness. One minute treating herself to a new three-piece suite and wallpapering a bedroom, then writing and telling me about it with the cat on her lap. The next telling me she feels as weak as a kitten. In the last letter I receive she mentions that she had a bit of a blackout and fell off her bike in the High Street.

Did I want access to her medical records? Did I want to see a list of prescriptions, the names of all the pills and what they did or mostly didn't do for her? No, thank you. I saw enough of them stacked on the pantry shelf. Did I want to read all the evidence of depression rendered in a doctor's barely legible script? Again, no thanks. I'll remember her for all the good things she was, for all the thankless tasks she did, for the bright girl who couldn't afford to go to college, for all the meals she put on the table and the ones left warming in the oven when any of us were going to be late back. I'll remember her for the person she managed to be when she wasn't submerged in medicated fog and dusk-light gloom.

****

The week Dad died, my parents had arranged to come and visit us in our cramped little housing-association flat in Clapham. They hadn't visited as a couple since we'd got married and moved to London. Mum and my sister Christine had been once the previous year. We lived in an attic flat in Putney then. The world snooker final played silently in the background as we chatted. Cliff Thorburn versus Alex Higgins. May 5th 1980. Mum's 50th birthday. On the way back to Kings Cross their bus was diverted in South Kensington. They heard a muffled explosion and what sounded like gunfire in the distance. At home we sat watching the televised conclusion to the Iranian Embassy Siege. "How's Dad?" I'd asked Mum. "He doesn't think he's done enough for you," she said. That surprised me. All of us who sat the 11+ passed it, and three out of four of us went on to higher education. That was entirely down to them, their aspirations, their intelligence and a fiercely instilled insistence that we never act thick and that we make the best of ourselves.

A few weeks later I wrote Mum a letter, knowing that Dad would read it, making it clear that I thought he'd done more than enough for us. You should always do that. Even if you don't tell them directly you should always make sure they get the message somehow. Lightens the load immensely. There's enough purgatory to deal with as it is.

Four days before they were due to come and see us, one day before he died, Dad phoned to finalise the travel arrangements. I gave him details of the tube journey from Kings Cross down to Clapham. Not sure if he was familiar with the fare structures I told him to get return tickets not singles. Those were the last words I ever said to him, "Remember to get return tickets."

****

Mum in Trafalgar Square 1953. A year before I was born.

Dad a year before he died.
Giving me his best fool suffering smile.

****

In Paul Morley's *Nothing*, by far his best book, he weaves a compelling narrative around his father's suicide. I warmed to the incidental details as much as I did to the poignancy of the central storyline. Like his Dad, mine smoked Guards cigarettes. Like Morley, I mourned the death of racing driver Jim Clark as only a small boy can, as he paddles in the shallows of incomprehension. The parallels in our lives began and ended with those incidentals. My Dad didn't seek out a favoured spot in Laurie Lee country to hang himself like Morley's did. Mine died of a dodgy ticker and too much hard work. Apart from the cigarette brand thing and the Grand Prix thing and more than a little of the pop thing, there was nothing much to connect my southern rural upbringing with Morley's northern industrial one. But there was one part in his eulogy that cut me to the quick. The bit where he reflected on how well he did in the period immediately after his father's death, the bit about how his own life took off with *Zang Tumb Tuum* and *Frankie Says* and the rest of it.

I contrasted Morley's art life to my own state of affairs in the early 1980s. In the aftermath of my parental loss my life turned to shit. I lost all sense of who I was, all sense of self and self-worth.

What kept me going? At 25, the sheer momentum of life keeps you going. Later you have to create that momentum for yourself, but in your mid-20s the automated sidewalk of existence just carries on moving, indifferent to fate or fortune. I liken the experience to those travelators you get at airports. One minute you are purposefully gliding towards your destination gate, the next minute death reaches over from the opposite walkway and punches you hard in the solar plexus, or delivers a stab wound to the rib. There is nothing you can do about it. It's no good turning round to try and catch a glimpse. Death already has its back to you and is heading in the opposite direction, reaching across to some other poor unsuspecting innocent. You stumble on in a dreamlike state, clutching your side in excruciating pain, all the while vaguely aware that none of the other people on the walkway have even noticed your plight. And all this while the moving sidewalk of life continues to propel you forward, regardless of whether you are emotionally equipped to go on with the journey.

You learn to take the grieving one hour at a time, then one day at a time, until eventually there comes a point when you realise you haven't actually thought about death for over 24 hours. You experience a twinge of guilt as you realise this, but you also acknowledge that the healing has started. I can remember exactly where I was when I first thought this. I was hauling my bike down some railway-bridge steps, heading for another of life's station platforms and another of life's late-running trains. It doesn't matter which station platform it was. The location is irrelevant. The incidental details are as mundane as the life I was leading at the time. It's the healing that's important.

The other thing that kept me going was music.

The day after we buried my Dad, BBC2 showed the 1975 film version of Eric Blau and Mort Shuman's off-Broadway Revue *Jacques Brel Is Alive and*

Well and Living in Paris. Brel himself had a walk-on part in his own life story, looking on with impeccable detachment as others interpreted his songs about love and death. Watching it was a cathartic experience. That evening, too numbed with grief to do anything other than feel like I had a walk-on part in my own life, I was probably more psychologically attuned to the depth and resonance of those songs than I ever will be again. I empathised in a way that I had never empathised before. The emotions writ large in those songs – *Alone, I Loved, My Death, Old Folks* – were now absorbed in a new way. It was the first indication that something had changed. Without you even knowing it, there is a sudden perceptual shift in how you view your past and the music you've grown up with. The songs remain the same but you inhabit them differently, they inhabit you differently.

As a kid you assimilate pop music piecemeal. The culture is making itself up as it goes along and so are you. By the time you reach the second half of your twenties the past is being sold back to you in a form you barely recognise. What began as impulse and ad lib has been infiltrated by a repertoire of conditioned response and cliché. Private joys and sorrows are devalued and belittled by received wisdom and the institutional construction of nostalgia. The mythical sixties, rather than the sixties you lived through, has been invented. The audio theme park of oldies radio regurgitates the Top 30 as selective tradition. Simon Bates's *Golden Hour* plays the pop charts of your youth, sometimes in sequences that are life-affirming, at other times in a way that is repellent to everything you cherish.

In the immediate aftermath of my parents' death I wrote a book. I threw myself into it as a way of typing my way out of despair, and in the process I learned how to write long-form. The book began with a comparison between rock'n'roll and the Cubists and ended (because things have to end somewhere) with *Apocalypse Now*. It was called *Dansette Heaven: Dollar Hell* and I still have a very nice rejection letter from Miles at Omnibus telling me that it deserved to be published. Some of it was used later as I fed my thoughts back into the culture that had fed me, via music journalism, CD sleeve notes and eventually books that did get published. There's an old scholarly truism that says all academics have just the one lecture that they go on giving all their life. If you live long enough you get to fully understand the joke.

In the 1980s, some of the more enterprising independent record labels and bootleggers began to issue compilations of hard-to-find curios from the past. In doing so they helped me reconfigure my 1960s. All those psychedelic pop gems I'd heard just once or twice in the radio-rationed post-pirate years gained a new lease of life. Other aspects of my pop past were reinvigorated too. Through the Boy's Own barter system of cultural exchange I traded all my early copies of *ZigZag* magazine with a guy in Aldershot who gave me an entire 1967 run of *NME*s in return. These too were eventually traded on, but during the course of our conversation the topic of the offshore stations came up. "Oh, you like pirate radio do you?" he said. "Only I have a box of old tapes in the loft. They belonged to my Dad." And so began a decade-long journey into the world of radio anoraks. I began placing small ads in *Exchange & Mart, Private Eye*, local newspapers, anywhere outside of the regular channels that might prise out long-forgotten mildewed tape reels from lofts and sheds and farm outbuildings. By the end of the 1980s, the sum total of all this sleuth work was a massive tape archive, much of which I still have and which led indirectly to me doing my Master's Degree on the subject, and soon after that to my first published book, *Selling the Sixties: The Pirates and Pop Music Radio*. In the same way that I heard far more 1960s music in the 1980s than I ever did in the 1960s, I spent much of the 1980s listening to the pirates in far greater quantity and quality than I ever did during the original offshore era.

A decade that had begun with death and desolation ended when I met my soulmate and second wife Caroline, and we eloped to Acid House together. By 1991 we were living in Manchester. A year later *Selling the Sixties: The Pirates and Pop Music Radio* was published by Routledge. I phoned Caroline at home to tell her I was now officially a published author. "Your Mum and Dad would have been proud," she said. It was all she needed to say. At the same time Routledge also published *The Space Between the Notes*, Sheila Whiteley's musicological study of the counter culture and its psychedelic soundtrack. Dr Whiteley, the first bona fide Professor of Pop to use her full title, was a kindred spirit at Salford University where we were both working at the time. On the day of their arrival at work we peered into the freshly delivered boxes of books and giggled to see our names in print. "Let's skip down the corridor," said Sheila. So we did.

ACT THREE.
FADE

I feel, in myself, the river run, the ocean swell/
And miles above me, a strange stairway.
(Bill Fay, *Strange Stairway*)

THERE'S A GHOST IN MY HOUSE

When I was young, rural communities could always find gainful employment for what in differently enlightened times were called the infirm and feeble-minded. For as long as I remained connected with the town of my birth, my not all there next-door neighbour but one Jacob continued to be the grateful beneficiary of an unspoken, unregulated protection scheme. There was always a factory or small manufacturing company that would thrust a broom into his willing hand, always a handcart that needed to be trundled somewhere for cash wages. I often used to see him cycling his big fixed-wheel bicycle round town. "'Ello, Robert," he would call, face side on and creased with effort as he bent into the wind and pushed against the pedals. During the summer of 1974, after I'd finished my A levels, I was working at a local industrial ceramics firm (long since "dissolved"), and there, in overalls, was Jacob, reliably dependent, conscientiously pushing a broom. Like most student shirkers, secure in the knowledge that there would always be holiday employment and a generous tax-free threshold for the remainder of my days, I seized every opportunity to skive off and found ever-more-inventive ways to avoid the floor manager's radar. On my numerous circuitous routes to the safe haven of the toilets, I often chanced upon Jacob sweeping away. I would assume invisibility, drift innocuously by and hope for the best. On almost every occasion he would follow me to the toilets a few minutes later and as I sat in a cubicle reading three-day old cricket scores or availing myself of the establishment's impressive stash of pornography Jacob would stand by the entrance, and sotto voce in tones untainted by adulthood, would announce: "And I told Robert. I told him you'd better come out of there fast because if the foreman sees him he'll get the sack. You're not supposed to skive off are you? I told him." Keeping up an imaginary unconvincing conversation with someone who wasn't there, reasoning with his own obedience and let that be a warning Robert in case the bosses they do come.

Many years later I was in the town library. I looked out of the window and there was Jacob, middle-aged now, stockier, slightly hunched but still about. He was standing in the Market Square, smartly dressed, talking to two women who were admiring the beautiful golden retriever sat beside him. There he was, dependable as ever with man's most dependable friend as his companion. A forever fixture of that town and my memories and those times.

More recently, for reasons not entirely unconnected with this book, I ventured a curiosity Google or two. I plucked names arbitrarily from the memory bank and watched them flash by in random mouse manoeuvres. I found one of the two murderers I knew as a child – they weren't murderers then, but they grew up to be. This one, if the pressure-group petition was to be believed, was killed in custody. Alternately he died of "natural causes", if the Gov.org records were correct. I also chanced upon the obituary of a slightly older school friend who I knew to be gay probably before his parents did, perhaps not long after he did, as I briefly became the recipient of his rough-and-tumble affections when it was too wet to play outside. I'd bumped into his mother when I briefly returned to live in my hometown in 1983 when my first marriage ended. His mum had known my mum well. "He never married," she offered knowingly, twirling the mother of colloquial pearls.

As I continued to peruse the obituary pages, there also *In Memoriam* lay Jacob. The newspaper announcement said that he had died a few weeks before his 65th birthday. I worked out that he must have been ten or 11 when I used to play with him. I'd always assumed him to be younger, maybe six or seven. I'd clearly miscalculated the mental-age conversion rate of what people used to call "backward". The obituary was accompanied by a photo, obviously taken in later life but instantly recognizable as the Jacob I knew. Lips slightly parted, rictus half-smile. Collar and tie. Powder-blue jumper. Neatly turned out for the camera, but evidently not tailored by a kindly aunt or sister, his family having long predeceased him.

My chance Google had led me to his demise and now Google Earth gave him an afterlife. I entered a postcode and followed the guiding arrows along the A1 to that tumbledown cottage where I grew up, still there, still tumbling, paint and plasterwork flaking away. There too, to my astonishment, was

Jacob, ambushed by the roving camera's lens, stood behind his garden fence, shoulders rounded, back slightly hunched, side on to the passing traffic. The camera caught sight of a well-tended garden, finely tilled sandy soil, an abundant crop of onions by the look of it. I stared at the frozen image and thought of Jacob remaining tethered to that house all that time. I thought of our Wubbse's harvest gatherings, Wubbse's long since gone, and now also gone the first person I ever spoke to who wasn't my Mum, my Dad or my Mum's Mum and Dad.

Search engines replenish themselves with brutal disregard for sentiment. They erase familiar landmarks and realities, taunting us with a reminder of our impermanence. When I returned to the street view a few months later Jacob had vanished. His garden fence had been torn down, the crop soil replaced by shale and plastic sheeting. A car now occupied the concreted space where Jacob once stood, hoe in hand, tending his crops. A buddleia was in full bloom by the front-room window, blocking out the light of the late afternoon sun.

****

A newspaper cartoon, the source long-forgotten, has lingered in my mind ever since I was a kid. It was a four-box strip depicting a stereotypical spatter-and-daub painter. In the first box, with the canvas laid flat on the studio floor, Jackson Pollock-style, the artist pours paint directly from the tin. In the second and third, he adopts standard action-painting techniques, bicycling and roller-skating across his abstract creation. In the final frame he props the canvas on an easel and steps back to admire his completed work, which is revealed to be a traditional landscape with trees and flowers and a meandering stream.

No doubt I have misremembered some of the details. Tony Hancock in The Rebel seems to have forced his way into the scenario somewhere along the line, but the principle and punchline remain faithful to memory. Latterly I come to realise that this cartoon symbolises my life. Out of all the chaos and random I have somehow fashioned a linear landscape.

Mine is a three-act life, equally divided into quarter-century stages. The first act ended at 25 with the death of my grandmother and my parents. The second act concluded at 50 with equally far-reaching consequences. By this calculation I expect to live to 75. Anything after that will be encores, curtain calls and codas.

As I approached 50 I had little desire to celebrate my half-century. Caroline and I had been to a few parties where friends or workmates had celebrated what they insisted on calling "the big five-oh" with what they equally distressingly referred to as a "bit of a bash", at which we were invited to "boogie on down". I learned a salutary lesson or two from these otherwise agreeable affairs. One was that nobody from my generation (or nobody that I was acquainted with at any rate) knew how to dress up any more. We made the effort, my gal and I, to put on our spiffiest glad rags and scrub up adequately, but upon arrival we invariably walked into function suites or upstairs pub rooms to be greeted by an array of shapeless Levis, baggy gardening jumpers and crumpled casual wear. And the men were no better. The second thing that remained inescapable, both from the house-band repertoires and the Dave Double Decks disco selection, was that few of these 40 or 50-somethings had updated their musical reference points in the past 20 or 30 years. The music of their youth validated them and justified cultural identities forged when they were in their teens and twenties. And as for the dancing! I don't wish to sound overly churlish, and we certainly didn't have an unpleasant time most of the time. Rum in strong measures is an excellent panacea for all kinds of ills, but the Wood's 100 couldn't altogether numb the pathos and the sense of stagnation that characterised these occasions.

Or perhaps the occasions had nothing to do with it. Maybe the emptiness emanated from elsewhere, from somewhere closer to home.

As I too edged towards my half-century I was acutely aware that I was approaching a sombre landmark in my life. Mum had died aged 50 years and two months. If I lived until the end of January 2005, I was about to surpass her time spent on this planet. I experienced considerable psychic turbulence at the thought of this and began to dream about her regularly. She was a quiet presence, sometimes standing on the upstairs landing, sometimes drifting aimlessly about the house. The unreality of these dream vignettes was reinforced by the fact that not once did she pick up a hoover or duster. We never directly communicated during these encounters but there was always a hint that something unspoken was passing between us, a suggestion that she was watching over me, waiting for me even. There was a sense of greeting in the dreams, guardian-angel stuff.

Just a few months earlier I'd been back to Albion Sands for the first time in years. That was the time I glanced across the road from the window in the town library to see Jacob holding court in the Market Square, faithful golden retriever by his side. I on the other hand was retrieving little or nothing. All that greeted me were the ghosts of long ago. Vaguely familiar faces passed me in the streets. Some struck me as being remarkably well-preserved until I realised they were the sons or daughters of people who had been my childhood friends. Everything else was old flames and memory embers. Every last market gardener's plot and haulage yard had been infilled, replaced by ticky-tacky little boxes and horse-shoe cul-de-sacs of new housing. One of the streets was named after the birds that would once have nested in the trees that lined the field where the houses were built before they were chopped down to make room for the houses.

In the evening I went for a walk up the sand hills. The atmosphere was pure *Blow Up*. I was David Hemmings looking for confirmation of what he might or might not once have witnessed. There were the same rustling leaves in the breeze and a similar uneasy ambience. Not sinister as such, but unnerving nevertheless, a feeling that unseen eyes had me under surveillance. A woman walking a dog eyed me warily and suddenly I saw myself as she might have seen me, not as a former resident treading the backward path, returning to boyhood haunts, but as something altogether more furtive – a man approaching 50, lurking suspiciously without apparent purpose. For all my innocent intent I might as well have been cruising for cock.

Late that night, reluctant to endure the ascetic confinement of my grim bed-and-breakfast lodgings, I walked in dimly lit darkness through Dog Shit Alley. Faithfully adhering to old habits learned long ago I trod tentatively in fear of the sudden misplaced footstep that might skid upon landing, or even worse land silently. I skirted the perimeter of the housing estate that now stood where Feltwell's Field used to be and found myself drawn one more time to my old road. Conspicuously alone in the midnight quietness, there was something I felt compelled to do, something that had come back to nag at the veracity of my memory after all these years. I have always credited my ability to pitch a cricket ball on a reasonable length to the fact that the distance from crease to lamppost where I first learned to bowl overarm as a boy measured exactly 22 yards. For old time's sake, I decided to pace it out once more, just to confirm or disprove the attribution of a skill long since abandoned. The lamppost was no longer there, although a square-foot smudge of concrete clearly marked the spot where it had once stood. But the line of the bowler's delivery, that was still there, still rolled out in a strip of tar from kerb to kerb, just as it was when I was a kid. Anyone peering through their front curtains at that late hour would have seen a shadowy silhouetted figure pacing 22, yes precisely 22, carefully calibrated footsteps that rooted him once and for all to the reliability of his recall. I can't be sure but I think there was a twitch of a curtain in an upstairs window. "Bill, come and look at this."

In the morning before I headed home I went for a walk up the Rec. It was trying to rain and the children's playground was deserted. The area around the swings and slide was paved with that absorbent padding which all play areas are now required to have, health and safety precautions sanctioned by those who refuse to believe that a bump on the head, a skinned knee or a bruised elbow are character-building. Instead children are immured from hazard and mishap – all pain must now be instantly swaddled or inoculated. The wrought-ironwork roundabout, where my Mod allegiances were sniffed out by older boys – that was gone. So too was the walled-off sandpit, although that was no bad thing as it never served as anything other than a canine toilet. I don't ever remember children building sand castles in there amidst the turds and the dog piss puddle craters.

Also gone was the curvature of the wooden fencing at the top end of the Rec, replaced by a uniform row of panels which ran straight and true from one side of the playing field to the other. As a result, the top of the Rec had been robbed of its unique psycho-acoustic properties, a natural echo that you could hear from streets away when I was a kid. I shouted a habitual "Oi!", croakier now than in my youth, but delivered with an instinctive modulation faithfully retained from a long lifetime ago. There was no echo. I oi'd again, louder this time. Still no echo. I clapped my hands, but instead of the rimshot that would once have ricocheted across the Rec there was just the muted slap of a man standing there in the fine drizzle, bereft of purpose, alone with his fading thoughts. Nothing much echoed at all after that.

The low perimeter wall where I sat as a boy of 12 one afternoon in the early springtime of 1967 and heard *Arnold Layne* playing on the pirates, that was still there, weathered and leeched with moss. I strained to hear the knowing voices of my youth. My mate Rees looking up from his transistor radio and saying: "They're called the Pink Floyd. They're going to be big." An old lady bicycled by. Basket and bell. I went and got my train.

As you grow older, you hope to turn into the best aspects of your parents rather than the worst. I have inherited some of my Dad's inverted snobberies, most of his radical politics, his itinerant employment record and more than a little of his selective sense of humour. I know also that I have inherited some of Dad's frustration with life, along with his tungsten-coated tenacity in dealing with those frustrations. "Them's high walls," as Hardy puts it in *Jude the Obscure*, as Jude is reminded of the sheer complexity of his quest.

I have also inherited Mum's propensity towards depression. During the winter months of the early years of the new millennium, with my seasonal affective disorder kicking in and the melancholy more immersive than usual I often found myself sitting in an armchair in the late afternoon, forehead cupped in the spread of my fingers, just as Mum sat when the black tide surged. I started having regular 3am consultations with the long dark night of the soul as my inner voice asked me, "What if none of this comes to anything?" "What if all of my creative endeavour has been for naught?"
By 1998 I'd been heading for that most tedious of middle-age clichés, burn-out. I was ostensibly making a living as a university lecturer, a broadcaster and a music journalist. But all I really wanted to do was concentrate on my writing. Caroline, gainfully employed at the BBC, told me that even if I didn't earn a penny she could support us. It's amazing how creative you can suddenly get when your partner tells you that. I sacked the teaching, the broadcasting work dropped off too (and in truth I never found my radio voice in the same way that I found my writing voice), leaving just the music journalism and the book-writing to keep me occupied. I wrote and wrote and wrote. A leading independent publisher sat on a novel of mine for over a year, saying "Maybe, maybe" – until eventually they sent me a letter that said "Unfortunately". Undeterred I battled on. I continued to write and write and write, but none of it seemed to be going anywhere. Six years on from my partner's generous sponsorship deal I had little of substance to show for it. And then something happened. I had, I'd hesitate to call it a premonition as such, but there was a sense of something premonitory nevertheless, a feeling that something foreboding lay up ahead.

I was lying on my bed one afternoon, reading, and my thoughts drifted to the autobiography that John Peel was writing. I have some previous with this topic which you probably don't need to know about, but I have to tell you anyway in order to explain what happened on that bed. I'd suggested to John Peel in the early 1990s that he should write his autobiography, and made it clear that if he didn't I would be happy to write the story for him. He informed me politely, but with detectable weariness, that several publishers had made similar overtures over the years, and that his long-suffering agent was permanently attempting to get him to draft something resembling a synopsis. Subsequently I raised the topic on numerous occasions, but Peel would always counter my enthusiasm with practised sangfroid and we were never any further forward by the end of the conversation than we were at the beginning. I mentioned my proposal to John Walters in February 1993 when we were both speaking at a radio symposium at Manchester University. "Oh, you should do it," he bellowed jovially above the noise of the conference hall. "He'll never get around to it. It's all tied up with his Dad." That tantalising aside was never satisfactorily elaborated upon, but Walters did allude to there being unfinished emotional business there. I took this as my cue not to intrude any further, but also to continue to monitor the situation, should there be any "change of circumstances".

Over the previous three decades I'd met John Peel as a fan, as a musician, as a fellow broadcaster, as a radio historian and latterly as a music journalist. I never knew him well, but I knew him well enough to be on nodding terms. The first time I spoke to him was at the CND benefit concert at the old Alexandra Park racecourse in 1971, when I was still at school. That was the first time I spoke to Kevin Ayers, too. "Thank you," said Ayers, when I handed him back the shades he had shaken off during a rigorously trance-y rendition of *We Did It Again*. It was Ayers that Peel and I spoke of as I took the opportunity to squat on the unoccupied patch of grass next to him as he sat, no doubt thinking beautiful Peel-like thoughts at the back of the main stage. The gist of our short conversation was that neither of us could understand why Kevin Ayers wasn't famous, why he wasn't in the pop charts, why he was considered "Underground". (Years later I raised the same query with Ayers himself. "The Underground is where you end up," I suggested. "The Underground is where they put you," Ayers responded.) Peel was as approachable and as courteous to a 16-year-old pop kid as you'd imagine he would be in 1971.

I didn't meet him again until 1979, when the band I was in, Glaxo Babies, played the famed John Peel roadshow on our home turf in Bristol. He said he thought I looked familiar, although I doubted that he remembered our previous meeting almost a decade earlier. I reminded him of the Ayers conversation. "Yes, I always used to think that about Fairport Convention as well," he said, at which point I remembered that he'd said that at Alexandra Park too. Uncanny.

When I met him for a third time at the Moonlight Club in West Hampstead, he didn't remember the second occasion. We had a good-natured disagreement about the artistic merits of Sheena Easton, and then the drummer from a B division indie band crashed the conversation and bored the pants off us both of us by enthusing about the production values on the new Joe Jackson LP. I saw Peel's eyes glaze over. He must get a lot of this, I thought.

During the second half of the 1980s, when I was researching and writing my book about pirate radio and the early days of Radio One, I was around the BBC quite a bit. I frequently bumped into both Peel and Walters in the corridors of Langham Place. The first time it happened I reintroduced myself to Peel and explained why I was there. He smiled at the reintroduction and made it clear that he knew who I was. When I said, without false modesty, that I never took that sort of thing for granted, he replied that he was the same and only recently had reintroduced himself to Bernard Sumner of New Order, presumably on the off chance that Sumner had forgotten who he was. It told me a lot about the modesty of the man.

My interview with John Walters for the radio book ran to three hours and took up two whole C90s, and I still only got a fraction of the story. Holding court on stage at that Manchester radio symposium, Walters was touchingly generous about the resulting publication. "When this guy first approached me, I thought he was just another anorak," he announced in that sing-song jeer of his. "But when I read the book I thought '*Actually* he's got it right'." (No-one could stress an adverb quite like Walters.) I had interviewed Peel for the same book on a glorious summer's day, sitting on a wall in Langham Place. At one point a Danish tourist interrupted us to ask directions. He sought advice from Peel, not me. "I think I have one of those kindly faces," Peel said when the Dane had departed. "He probably thought I was interviewing you." The date of that encounter is permanently etched upon my memory. When I went back into the building to seek out my second interviewee of the day, Johnnie Walker, he was preoccupied with the news coming out of the radio. "Have you heard about this maniac that's on the loose?", he said. Michael Ryan. Hungerford. August 19th. 1987.

When I passed Peel's office his door was ajar, but he was already back in obsessive work mode. "Have you heard about this maniac on the loose?" I said. He looked visibly distracted. I had clearly interrupted the carefully crafted flow of his record selection. "It's getting more like America every day," he said.

I let my fan-boy tendencies intrude just once during this period. In April 1992 I asked Peel if I could satisfy a long-held desire to sit in on the programme as he presented it. He agreed to this without hesitation, and so fan boy got to watch the Friday night 11pm-till-2am programme as it went out on air. Before the show I joined Peel at a pre-arranged meal at a restaurant just around the corner from the BBC. Also there were Rough Trade publicist and promoter Scott Piering, a bespectacled lady from Steve Wright's posse, and a couple of Peel's own programme assistants, who occasionally guided the conversation towards issues that seemed to matter a great deal to the procedural requirements of the radio show, but not unduly as far as I could detect to the man who presented it. During the meal, I gave the topic of the autobiography another nudge. "Look," said Peel, forcing himself, if not me, towards an ultimatum. "I'll tell you what. If I haven't started it by this time next year I'll hand it over to you. OK?" That seemed more than fair and we left it at that.

Walking back to the BBC, Peel mentioned that he had recently watched an afternoon rerun of *It's Trad, Dad!* on Anglia TV. "I'd completely forgotten that Alan Freeman was in it," he said. We talked about our mutual admiration for Fluff, and when we got back to Langham Place the man himself was in the production studio preparing his Saturday night rock show. The air was thick with his cigar smoke. Taller than I had imagined and casually attired in a flowing white smock of the type adopted by Timothy Leary during his psychedelic heyday, he was beatifically amiable. I mentioned *It's Trad, Dad!* to him. "Was I in that?" he exclaimed in THAT voice. "Can't remember a thing about it."

One thing I noticed during Peel's show was that he occasionally scribbled down little comments and phrases which he then used in his on-air links. During one of the lengthier records he took the opportunity to phone his wife Sheila at home. The conversation moved from chatty to what can only be described as fruity. Sauciness was clearly being exchanged and Peel's voice dropped to a near-inaudible mumble. "Wrong number?" I joked, when he put the phone down. Peel smiled and repeated a sentiment I'd heard him express publicly several times over the years. "She saved my life," he said. Yes, we all need someone like that.

Early on in the programme he played something a bit hardcore and thrashy. Gesturing to the adjacent studio where Tommy Vance was gathering up his belongings after presenting his Friday-night rock show, Peel said: "I can't understand why Tommy doesn't play more stuff like this." Still inclusive and expansive after all these years. Still wondering why everyone doesn't want to share the joy, still concerned that not everyone seems to get it. I was happy to sit quietly and fetch coffee when asked. I was referred to on air as "the posse" whenever Peel sought confirmation that the record he happened to be playing was as splendid as he suspected it was. As the hour grew late, I marvelled at the sheer stamina of the man. I was visibly wilting and I wasn't the one presenting a three-hour radio programme. "You look tired," said the man 15 years my senior. I left for my hotel bed at about 1am, happy to have fulfilled a dream. I would have been sound asleep long before Peel drove home to Suffolk through the night.

In December 1991, a few months before my fan-boy rendezvous, John Arlott had died. And it was while in belated contemplation of Arlott's life, and death, that I finally decided to abandon the idea of writing the Peel book. But first I had to write a letter. Like Peel, Arlott had been a mainstay of my youth. That voice (again, the voice) had guided me bucolically through countless hours of test-match commentary. The great man retired from active duty a month after my Dad died and I was still raw with emotion when he spoke his final on-air words. In the time-honoured manner of many test-match devotees, I had the TV sound down and the radio commentary on when he innocuously announced his send-off. "Nine runs off the over – 28 Boycott, 15 Gower, 69 for two – and after Trevor Bailey it will be Christopher Martin-Jenkins." I didn't realise the significance of that routine summary until his fellow commentators began to clap. On the TV I watched Arlott unsteadily make his way down the steps from the press box. The game came to a halt as both spectators and players stopped to applaud him. I thought of the times. All those times.

Later that day, still numb with the grief of my greater loss, I contemplated writing a letter to Arlott to tell him how much he had meant to me, but I didn't, and I'm glad I didn't. It would have been too entwined with the death of my Dad, overwrought, overstated and everything else that John Arlott – in public life at least – was not. When he died in 1991, the Guardian ran a fulsome obituary. Among the many tributes was a letter from a listener, who stated that when that final test-match commentary concluded in 1980, he had to pull his car over to the side of the road as he was overcome with emotion. "I thought of writing him a letter," he said, "But I didn't."

In 1992, a few months after I'd sat in on John Peel's radio show, I decided to finally write that letter. In cautious, carefully weighted tones I told him how much he had meant to me, how his programmes had provided a great deal of my musical education, my education full stop at certain points in my school-refusing teens, and how he had been, if not a second dad, then certainly a hip uncle. I also said that I had come to realise that it was he who had to write that book, and how could I have even been so presumptuous to think I was equipped to tackle the job in the first place. I've no idea if he read or even received the letter. He didn't respond and I gave him no reason to, but I was glad to read soon after that that he had finally started to write his autobiography.

The last time I spoke to John Peel was in the summer of 2002. I was writing a piece about Tyrannosaurus Rex for *Mojo* magazine and wanted to talk to him about his involvement with the band. Among other things, I was keen to hear his reflections on the way that Marc Bolan had so comprehensively discarded him the moment he got famous. I had Peel's home phone number, but was wary of intruding upon his family life and simply wasn't pushy enough just to dial him up and impinge upon his domestic arrangements. So I phoned his agent Cat Ledger instead. "Leave it with me," she said. A week or so later I phoned back. "He doesn't often say yes to these things," she began unpromisingly, "But he said seeing as it's you he'll do it." Those words will gratify me for the rest of my days.

During our phone chat, when for probably the nth time he politely reprised the rise and fall of his relationship with Bolan, I asked him how the autobiography was going. "I feared you were going to ask me that," he sighed, with a defensiveness that surprised me. He briefly elaborated upon the book's lack of progress but, as with my tentative enquiries a decade earlier, we were no further forward by the time I put the phone down. I was somehow left with the feeling that the writing wasn't going smoothly. Nothing tangible, nothing I could put my finger on, just that slight hint of irritation, with himself as much as anything else, during an otherwise cordial chat.

A few months later Caroline and I were tidying a messy bedroom, putting clothes away and generally rearranging the sprawl and clutter of our daily lives. The radio was lying on its side, half-buried in the contours of the quilt from where Peel was burbling away about whatever thoughts he was having, which may have been but in all probability weren't related to the record he had just played. As tangent heaped upon tangent and he continued to ramble magnificently into the night we had one of those shared staring at the radio moments. Both of us smiling fondly at the inconsequential eloquence of the words emanating from the mounds of an unmade bed. It was easy at such moments to imagine that he would go on broadcasting forever, always the hip uncle to somebody somewhere.

But as I lay on that same bed one idle Saturday afternoon, not so long later, that premonitory moment engulfed me. I thought again about the Peel book, the book I didn't get to write and the book that was now finally being written. I thought once more about the sheer magnitude of this man's input into my cultural life, cherished records he turned me on to when my brain was pliable and my tastes were being moulded on a weekly basis by what he played. *Defecting Grey* by the Pretty Things. *Skeleton and the Roundabout* by Idle Race. *Graveyard* by Forest. *Please Sing a Song for Us* by The Humblebums. *Him or Me* by Paul Revere and the Raiders (you need to have been a dedicated early listener to realise the significance of that one). Those Saturday afternoon Tyrannosaurus Rex sessions. Those Sunday evening Pink Floyd sessions. Those *Trout Mask Replica* recitals when he played three tracks a week until he (and *Trout Mask Replica*) had completely reconfigured the way I thought about music. And all those other moments that we as a listening community have shared and hold dear in our memory.

I thought of all this, and simultaneously I thought: "This book will never happen." I felt that something was lurking up ahead, just over the horizon, just around the next bend, and my abiding thought was: "I will not get to read this book." I mused on the idea of reconnecting with John Peel in old age in whatever circumstances that might entail, but all I could conjure up was emptiness and absence. This feeling startled me. I am not given to premonition and extrasensory perception. My Dad was, but not me. Dad said that he'd heard the ghost planes roar as we stood one time on the long-abandoned landing strip at Tempsford Aerodrome, as he made his one futile attempt to teach me to drive. Those fly boys are attuned to the metaphysical in a way that no other armed forces are, and I have no reason to disbelieve the evidence of his ears. On another occasion he claimed that he had been at a church service when with inexplicable prescience he predicted each of the hymns that would be sung before they were called out. I noticed however that this gift always deserted him when it came to doing the football pools. Here, his bizarre "system" of selecting eight obvious home wins and then putting them down as eight aways hadn't once reaped a 24-point dividend.

I felt Dad's own presence twice after his death. The first time was in 1984. I was playing tennis with a work colleague on a bright summer's evening. A faint rustling of the leaves, the wind dropping to an eerie hush. Something spoke to me, an invisible voice among the branches. I mentioned this to my tennis partner, the funniest and campest man I ever worked with. "Oh, you're just saying that to make me think you're deeper that you actually are," he said. I shrugged off the psychic intrusion and we got on with the game.

This time, though, the presence – or rather the absence – was darker and far less larky. Whatever lay up ahead, it wasn't going to be an autobiography, not in the way that I had envisaged it. On the afternoon of October 25th 2004, a friend phoned and uttered the simple words: "John Peel has died." "Oh God, I had a premonition about that," I blurted back. He was understandably taken aback by my response. But couldn't he see the reasons for my reaction? That's what all my dark thoughts had been about. That's what they had been predicting, surely? Peel's demise. But they weren't predicting that at all. I hadn't read the tea leaves correctly.

A couple of months later, a few days after Christmas in fact, I was having a piss, and in that instinctive manner that men have when they feel compelled to do something with their spare hand I felt around my jawline to see if I needed a shave. A gland in the left side of my neck felt less supple than it should. There was no bulge or detectable swelling, just a hardness, like the veins were silted up. "What do you make of this?" I said when I went downstairs. "Better get that checked out," said Caroline. "Just to make sure it's nothing sinister."

Part of you knows already. Knows right there and then, it's just that it's the part of you that doesn't yet know that it knows.

It took a full five months to come up sinister, but come up sinister it eventually did. I had a blood test, a needle biopsy, and an ultrasound scan, but none of these revealed very much. When I went for the blood test (at Trafford General, the very first NHS hospital), I took my ticket and waited in line like everybody else. My ticket number matched my age: 50. I took this to be an omen. My number had come up. I swiftly disregarded this as hokum and reassured myself that everything would be all right. A week later, as I sat in the doctor's waiting-room waiting for the blood-test results that would tell me no abnormalities had been detected, a baby began to cry. I pondered that too. Was this symbolic of a future that I would never know? Was it telling me that my own life would be renewed? Over the next few months I sent myself half fucking crazy with such thoughts as my emotions see-sawed between "Everything will be all right" and "Oh, God, what if everything is not all right?".

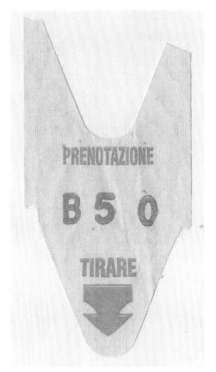

When your number comes up your number's up.

I became a regular fixture in that doctor's waiting-room, flicking through a newspaper or magazine with as much attention as I could muster, watching the electronic display for my name to come up, reading the accusatory message pinned to a noticeboard on the front of the counter, appointments missed this week, appointments missed this month, cost to the National Health Service. During one visit the name Marie Brennan came up on the display. I scoured the room with interest. On the wall in the alley between my street and the main road someone had scrawled "Marie Brennan is a babe". I passed it every morning as I walked to the paper shop, and grew curious as to whether the object of the writer's affection was indeed a babe. She certainly sounded like a babe in a way that Deirdre Braithwaite didn't. If I'd still been at school there is a fair chance that I would have fancied someone called Marie Brennan. I'd walked past that wall many times and was now finally going to find out if the graffiti spoke the truth. Alas, no Marie Brennan stood up in the waiting-room. Just another unkept appointment to be added to the list. The next name to flash up was Val Parnell.

The weeks wore on. Complacency turned to uncertainty. Positivity would unravel at a moment's notice. "I'm afraid that a needle biopsy is an unreliable indicator when it comes to detecting cancer," my doctor told me, after I'd rather, uh, pinned my hopes on it. (Caroline, not wishing to be deterred from an optimistic disposition, immediately christened him Dr Doom.) The specialist who did my ultrasound scan had a student observer with him and irritated me by playing to the gallery throughout, upbraiding his young charge over some terminological inexactitude rather than explaining to me what that curious shading was in my lymphs. "I know what it's not but I can't say for certain what it is," he offered circumspectly when pressed. He knew that it wasn't was a cyst, that's all he was prepared to tell me. At this stage I did what any rational lay person might do. I scared myself witless by reading up on neck lumps on the internet. The news was not good. Statistically, for all ages, if a lump hasn't gone down after a couple of weeks, start worrying. The negative to positive ratio increases with age. By the time you get to 40, doctors will proceed on the assumption that a sudden unexplained lump is malignant. By the time you get to 50, as I was by then, all bets are off.

At the beginning of May 2005, I went to see the re-formed Cream at the Albert Hall. I'd been too young to see the trio at the height of their fame, and I'd never been to the Albert Hall, and even though I wasn't much of one for rock-god reunions I was happy to go along and review the gig for *Uncut* magazine. By this time the lump in my lymphs had swollen to the size of an apricot stone, but that night I was in full denial mode and up for a good time. I found myself in an upstairs press box seated next to Paul Morley, who was reviewing the gig for the Observer. We traded pleasantries, about Laura Nyro for some reason, and about his evisceration of Robert Elms on an episode of *I Love the '80s* which my other half had worked on. I told him how much I had enjoyed his *Nothing* book and about how my Dad had smoked Guards too. He indulged me in that way that music writers of a superior mien do, but he didn't warm to the subject of discussing his *Nothing* book further, or perhaps he was just mildly alarmed at a man who appeared to have an apricot stone poking out from the top of his polo neck. Cream were hugely enjoyable. They shambled on with their shirt tails hanging out and treated the whole affair like it was just another night down Klooks Kleek, circa 1966. From our balcony vantage point the *Nothing* man and I noticed a young 20-something in the front row who was enthusiastically waving his vinyl copy of *Disraeli Gears* at the performers. We pondered what his motives could be – "You made this! Look!" – and traded non-sequiturs on the strangeness of fandom. Earlier Morley had mentioned Laura Nyro's collaboration with

Labelle, an album I hadn't heard at that point. I admitted this almost shamefully. "There's time enough for everything," said the *Nothing* man reassuringly. Let's hope so. Let's all hope that.

Dr Doom offered me an appointment for a skin biopsy on Monday May 16th, but I already had a prior engagement with the Times newspaper to interview Jim Webb on that date. We rescheduled the biopsy for the following Monday, the 23rd. I reasoned (possibly erroneously) that if the game was up then seven more days wasn't going to make a great deal of difference to the outcome. And anyway, I wasn't about to turn down a chance to meet the man who wrote *Wichita Lineman* and *Where's the Playground Susie*. In the great trade-off between my mortality and the immortality of those songs there was only ever going to be one winner.

I went to the interview knowing full well that it might be the last one I ever did. Jim Webb was a generous host – accommodating, expansive and full of southern courtesy. He referred to Frank Sinatra throughout as "Mr Sinatra". He was self-effacing about his abilities to interpret his own compositions (a shade above Burt Bacharach I'd say but several sea fathoms below Laura Nyro). I told him a story about Maurice Ravel having a similar lack of faith in his piano-playing, thanking those who had tolerated one of his recitals with a grateful: "And as you have all been so polite I will play you some Liszt." I would happily have listened to him all afternoon, but our pre-arranged 60 minutes was truncated to 45 by a PA who had to hastily reschedule Webb's next appointment at the BBC. Hers was the last voice I heard on the interview tape when I transcribed it, tersely ignoring my plea for just five more minutes. A bowdlerised 1,000 words from that life-affirming encounter subsequently appeared in *The Times*. I'm grateful that I got to read them.

I'd pretty such diagnosed myself by the time my skin biopsy came around. And still the dreams persisted. There was Mum, always waiting silently on the landing as I slowly ascended the stairway. January had come and gone, but the moment I outlived her barely registered, so fear-stricken was I at the thought of what might have taken up residency in my neck. The dreams gave me no reprieve and became as feverishly, nightmarishly disorientating as the ones I'd had after Dad died. It was during one such nocturnal visitation that my unconscious mind diagnosed me. The *Twin Peaks* dwarf, the actual Black Lodge talking-backwards dancing dwarf, leaned into my ear and in deep foreboding tracheotomy tones said: "It's cancer." My unconscious mind knew weeks before I did.

I'd imagine a fair few people knew before I did. The morning after my invasive and painful skin biopsy, the one that eventually located my Black Lodge malignancy, a huddle of junior doctors paused briefly by my bed as the surgeon did his rounds. Forming a routine phalanx before they passed briskly on to the next patient I saw one of them, eyes fixed firmly on my neck, lean to his left and whisper into the ear of a colleague. He barely registered me, he just saw a skin full of symptoms. It was something in the way his gaze never averted from my swelling and the conspiratorial nature of his whisper that convinced me that he wasn't discussing lunch arrangements.

I was sitting in another of life's anonymous waiting-rooms, half-way through reading the Guardian obituary of the artist Mark Boyle, when I was called into an office to hear a sentence that began with the word "unfortunately". The other three words in that sentence were "cancer was found". We had been to Majorca a few weeks earlier. I had a sun tan. I was the healthiest-looking person in the place. And now I had cancer. Caroline was in bits, as no doubt I would have been had the positions been reversed, but it's always calmest in the eye of the storm. Something settles the moment you are diagnosed. That see-saw momentum between OK and "Oh God", between uncertainty and something approaching insanity, just grinds to a halt. Equilibrium of a sort is restored. You know now. Language itself becomes superfluous. It was certainly found wanting in the mouth of the consultant who began his sentence with the word "unfortunately". "Sometimes life is like this," he concluded with a shrug as he got up to leave us alone with our legacy. It was profoundly Chekhovian in its banality.

Dr Doom entered the room moments later and immediately transformed into his alter ego, Dr Reassuring. "This kind of cancer has a 70-80% clear-up rate," he said, crouching on his haunches as if addressing a nursery-school child, a posture I appreciated in the circumstances, as I was now as dependent as any infant. My first words to him were: "OK, what happens now?" My first words to Caroline when he had left the room were "Sorry", followed by "We'll get through this". I wasn't being brave. It wasn't just fighting talk. I meant it. I had been certain that something dark and foreboding lay up ahead. Having now arrived at my (pre)destination I was equally adamant that I would get through this.

I won't say that it was comforting to be diagnosed. As a sympathetic friend later put it, nothing quite lands in the In Tray of life with such a heavy ominous thud as the package marked C. But the knowing was better than the not knowing. Once you know, you have finite options and a game plan. Which in my case was surgery, to be followed by a month of radio and chemotherapy. "Slash, burn and poison", as it's known in the trade.

As we walked down the long hospital corridor and out into the bright midday sun Caroline linked arms and held me as she had never held me before. It reminded me of how I held onto Mum as we walked up the gravel path of St Swithun's Church behind Dad's coffin. In the afternoon we went to a garden centre and bought bedding plants. No point ruining anyone's weekend by phoning them up and telling them you've got cancer. Dignity was maintained. I felt strangely reconciled to my situation. Admittedly I had a slight wobble on the Saturday morning while I was in the shower listening to Vaughn Williams on the radio, but that English pastoral will get you every time. My abiding thought that morning was if: "I do die I won't get to see Cristiano Ronaldo fulfil his potential."

A few World War Two analogies came in useful, I found. The period I was in now, post-diagnosis, pre-surgery, was the phoney war. We both knew that blitzkrieg was coming but there were no planes on the horizon as yet. Surgery would be Dunkirk, I decided. The necessary evacuation. Radio and chemotherapy I regarded as the D Day landing, with VE day to follow at the end of my treatment. As it turned out those 30 days of slash and burn were not VE Day or D Day. They were Dresden.

People's reactions vary when you get cancer. Some head for the hills. Some plaster on the kind face, the condescending "Does he take sugar?" face, as if you half aren't there already. Some hide their own fear of mortality with embarrassment, embarrassment at their own perceived and often self-confessed inadequacy, embarrassment that the subject has arisen at all. One or two music writers got in touch to offer reassurance and best wishes. Music journos usually only get in touch if they want something and what they usually want is your address book, but John Mulvey from *Uncut* and Mark Ellen from *the Word* both offered strong words of encouragement when they were needed most. People I barely knew in the record industry, or thought I barely knew, sent cards and got everyone in the office to sign them.

Best of all were the friends who treated the whole affair with a huge dollop of irreverence. The BBC workmate of Caroline's who said, "Oh, God, he's not going to do a blog, is he?", which made me hoot, or the old Polytechnic friend who had moved to Japan and who I hadn't seen in years. His own cancer had lodged between his large and small intestine and was only diagnosed when he fell off his bike on the way to work. This being Japan, he didn't have to wait seven months like I did. They had him in that operating theatre before you could bow gracefully. He phoned out of the blue one Sunday morning from his Sunday night and greeted me with a bright and breezy: "Ah, Rob, I hear you've joined the cancer club." Best of all was my old schoolfriend Danny, who had previously re-established contact through *Mojo* when he recognised himself as the significant other in my tale of seeing Syd Barrett's Stars at Cambridge Corn Exchange. "Rob, I don't want you to think I'm just phoning because I think you're going to die," he opened with a belligerent panache that had clearly not deserted him down the years.

Caroline, however, did think I was going to die. She only told me that much later. During my see-saw months she clung steadfastly to the coastal rocks of optimism, determined not to be washed away on a tide of Catholic fatalism, but when the decree came she buckled and the undertow took her out to sea where she floundered for a long time. She's a strong swimmer, though, much stronger than me, and she made it back to the shore.

On the penultimate Sunday before my radical neck dissection (as I learned to call it), we drove to Edale and climbed to a grassy summit. The sky was blue, a paraglider took a call on his mobile as he swirled in an air pocket high above us. Barely yards from where we sat a lark ascended from the bracken and trilled jubilantly. I thought of Dad.

Because life cannot possibly get any more tragicomic in such circumstances, we went to see Alan Carr at the Lowry 48 hours before my operation. I had a double booking with the MacMillan nurse and we had to get special dispensation from the hospital. The nurse told me that all being well, my cancer would be in a bucket by Monday afternoon. I thanked him for the graphic summary. He responded that he thought I was the kind of person who would want to hear it like that. I'd obviously toughened up more than I thought. Alan Carr was still only semi-famous then and hadn't yet turned into his pantomime mask. He and Caroline shared both a Northamptonshire upbringing and a Stretford residency, and they got into a bit of banter about landmarks and "local Arndale characters". The dialogue entered the rambling realms of the surreal after a bit and Carr had to bring things to a close with an abrupt: "Anyway, sorry love, I'm working at the moment." Afterwards Caroline thought she had made a fool of herself. I thought it was priceless, and magnificently diverting.

On 2pm on Monday July 11th 2005, the doctors came and took the shit out of my neck. On Tuesday July 12th, 24 years to the day since Mum passed away, I was sitting up in bed with an untouched morphine drip and a blood bag by my side. I was grateful that I still had my sense of taste and movement in my facial muscles, both of which I had been warned I might lose. I was grateful that I was here at all.

On the Monday lunchtime, an hour before I was taken into surgery, I listened to the one o'clock concert on Radio Three, three Bach violin partitas live from London's Wigmore Hall. At the start of one, the violinist broke a string. I pondered the omen and settled into my plumped-up pillows. If Johann Sebastian Bach was to be the last music I heard on this earth, so be it. "Are you ready?" said my surgeon as he entered my room on the stroke of 2pm. "Get this shit out of my neck," I replied. "That's what I was hoping to hear," he said. Earlier that day he'd popped in to see me in order to explain the procedure. "This is routine stuff to me," he said. "I do two or three of these a week." That was exactly what I needed to hear. I'd already had the list of what can go wrong (loss of taste buds, drooping mouth, facial paralysis etc), I didn't want to know any more about the intricacies and side effects. I wanted all further procedural matters to be relayed to me with the dispassion of a car mechanic surveying some dented bodywork.

Within minutes of being transcendentally transported by Johann Sebastian Bach I was all wrist-banded up and ready to go. Trussed and tied in one of those backless gowns they give you just in case you had been hoping to hang on to a shred of dignity, I was positioned at the end of a long corridor leading to the operating theatre. As I trudged the slow lonely trudge of the condemned man, the orderly who was guiding me turned and said, "So, what would you normally be doing today?" That's when I went. He was only doing his job and making what he assumed to be reassuring small talk. Of all the things he could have asked me, he had to go and ask me that. Please don't lead me to the anaesthetic I might not wake from with seven months-worth of eagerly replicating body-snatching malignancy in my neck, and then casually enquire as to what my domestic arrangements might have been in a parallel existence. The answer to your question is "ANYTHING BUT THIS!". I think I may even have attempted an answer – something about writing, I suspect – but all I could think about was Caroline at work, glancing at the clock, possibly doing something with rosary beads.

I was in pieces by the time I walked into the theatre. "Look after me," I sobbed as I lay on a stretcher and awaited the sleep juice. As I breathed deeply and counted to ten, the anaesthetist fumbled with my face-mask. "What's wrong," I garbled. "The automatic readout isn't working. I'll have to estimate manually," he said. Those could have been the last words I heard on this earth. Someone leaning into my face, gaze distracted by his malfunctioning implements, relying on instinct, chancing it a bit. That's how things may well end anyway. One day.

Once you've stared down both barrels at your own mortality it changes the way you hear music. That highly strung Bach partita wasn't even the start of it. While I was still at the "Better get that checked out in case it's sinister" stage, I continued to review the odd record for the music mags. Mick Houghton at Rhino sent me a couple of beautifully packaged CDs, *Hallucinations: Psychedelic Pop Nuggets* and *Come to the Sunshine: Soft Pop Nuggets*. I enjoyed both immensely, the Soft Pop one slightly more. As long as I soothed myself with the sugar balm of songs with titles like *Candy Apple, Cotton Candy, Silver and Sunshine* and *Trip to Loveland*, I could put all this to the back of my mind.

At times music acted as a mild palliative, a placebo, a pleasant distraction. At other times it was merely an irritant. I remember one day in particular, walking round the shops with the wind whipping up dust in the precinct, ELO wafting out from a clothing store, when the part of me that didn't yet know that it knew could almost feel the presence of malignancy depleting my healthy cells. ELO had been a key player in my ongoing Post-Punk revisionism. I'd finally been convinced of their magnificence when with a masterly flourish producer Paul Thomas Anderson chose to end his movie *Boogie Nights* with their 1976 hit *Livin' Thing*. My previous disdain for ELO had been built purely on irrationality. I associated them with the perm-heads in their non-biker leather jackets who used to frequent one of the soul-sapping local pubs we sometimes drank in during the Punk summer. The perm-heads had a habit of congregating thuggishly around the jukebox, where they would monopolise the record selection with their shit tastes. Any attempt to squeeze past them to put on *Gary Gilmore's Eyes* or *Something Better Change* was met with jeers and jostling. I'm not sure they even liked ELO, in fact I don't remember there being any ELO on the jukebox. The perm-heads' idea of a cutting-edge record was *Davy's on the Road Again* by Manfred Mann's Earth Band – but they looked like members of ELO, or at a pinch ELO roadies, and that was enough to pariah them during the 1977 style wars. By 2005 I had long since shed those Year Zero tendencies. But with the sinister now embedded, and the Black Lodge backwards-talking dwarf waiting to sleep-greet me, everything conspired once more against Jeff Lynne and his Brum Beatles. The cold spring weather, the ugly Goober-wear fleeces on the carousel rack outside the clothing store, the wind whipping up a vortex of debris, the utter uselessness of ELO telling me to hold on tight to my dreams – on days like these I carried my cargo like a beggar carried leprosy.

Some music was far too strong for medicinal purposes. It screamed my mortality back at me when all I sought was solace. I've never been a fan of country music, but Hank Williams has always been more than a country singer to me. He walks like a metaphysical prophet among the Grand Ole Opry pickers and grinners. I mistakenly thought his songs of faith would sooth me. I played *Lost on the River, Alone and Forsaken, Thy Burdens Are Greater than Mine, When the Book of Life Is Read*. All I wanted to do was linger awhile among the lonesome and blue that spilled, so tired yet so timelessly, from his lips. These were my songs of praise, my hymns in a man's life. I craved reassurance, but was confronted instead with eternal darkness. The feeling was akin to opening the back door in the dead of night and hearing somebody out there on the prairie, howling his sermons into the void. Hank Williams's lonesome moan scared the living crap out of me.

Albert Ayler was even more terrifying to contemplate. *Spiritual Unity? Spirits Rejoice? Music Is the Healing Force of the Universe?* I fumbled like a blind man through the Braille of those titles. All I could hear in Ayler's spectral sobs and sanctimonious wails was the apocalyptic contemplation that led the saxophonist to hurl himself into the freezing cold depths of the East River in November 1970. I didn't listen to any free jazz for a long time after that.

I woke up with my cancer in a bucket and 44 box-crate staples running neatly down a scar line that started behind my left ear and stopped just short of my Adam's apple. "Look, I can still smile and shrug my shoulder," I said to Caroline. She starred horrified at the Herman Munster stitchwork that ran like railway tracks across a relief map.

"You haven't touched your morphine drip," said my doctor the following morning, amazed that I'd gone cold turkey with the pain as the anaesthetic wore off. My life-saving surgeon leaned in and admired his previous day's handiwork up close, as he was well entitled. Every morning Caroline brought me a newspaper, fresh flowers from the garden and mint tea in a flask, before heading off to do a full day's shift at the BBC. In the long hours between her visits I stoically suffered the hospital food. I was given a nutritionist's pamphlet which recommended cheesy quavers as a source of sustenance. I squeezed my buzzer in the dead of night and a softly spoken middle-aged Asian nurse quietly administered painkillers. When I was ill off school, Mum would often buy me an extra music paper in addition to the ones I had delivered. All you really want at a time like that is Mum, any mum will do, and for all that week spent in hospital, my kindly nocturnal bed visitor, she was mum, metaphorically bringing me a *Disc and Music Echo* to soothe whatever post-surgery ailment was aching.

Anyone who has spent any amount of time in hospital will know that at 6 am they display all the tranquillity of a rail terminal at rush hour. I savoured the peace and quiet of the night-time, because every day bang on cue the ward would explode into life before the birds had finished their dawn chorus. An irritatingly bright and breezy duty nurse sang Blue Mink's *Good Morning Freedom* with lung-busting gusto as she bustled from room to room. I suppose I should have been grateful to hear her. As decreed by the Law of Sod, it was the hottest week of the year, and once the sun hit the south-facing greenhouse windows of the ward the heat became unbearable. Caroline had bought me brand-new stylish Paisley nightwear, but it went unworn. I took to wandering about the corridor in little more than a toga towel, clutching my blood-bag accessory. It was on one such walk back from the toilet that I saw my bed, with my clothes and belongings unceremoniously piled on top, being wheeled out of my room and into a shared ward. Later I learned that this was a breach of protocol and that I should have received warning that this was going to happen, but when I saw the young ghost of a guy who had taken my place, looking closer to death than I ever was, I understood the brutal virtue of the pecking order. In the evening I offered him a thumbs up as I walked past the room. It was one of the most futile feeble gestures I have ever made. He was gone by the morning.

I only spent one day and night on the group ward but it was, shall we say, eventful. Things began innocuously enough. A couple of old guys seated on opposite beds by the window put down their *Daily Mails* and bonded over their imminent hip replacement. A young guy in the bed next to me sat morosely watching as his girlfriend put new apps on his phone and recited the name of each one in a flat Mancunian monotone. Late in the day after visiting hours were over another young guy was wheeled in, all dripped up and bandaged. This being Manchester I was woken up in the middle of the night by the sound of him on his mobile issuing instructions as he quietly plotted revenge on his attackers. "I fooking know who it was, right," was the whispered gist of it. The dramatic tension took a sudden turn the following morning when his father came in to visit him. "They turned up in the night and torched your car, son," was his opening gambit. "Me and your Mum have had enough. You're going to have to move out." When I returned from the toilet ten minutes later the ward was bustling with nurses. Another came in to ask why she had just seen a patient storming off down a corridor with drips and tubes still attached. I was back in the sanity of my own room by late afternoon.

On the Friday they were reluctant to release me. "We're not willing to let you go home until you start eating properly," said my life-saving surgeon as the early morning posse gathered by my bed. "I'm not going to eat properly *until* you let me go home," I replied. They accepted the logic in this and were no doubt grateful for the freeing up of a much-needed bed. By lunchtime I was walking out into the bright summer sunshine once more, my soulmate by my side. I got into the car, drowned in the scent of the bouquet of lilies she had placed on the back seat and burst into tears.

An hour later I was crouched on the back doorstep, brand new night attire flapping unceremoniously in the breeze, as I tried to read the ring number of the racing pigeon that had landed exhausted on our drive. "Get back in bed. You're supposed to be resting," ordered Caroline when she returned from the shops. Having convinced her to help me establish the pigeon's ID, I phoned the appropriate national organisation. "We're not really supposed to disclose members' details," a lady explained, but gave me a phone number anyway. "Don't feed it,' she advised. "You have to be cruel to be kind. It'll fly off of its own accord."

I phoned the number in Leigh, Greater Manchester, and the owner sounded relieved but resigned. "It was a first chuck for most of them," he said, acquainting me with pigeon fancier's lingo. "Only seven out of 32 have come back." "I could probably entice it into a box with a bit of bird food," I said. "But I can't really bring it to you. I've just got out of hospital after a major operation." "And I can't come and collect it," he replied. "I'm 82." Birdy took refuge on our garage roof and hung about for a couple of days, but he had gone by Sunday lunchtime.

That same Sunday Michael Berkeley's guest on Radio Three's *Private Passions* was Scottish poet Don Paterson. He chose as fine and eclectic a selection as I have ever heard on that programme, Antônio Carlos Jobim, Boards of Canada, a Satie nocturne, a Bartók string quartet, and *Sea Song* by Robert Wyatt, which moved me to tears in a way that it had never done previously. I've always regarded *Sea Song* as one of the finest love songs in the English language. I love the way the aquatic imagery of the first verse gives way to the irreverent "joking apart, when you're drunk you're terrific" of the second without making the first verse seem like a joke at all. Many are the ways to treasure an intervention like that, not least of which is the use of the shamefully underused adjective "terrific" in a pop song. There is something recognisably life-affirming about the sentiment when you too have shared time with someone who is also undeniably terrific when a little bit squiffy. Driven by that quivering four-octave Riviera organ sound (Wyatt's Kinder toy equivalent of Marc Bolan's Pixiphone), *Sea Song* inhabits the very ocean bed of my soul. I've been listening to that song since the *Rock Bottom* LP was released in 1974. But sitting there that Sunday afternoon with 44 box-crate staples in my neck and the breeze gently rustling the bedroom curtains, its stark plaintive beauty was revealed to me as if for the very first time. Granted my emotional defences were down, but I blubbed like a baby all the same. It might just have been the medication, I suppose.

Joking apart, listening to *Sea Song* that afternoon made me think about the music I liked in a way that I'd never considered before. The essential question I contemplated was this. Do your music tastes reflect the person you are, or do they create the person you become? To put it another way, does repeated exposure to those life-affirming bursts of organised sound shape your emotional landscape or merely validate what you always were, or were in the process of becoming? In other words, is music an anticipation or a confirmation, an impression in the mould or the mould itself? Immersed in the splendour of *Sea Song* I reconnected with the younger soul-searching self who was always waiting for something that sounded like this. It's more than a little presumptuous to reduce someone else's creativity to a mere evolutionary particle in your destiny, I know, and for all my post-surgery speculation the matter remained, and still remains, pleasingly unresolved – but as I lay there bathed in tears listening to Robert Wyatt serenading the next full moon I was comforted by his reassurance that things would be different in the spring, and that his lunacy fitted neatly with my own.

I've come to realise that there is a reason and a season for everything, and if your motives were pure when you first encountered the music, or when it first encountered you, it will look after you. It will nurture you through the good times and sustain you through the bad. "Growing to gather the good of each other," as Syd Barrett sang on *It Is Obvious*. In

1996, when I interviewed the various members of the original Soft Machine for a feature for *Mojo* magazine, they all had interesting and astute things to say about each other. Daevid Allen was particularly insightful about Kevin Ayers. "The thing with Kevin is that he is still outwardly quite shy," Allen told me. "And when he isn't supplanting that with hedonism he goes away and reads all these books and gets very involved. There is still this secret side of Kevin which he tends not to talk about. He prefers to let that social persona be one of expanded extravagance." "Remind you of anyone, Rob?", I thought. In essence that's me too, pretty much every word of it. Daevid Allan's words made me realise that there are fundamental reasons why you are drawn to the music you like. More often than not they lie beyond articulation. After a while, without you even noticing, the music becomes you and you become the music. "Things don't happen, they just occur," as Kevin Ayers once sang. I firmly believe in the alchemy of that. You can hear the same assemblage of notes a thousand times, and without warning the thousand and first will suddenly make you tearful. You will simultaneously feel fulfilled and bereft, fulfilled by what has endured, bereft at what has been lost along the way. I suspect that's what was going on with *Sea Song* that Sunday afternoon – these things plummet subliminal and deep.

"Oh, you'll do a lot of crying," confirmed Tim, my Japan-based member of the cancer club. He had the same reaction to the Pet Shop Boys' *Being Boring* when his psychic defences were down. Yeah, that would do it. Particularly the bit about finding inspiration in every one who's ever gone, but even more so in the bit about never dreaming that you would get to be the creature that you always wanted to be. You have to live a lifetime to fully understand how that one pans out.

Barry White was playing on the radio when they fitted my bespoke moulded face mask in preparation for my impending radiotherapy. It was one of the hits, can't remember which. It was a Friday afternoon, the radiotherapy suite was cold and cavernous, and although attentive to their task I detected that the radiographers were demob happy as they made their weekend plans. I lay on my back, all masked up. The equipment was put through a test run, measuring to a milli-thou the trajectory of entry and exit points as I was primed to be zapped with radiation. I'd asked the staff to talk me through the procedure via the intercom as the machinery whirred menacingly around my head. They assured me they would, but they didn't. I was only in the mask for a few minutes but it seemed a lot longer. The one thing that kept me focussed and claustrophobia-free was

Barry White on the radio. "Will I be able to bring in my own music?", I said. Sure, they replied, and went on organising their weekend leisure time. If the radio hadn't been playing it wouldn't have occurred to me to ask.

And so for the entirety of September 2005, for the 20 weekdays that I was zapped by the Ray Gun I was the curator of my healing. I chose music that leaned towards the meditative and reassuring, nothing that would move me, physically or emotionally, nothing that would necessitate choking back tears or having to clear my throat as I lay there constrained in my mask. Surgery had robbed me of vital salivary glands and my newly restricted throat passage now fluctuated between parched and clogged, making eating a whole new masticatory, not to mention masochistic, experience. It was imperative, therefore, that I remained tranquil and still while the life-extending machinery did its work.

I don't know how I would have got through that gruelling month of burn and poison without my music. Only on one occasion did they forget to play my selected CD. The truth dawned on me 20 seconds into the whirring and buzzing, and I lay in blind mute panic for the entire meticulous procedure. When the nurse came in and removed my mask I shot bolt upright on the table with a rapidity that would have impressed Linda Blair in *The Exorcist*. "Don't ever do that again," I blurted, more in shock than anger. They didn't do it again. On the very last day of my treatments I took in Minnie Riperton's *Les Fleurs* as my valedictory music of choice. Normally the volume was set at respectful, but on this final morning I asked if it could be played loud. I meant through my headphones. I didn't realise they were blasting it out in the control area too. Caroline told me it could be heard clearly in the waiting-room. Patients and staff alike were asking what the music was. I'd like to think I turned a few people on to Minnie Riperton that morning. The young Senagalese nurse who had led me to and from the treatment room every morning walked me along the corridor for the final time and said: "Don't take this the wrong way, but I never want to see you again."

If you are going to get cancer anywhere in Great Britain (and one in three of you will) you could do far worse than get it while living in the catchment area of the Christie Hospital in Manchester. When I first took my place in the waiting area for Machine Three I used to wonder why there were so many thank you cards lining the shelves and pinned to the walls. After a couple of weeks I fully understood why. "Oh, you're ulcerating up nicely," said my nurse Cathy approvingly, as she shone a torch into my obliterated mouth. You don't feel the effects of radiotherapy at first, a mild scorching

september septembre • septiembre • september 2005

1 THU · jeu jue die — C2 R1 Minnie Ripperton

2 FRI · ven vier bø — C3 R2 John Fahey

3 SAT · sam sáb sam — C4 New Moon

4 SUN · dim dom son — C5 *Father's Day (AUS, NZ)*

5 MON · lun lun mon — C6 R3, Beach Boys Friends *Labor Day (US) / Labour Day · Fête du Travail (CAN)*

6 TUE · mar mar die — C7 R4 FLO

7 WED · mer miér mit — C8 R5 Dmitri From Paris

8 THU · jeu jue die — C9 Air

9 FRI · ven vier frø — C10 Remembered Drive

10 SAT · sam sáb sam — C11

11 SUN · dim dom son — C12 First Qtr *World Trade Center Remembrance*

12 MON · lun lun mon — C13 Ravel Le Tombeau

13 TUE · mar mar die — C14 Scriabin

14 WED · mer miér mit — C15 Rodrigo

15 THU · jeu jue die — C16 Nick Drake *Noche del Grito (MEX)*

16 FRI · ven vier frø — C17 Sibelius *Día de la Independencia (MEX)*

17 SAT · sam sáb sam — C18

18 SUN · dim dom son — C19 Full Moon *Chinese Autumn Moon Festival / Chuseok begins (KOR)*

19 MON · lun lun mon — C20 The Irresi *Respect for the Aged Day (JPN)*

20 TUE · mar mar die — C21 Os Mutantes

21 WED · mer miér mit — C22 JOHN CAGE 4" 33" / SILENCE

22 THU · jeu jue die — C23 Ravel - Bolero

23 FRI · ven vier frø — C24 *Native American Day (CA)*

24 SAT · sam sáb sam — C25

25 SUN · dim dom son — C26 Last Qtr

26 MON · lun lun mon — C27 Lou Christie

27 TUE · mar mar die — C28 Morricone *Fête de la Communauté française (BEL)*

28 WED · mer miér mit — C29 Minnie Ripperton.

29 THU · jeu jue die — Charity marathon. yeah right.

My music choices while I was undergoing radiotherapy.
Note ironic John Cage reference the day they forgot and equally sardonic entry for
the day after my treatment ended.

at most, a little discomfort in the neck area, but diet and digestion, bland and precautionary though they were, were actually beginning to resume some semblance of normality as my operation scar began to heal. At the start of the second week of my radiotherapy the most difficult thing I had to digest was the introduction of the *Guardian*'s new Berliner format. But the following weekend, bang on cue according to the literature, soft boiled rice began to taste like razor blades and I started to complain about the "bits" in my vanilla ice cream. Uh-oh.

I adjusted my World War Two analogies accordingly. The period before surgery wasn't the phoney war. The first two weeks of radiotherapy was. In the bigger "slash, burn and poison" scheme of things, surgery was a doddle. I was back at my computer two weeks after my operation, tappity-tapping away. I'd resigned myself to the fact that I'd never bowl left arm over the wicket again – the missing shoulder nerve and muscle impingement saw to that – and my singing voice had been reduced from two-and-a-half octaves to barely one, as I subsequently discovered once I felt like singing again. The physical pain, such as it was, was localised and minimal, and easily subdued with painkillers. Surgery is one thing. The body soon recuperates. Radio and chemotherapy is a whole other bombsite.

"Are you taking your morphine?", asked Cathy, as she examined my ulcerated mouth. "No," I started to answer. "I'm trying to avoid dependency – ." Cathy cut me short. "You have to take your morphine," she ordered. "Make him take his morphine," she said to Caroline. I started taking my morphine.

You don't "fight" cancer. And you certainly don't fight a simultaneous dose of radio and chemotherapy. A fight implies a two-way tussle, a duel. There is no adequate battle plan when it comes to having your body systematically pummelled by waves of radioactivity and the poison pills you force down three times a day, seven days a week. It's like going 15 rounds each day with a psychopath. You crouch into a foetal ball, cover up your extremities and wait for the beating to stop. You recover your composure for just long enough to get some breath back and the next day the pummelling starts all over again. You take your morphine.

During that gruelling month I took my compensations where I could. I compared and contrasted myself with high-profile cancer cases to see how those 70-80% survival odds might play out. The cricketer Geoff Boycott had been diagnosed in 2002, and he was still with us. I began to take a keen interest in his visible radiation scar when I watched him offering post-test-match punditry on TV. Former jockey Jonjo O'Neill had been diagnosed with non-Hodgkin's lymphoma in 1986 and he was still training horses, a little frailer in interviews I thought, but still here to greet each day. I was not unaware of the shortcomings of this approach. "Fifty-four's not very old," I thought when Peter Sellers died of a heart attack on July 24th 1980, exactly a week before my dad died at 53 of a heart attack. When Harold Pinter died in 2008 I reined in my optimism accordingly, but here I still was, and as the radiation and chemo took hold I repeated the mantra of all who undergo such torture. Just remember this is making you better.

All this time *The Times* continued to offer me titbits of journalism. I had been a freelance contributor to the paper since the late 1990s, music and book reviews mostly, plus the occasional feature (Joe Meek, Kathy Kirby, the Jim Webb thing). I'd successfully ridden the changes as three different music editors came and went, and the Saturday review supplement underwent a similar number of style makeovers and name changes. When an e-mail arrived in late July asking if I liked the Brazilian psychedelicists Os Mutantes I assumed that I was going to be sent a CD to review, but two weeks after my neck surgery I found myself sitting on the steps of the Paris Opera House with Sérgio Dias, the leader of the band, discussing where we might eat and do the interview. I could only ease food into the right corner of my mouth and apologised to my host for my ungainly table manners. Sérgio was beautiful about it, and offered me the kind of reassurance that could only have come from a man who had seen worse things in life and had survived a military junta. He told me about how Os Mutantes in their naivety couldn't identify the backward cymbal hiss effect on the Beatles' *Revolver* and replicated it on their own albums with a mosquito spray plunger. I told him how at 13 I thought Donovan got that voice effect on *Hurdy Gurdy Man* by patting his open mouth as he sang. "We were out to lunch, breakfast, dinner and tea," said Sérgio. They used that as the pull quote.

Blitzed as I was by the radio and chemo shitstorm, I didn't expect the commissions to keep rolling in. Vague promises regarding the first new Kate Bush album in 13 years had been put my way, but then it all went quiet again. As the autumn evenings began to draw in and my sleep patterns grew increasingly hibernatory due to the after-effects of the treatment, I managed to stay awake for long enough one night to watch the exclusive showing of the video for *King of the Mountain*. It was great to have Kate back, greater still to be here to witness it. When *The Times* ran a feature promoting the imminent arrival of the new album, I assumed that was pretty much it as far as my involvement went. "Oh no, we still want you to review it," confirmed my editor. "Can you come to London on Thursday?" And so it was that I found myself in a monastic, softly lit EMI listening facility in North London signing a solemn undertaking not to remove as much as a publicity sheet from the room, and being led to a comfy chair and a set of headphones. A helpful young assistant brought me a cup of tea and some razor-sharp biscuits (or biscuits as I would previously have known them). I said that I would forego the snacks – and told him the reason why – but if he could keep me supplied with a plentiful supply of weak tea that would be just great. Being a kind young man, he did.

There was only one other journalist there that afternoon, a smart-suited 30-something, stern of bearing and body language. He sat hunched at the listening console directly opposite me and didn't once meet my eye. I don't know who he was, but he seemed to be finding listening to music a deeply brow-furrowing experience. Was he hearing the same sounds that I heard? The sheer crystalline beauty of Kate Bush's new record gave fresh impetus to my recuperation. Aerial's meandering songscapes, and the singularity of their creator's artistic vision, offered the kind of nutritional sustenance that was otherwise denied me during those meal-deprived weeks. Released at a time when I was existing solely on a diet of melon and porridge by day, and euphoric De Quinceyan pocket ecstasies by night, I still hear echoes of my depletion whenever I play it. I put on Aerial the other day for the first time in ages. They were all still there. The dry-mouthed, energy-sapped, tumour-zapped memories of a shell of a man glad to be alive, and happy to hear Kate Bush turning into all the creatures she ever wanted to be and never being boring.

Johann Sebastian Bach sounded pretty majestic too. In the week before Christmas 2005, Radio Three devoted the entirety of its output to his complete works. I listened to as much as I could stay awake for (by December I could remain alert and attentive for anything up to three hours at a time). With the exception of the Lutheran cantata stuff I was enraptured by everything I heard. Bach too had been lingering up ahead all this time. He had been a light-entertainment mainstay of my youth, recited in prime time by Jacques Loussier and the Dudley Moore trio. He was there in Procol Harum's *A Whiter Shade of Pale* and Jethro Tull's *Bourée*, and now he was here in all his even-tempered variations for seven days and nights on Radio Three. Paul Morley was right. There's time enough for everything.

We were driving out to a Christmas market somewhere. I can't remember the piece. It might have been a Toccata and Fugue. It could have been the French Overture in B Minor or a harpsichord concerto. It could have been all or none of these but listening to Bach that day was like experiencing an endlessly replicating Mandelbrot fractal in 4D 16-bit, hi-res synaesthesia. Everything seemed to expand and fold in on itself in an infinite variety of patterns. Later that same week, drifting about during the Christmas sales, led safely from shop to coffee shop to car park by the dependable Caroline, I stood outside Arthur Kay the jewellers, on the corner of St Ann's Square in Manchester, gazing in awestruck wonder as shoppers merged with their reflections in the curved glass of the shop frontage. I marvelled at their ability to walk into and right out through the other side of the window like that without sustaining a cut or graze. That morphine was very strong.

The only real upside to cancer is that you do get your Gold card when it comes to the ready acquisition of Grade A opiates. Despite my initial reluctance to take my morphine I soon became a regular visitor to the serving hatch at the Christie dispensary. One morning, as pliable as a pillow and as skittish as a kitten, I floated into the empty waiting-room, assumed my familiar slumped posture at the tiny window and waited for someone to come and serve me. Everyone seemed to be gliding about their business as if on skate wheels. A nice young man finally came to the window. "Furbish me with your finest opiates," I proclaimed, summoning the spirit of *Withnail and I*. He smiled tolerantly and took my order. "Five minutes," he said. I turned round to discover that while I had stood there dribbling out my Grade A small talk the previously empty waiting-room had filled with customers.

The dreams I had during that period were the full Kubla Khan. There was one involving the Queen Mother, another where a magnificent Holy Trinity slowly took shape in a stained-glass triptych, the Holy Ghost bearing a strong resemblance to Jimmy as played by Geoffrey Palmer in *The Rise and Fall of Reginald Perrin*. The rest of the time you were all watering-cans walking down Tavistock Street. I awoke one opiated morning convinced that the true nature of existence had revealed itself to me in my sleep, but decided that I should cherish the precious essence for a few moments longer before I revealed its eternal radiance to Caroline. With hindsight I should have rambled my vision out there and then, but fatally I coveted it just a little too long, and like Coleridge's stately pleasure dome it rapidly crumbled into memory dust. All that was left by mid-morning was the outline of an aura.

That's how my cancer would come to seem in time, a fading aura – just the diminished luminosity of some bad dream I'd had. On the whole I agree with Alan Bennett, who declared: "Cancer, like any other illness, is a bore." He detested the idea of a "cancer club", and based his entire post-treatment strategy on hoping "to edge by and go unnoticed". That was me too. Didn't want the T shirt. Didn't want to do the fun run, just wanted to keep my head down, get better and hope malignancy wouldn't strike again. I began to celebrate each day I managed to have a phone conversation or send an e-mail without mentioning it. But first I had to recover, and the recovery process is slow going. You get better at a rate of one inch a day. That's what it felt like, driving a car an inch a day. The progress is virtually undetectable at first, but after a while you start to think: "Hang on, didn't that tree used to be somewhere in the distance, and wasn't that lamp post further up the road?"

Along the way there are all kinds of unforeseen hazards to negotiate. They give you a pamphlet and a cautionary list of side-effects when they first see you, and once you have digested that they give you another list of symptoms which weren't in the original pamphlet. And still there are more. Dr Reassuring clocked me in the Christie waiting-room one day, and I told him I had developed a severe blockage in my left ear. I joked that glue ear wasn't in the manual. "There's no manual big enough," he joked back as he led me into a room containing some brand-new auditory-canal equipment. "Oh, yes, quite a blockage there," he said as the screen image confirmed his diagnosis. Or at least I think that's what he said. I was told that the matter would resolve itself in time, but when the right ear blocked up too I was functionally deaf for several weeks. I had the telly up at 90-year old gran volume and bluffed my way through most adult conversation – although to be fair that was nothing out of the ordinary. One cold crisp afternoon in the back garden I blew my nose, something popped and suddenly I could hear a blackbird singing and the ambience of city traffic once more. Back indoors my long-suffering other half demonstrated with the aid of the remote control the room-shaking decibel levels at which I had been watching TV.

I also developed gynaecomastia, a painful swelling in the left breast which made even the mere accidental brush of a hand or the putting on of a T shirt an agonising experience. A helpful specialist assured me that it was not a sign of further malignancy but merely another side-effect of the chemical sand-blasting I'd undergone. Very common in puberty, he told me. Boys suddenly get very self-conscious about it. I reminded him of the time

I thought I was growing breasts when I was at Senior School. He was able to reassure me a full 36 years after the event that my adolescent swelling had nothing to do with the ingesting of dog biscuits or animal feed.

Time goes by. The hospital appointments change from weekly to monthly to three-monthly until finally after two years they don't want to see you any more. There's no grand send-off, no fanfare, the birds aren't singing a special chorus when you leave the building. The same grim apparitions are still hanging round the entrance having a final cigarette before they go in for their chemo. Life goes on in all its banal and beautiful manifestations. But that's all a long way down the line when you first set out on the slow haul to recovery. First there's the mornings to negotiate, the vomiting up of chemo poison as thick as gravy, so thick that it won't wash down the plughole. There's the preliminary preparatory sip of tap water through a straw to lubricate the throat sufficiently enough to manage a sip or two of tea (also through a straw). There's the porridge and melon diet, which is all you can eat for a while, and only the blandest of non-seeded melon at that. Meanwhile, because your other half is a sadist, she cooks herself delicious meals and eats them in front of you. You don't lose your appetite, you just lose your ability to eat anything other than pulp and mush. You begin to hallucinate with hunger. You experience cravings that you have never previously had for food combinations you will never eat even when you are well enough to try them – guacamole and chips for example. And then there's the reflux. Basically, your body has to learn to eat again. The NHS nutritionist tells you this when you ask her why you are having to wrap a towel around your neck and shoulders, boxer style when you eat anything stronger than mashed potato in order to soak up all the sweat that pours from your head. The mildest cheese will bring on a Vesuvius of the scalp. A curry is the stuff of dreams. That December, three months on from my treatments, I optimistically bought a celebratory bottle of wine. I managed one sip on Christmas Day. It tasted like Dettol. I tried a dark chocolate Bounty bar and promptly threw it up. The first time I attempted to eat chips in public we had to sit at the back of a near empty café in Leeds city centre with an ample supply of paper towels.

As we drove back to Manchester that same evening we listened to Radio Three. Over Christmas that year the station devoted a fortnight of programmes to lesser-known British composers. Broadcast every weekday between 5pm and 6:30pm, the *Made in Britain* series introduced me to the splendour of Alan Rawsthorne, Herbert Howells, E.J. Moeran and a whole cast of unsung provincial pastoralists, pacifists, theosophists and war casualties previously unknown to me. After a break of several years, my classical education had resumed on December 31st 1999, as Caroline and I drove around the Peak District looking for somewhere deep and meaningful to spend the final minutes of the nineteens and the first moments of the two thousands. Somewhere that wouldn't entail having to listen to Jools Holland tinkling, Noddy Holder bellowing, or any of the other seasonal options on offer as drunken gatherings counted down the seconds to the Big Ben chimes. As we drove around that New Year's Eve afternoon we listened to Radio Three, which was working its way at a sedate pace through the music of the previous millennia. Things had kicked off at 6:15am with a look back at what had survived from Egypt, Italy and Gaul. By the time we were scouting out isolated churches and suitable fin-de-siècle vistas, Radio Three had reached the 17th century. I quietly made a new year's resolution to listen to more Radio Three.

For our chosen rendezvous we eventually settled on an out-of-the-way chapel down a hilly incline deep in the Derbyshire woods, but when we returned later that night the chapel was in darkness and there was no sign of a service. Instead we saw out the nineteens in hastily improvised fashion parked up by a country lane on the outskirts of the town of Broadbottom, listening to a radio montage based on John Cage's 1937 lecture *Credo*. As midnight approached, we sat and gazed at nothing more exhilarating than a row of cottages. When the bells began to chime we got out of the car to breathe in the last-of-the-century air. Down the lane some children came out of one of the cottages and went next door, where in the accustomed northern manner a kindly neighbour accepted their piece of coal and let the New Year in. We held hands and watched this touching domestic scene for a few moments and then drove home. Making our way back to Manchester through former pit villages, we watched a succession of fancy-dress fairies wibble their way home, slightly the worse for drink. Some held cigarettes aloft as if keeping them away from flammable fairy wear. Others nursed drinks so as not to spill a drop. In that first hour of the two thousands we saw variations on this vignette enacted in every town or village we drove through as women (and it was mostly women) tottered on impractical heels away from pub or party and set their tracking devices for home. It was our version of Philip Larkin's *Whitsun Weddings*, New Year's Eve style. "And none/ Thought of the others they would never meet/ Or how their lives would all contain this hour."

I thought I'd detected something like disappointment in Caroline's voice when I suggested it was time to drive home. "Come on then," she said with a sigh as we got back into the car. Exactly a year later she told me she thought I'd dragged her all the way out there to propose. She admitted this a minute or so after I actually had proposed to her, which was what I'd always intended to do when the actual millennium arrived, rather than at the dress rehearsal one which the mathematically challenged pre-empted with their dismal Greenwich Dome. I'd long since decided that the first words I uttered in the millennium in which we all will die, you, me, all of us, would be: "Will you marry me?" Even if I have been robbed of a two-and-a-half octave singing voice I still possess a sense of cosmic proportion. She said yes. We went to the back window and stared at our little patch of winter wonderland. The security light was on, illuminating the snowman we'd built that afternoon with next door's little girl, whose parents had recently separated. The snowman looked cold and forsaken, as they always do at night. Caroline held me as she'd hold me five years later when we left the hospital on that fateful diagnosis day. Sometimes life is like this.

On July 7th 2006, almost exactly a year after my cancer operation, Syd Barrett died from a far more invasive strain of the disease. I wrote a lengthy obituary for Mojo magazine during the hottest week of the summer, and once the temperatures had subsided from the sweltering high 80s to the pleasant low 70s, Caroline and I spent a week revisiting some of my childhood haunts in Bedfordshire and Cambridgeshire. The only cassette we had in the car was a Ralph Vaughan Williams compilation, containing his best-known short orchestral works: *In the Fen Country, The Lark Ascending, Norfolk Rhapsody, English Folk Song Suite, Fantasia on a Theme by Thomas Tallis*, etc. It was a car-boot purchase, 50p, lovingly curated, and packaged with a hand-made inlay, a generic landscape view on the outer sleeve, a photo of "Rafe" on the inner, and a quaintly etched drawing of "the composer conducting his Sea Symphony in Leeds in 1958" on the cassette label. The C90 showcased the best orchestral performances of each work. Three Boults, two Beechams, a Boughton and a Handley. It remains the least clandestine but most treasured bootleg in my collection, compiled I would guess by some dedicated old classical buff, pleasingly ignorant of or indifferent to cross-licencing deals and the debilitating effects his actions might have on the future of live music. We had it on permanent play for the entire week. It was high summer. The harvest was mostly gathered in, pretty village cottages displayed their home-grown produce and put out an honesty box for payment, the air was ablaze with memory essence and orchestral colouration. I concluded that there were far worse places I could have grown up. There was none of the

Ralph Vaughan Williams
Short Orchestral Works

Oboe Concerto
In The Fen Country
The Lark Ascending
Norfolk Rhapsody No.1
English Folk Song Suite
Five Variants of Dives & Lazarus
Fantasia on a Theme of Thomas Tallis

Side 1
1. Oboe Concerto
2. In The Fen Country
3. The Lark Ascending

Side 2
1. Five Variants of Dives & Lazarus
2. English Folk Song Suite
3. Norfolk Rhapsody No.1
4. Fantasia on a Theme of Thomas Tallis

Side 1
1.3, English Symphony Orchestra / Boughton - Maurice Bourgne (Oboe)
2. New Philharmonia / Boult

Side 2
1. London Philharmonic / Handley
2. London Symphony / Boult
3. New Philharmonia / Boult
4. English Symphony / Boughton

ghost-zone neurosis and dislocation that had contaminated my previous visit a couple of years earlier. On Everton Road just south of the hamlet of Tetworth we pulled into a market gardener's yard and I tried to buy local potatoes to take home with us. Maris Piper madeleines, remembrance of meal times past, second earlies. The stall had lettuces as big as footballs, bunches of knobbly carrots and fruit in punnets, but no spuds. "Don't look so despondent, boy," said the old farmhand who served me. He said it in that familiar sing-song Bedfordshire I grew up with, the way my grandparents spoke, the way everyone of that generation spoke, despondent itself in a way, but wry with it, and articulate too, a vernacular passed down from previous generations of my family who farmed and poached these parts. I got back in the car, half-amused, half-bruised by what the old boy had said. "Yeah, you can look pretty despondent sometimes," Caroline guffawed. I'd been back in the neighbourhood a matter of days and had barely reacquainted myself with the lime-scaled kettles and the hard-water taste of the tea, and here I was being teased like I was 13 again.

In violet dusk-light we drove to the end of a dusty Tetworth track and found ourselves at an intersection of fields and derelict farm buildings that gave no hint of trespass or prohibition, and whose right of access seemed to us, both rural born, a given – based solely on their isolation. Walk a mile in any direction from the town where I grew up and they are everywhere, these uncharted sites: quarries, spinneys, copses, coppices and clearings that defy the surveyor's instruments and the speculator's gaze as they slip into anonymity and disrepair. An apple tree grew wild and unattended, bursting with ripening unpicked fruit. There was something a little Edenesque about it all. A breeze got up and wafted warmly through the evening air, the kind of breeze that only serves to emphasise the stillness. It was that time of high summer when the birdsong had stopped and the last of the fledglings had flown the nest. The distant hum of B Road traffic dropped to silence and I sensed the presence of my ancestors, grafting and surviving and snaring their way through these fields a century and a half before I was born.

On the final morning before we headed home we drove into Bedford. Willows dipped their branches in the wide-open Ouse. As we walked past Debenhams, or E.P. Rose's as it was when I was a boy, a woman exited the shop and walked directly into my path. If we had been cars she would have been guilty of feeding into motorway traffic at an inappropriately slow speed, occasioning preventative action. I clipped the back of her heel causing her to stumble slightly. "Don't you moind moi feet," she said with that familiar sing-song sob and perfectly weighted cadence, a life-long martyr to her corns and her pathos.

In the second year of my remission from cancer I finally had my redemptive Paul Morley moment. I had a novel published and a Syd Barrett biography commissioned. There was even sufficient Post-Punk interest in my band to warrant a reissue for all that old Glaxo Babies material. I wrote with singular passion about Syd Barrett, and meticulously documented the influence all those one-parent or no-parent authors – Lewis Carroll, Edward Lear, Hilaire Belloc, Kenneth Graham – had on his work. I noted also the preponderance of lone parents, divorced parents and deceased parents among Syd Barrett's peer group, but not once did I make any explicit attempt to place myself in the picture or draw any connection between the narrative arc of these lives and my own. By the time my Barrett biography was published in 2010, I had spent more time on this earth without my parents than with them. The situation had become utterly normalised. Anniversaries were duly acknowledged, then I got on with my day. I should be enjoying the luxury of them dying as octogenarians about now. Instead they've been gone for nearly five decades.

Reconciliation to absence is in the end the only viable survival strategy, the only way to make sense of the world – you'd go mad otherwise. This reconciliation has in recent times subtly coloured my perception of the music I heard in my youth. The twinge of recognition I get from hearing a pop song from my teens rarely has anything to do with tribal allegiance or empathy, but increasingly reminds me of a time when my tea was on the table and Dad was visible through that crack in the door. This emotional taproot threads all the way back to Act One of my life and connects me to a time when absence and loss had no emotional purchase.

Music remains for me the ultimate mediator of memory. Something endures in the resonance of the notes that time can never wholly diminish. I thought the faculty would have faded by now and that distance would have dulled the residual impact, but I only have to hear certain songs and I am immediately transported back to the square foot of Nowhere Land that I inhabited when that particular song was released. When I hear the opening eerie bars of David Bowie's *Space Oddity* there is always part of me that is walking up Bedford Road past the Rec on a warm Saturday evening in July 1969 when Pete Drummond first played it on Radio One. It was a week before we broke up for the summer holidays, and I went into school on Monday raving about this new song. *Space Oddity* was what was known in those days as a "sleeper". It didn't chart until September, by which time we were back at school, and most of my classmates were enthusing about it too. "That's the song I was talking about before we broke up," I protested to no avail, as boys of 14 affected the kind of indifference that only 14-year olds can. I still hear all this in the first four bars of that acoustic strum. It connects me to the part of my life that is forever bonded to the summer of 1969, all receptors open, all responses unfiltered, a boy so alive in the long ago. They lie in wait all the time, these trigger mechanisms, and they manifest themselves at the most unexpected moments.

Recently I heard the opening bars to the *Theme from Shaft* by Isaac Hayes, just as I must have heard them hundreds, possibly thousands of times before. *Shaft* has one of the most instantly recognisable intros in the history of popular music. I have absorbed that hi-hat and wah-wah so intravenously that I no longer hear *Shaft* as such, I hear an approximation, a sequence of multi-layered memory echoes. As it played once again I could have thought of any one of a number of things. I could have thought about Blaxploitation, a term that didn't exist when *Shaft* was recorded. I could have thought about sociopolitical context, history, heritage, legacy, Grammy awards, discographies, Funk revivals, session players, gatefold sleeves, CD re-issue liner notes, but I didn't – and in truth I rarely do think of any of those things when I'm listening to music, or on this occasion not even listening to music, merely being in proximity to it as it played on the radio. No, what I thought about was Christmas. I could hear December in those notes. I could feel the cold winter air on my face and the warmth of shops all glittered and tinselled up, going into E.P. Rose's Department store and buying, or perhaps shoplifting, perfume for my Mum. This reaction puzzled then intrigued me, so I went and got the chart books out and sure enough there it was. *Theme from Shaft*. Isaac Hayes. Week of Top 30 entry December 4th 1971. Top Ten for the rest of the month. *Shaft* was just another "back and to the left" moment, like so many others. The Dunstable row of shops. ACDelco. Good Vibrations. Music will do that. Music will always do that.

There are still ghosts in my house and I still dream about them now and then. I'm getting off a late-night train at the station at the other end of town and wondering if Mum will still be up. I'm pedalling a bicycle down some unspecified trunk road in Hertfordshire pondering the sheer improbability of cycling all that way back to Albion Sands. I'm forever not at home, wanting to be there, but never arriving. And even in the dreams I know that I won't arrive anyway. Rationality always intrudes and reminds me it's not my house to go to any more. Someone else lives there. The symbolism is obvious, the metaphor banal in the same way that most metaphors (and the majority of dreams) are banal. It's still always Mum though. Never Dad. He had to go that way now, as I too will go one day.

The last piece of music journalism I wrote was a feature on the Zombies. I met up with the surviving members of the band in 2008 at Abbey Road studios to discuss the 40th anniversary of their melancholic masterpiece *Odessey and Oracle*. We sat outside. It was a bright, crisp autumn afternoon and our conversation was punctuated by the sound of horse chestnuts falling onto the stone flagging of the restaurant garden. At one point, bass player Andy White took a Swiss Army pen knife from his pocket, acquired a piece of string and threaded a conker. The piece wrote itself. A few days later I transcribed the interview from an unmarked C90. With a minute or so of tape remaining, the conversation wound down to small talk. Concluding pleasantries were exchanged followed by the familiar muffled sound of me fumbling for an off switch. The final moments on the cassette were filled with what I'd just recorded over. A drawling, courteous voice could be heard thanking me for a most enjoyable chat. In the background a terse, impatient PA informed Jim Webb that he had to be at the BBC in 45 minutes.

Printed in Great Britain
by Amazon